WHITEWASH

COLOMBIA

Caribbean Sea

PANAMÁ

VENEZUELA

Santa Marta
Barranquilla
ATLÁNTICO
Cartagena

GUAJIRA

MAGDALENA

CÉSAR

CÓRDOBA

SUCRE

BOLÍVAR

Río Cauca

NORTE DE SANTANDER

Cúcuta

Bucaramanga

SANTANDER

ARAUCA

ANTIOQUIA

Medellín

CHOCÓ

Río Atrato

Río Magdalena

BOYACÁ

CASANARE

CALDAS

RISARALDA

Manizales

QUINDÍO

CUNDINAMARCA

BOGOTÁ

VICHADA

*Pacific
Ocean*

VALLE DEL
CAUCA

Buenaventura

TOLIMA

Cali

CAUCA

Neiva

HUILA

META

Río Meta

Río Guaviare

GUAINIA

San José
del Guaviare

GUAVIARE

NARIÑO

Pasto

PUTUMAYO

CAQUETÁ

VAUPÉS

Río Caquetá

BRAZIL

ECUADOR

AMAZONAS

Río Putumayo

Río Amazonas

Leticia

PERÚ

| | The Andes |

0   100   200 miles

0   100   200   300 Kilometres

SIMON STRONG

WHITEWASH

PABLO ESCOBAR

and the

COCAINE WARS

MACMILLAN

For my parents, Ma and Cristina

And for all those Colombians who have sacrificed their lives,
or their jobs and careers, in resisting the cocaine business

First published 1995 by Macmillan

an imprint of Macmillan General Books
25 Eccleston Place London SW1W 9NF
and Basingstoke

Associated companies throughout the world

ISBN 0-333-60235-8

1 3 5 7 9 8 6 4 2

A CIP catalogue record for this book is available from
the British Library

Typeset by CentraCet Limited, Cambridge
Printed by Mackays of Chatham plc,
Chatham, Kent

CONTENTS

ACKNOWLEDGEMENTS

The written sources I have used for this book are easy to acknowledge. They are to be found at the back. Most important were the works of Fabio Castillo, *Los Jinetes de la Cocaina* and *La Coca Nostra*. The former in particular is a classic, if rushed, piece of investigative journalism in which the dense, vacuum-packed information is compiled with dogged moral certainty. Castillo, of the *El Espectador* newspaper, wrote the book in two months in 1987 after an inter-media research group – which included a future presidential candidate – broke up in disarray when he shared his information about corruption related to the drug traffickers in the city of Cali. Castillo fled Colombia, not returning until 1993. The book became a bible for the United States' Drugs Enforcement Administration (DEA).

Two other important books to which I owe much thanks were *Kings of Cocaine* by Guy Gugliotta and Jeff Leen (published 1989), and *El Patrón, Vida y Muerte de Pablo Escobar* by Luis Cañon (published 1994). The authors assembled a formidable amount of material from interviews and documents. However, Cañon's account suffers in that it balks at nailing down political and economic corruption or attacking the Cali traffickers.

Other written sources to which I am immensely grateful are Colombia's newspapers and magazines, especially *El Espectador* and *Semana* but also *El Tiempo* and *La Prensa*. Unfortunately, Colombian nationalism, accommodation with government, the bribing of journalists and violent reprisals have increasingly caused

ACKNOWLEDGEMENTS

its newspapers, radio and television stations to limit their investigations and coverage of drug-related corruption. Crime stories are not followed through to the end – the country's labyrinthine legal and administrative processes often ensure that there is none anyway – and little attempt is made to provide family, business or historical context. Colombians are not encouraged to remember yesterday clearly, even if they wanted to, which many do not. And in Colombia, family links matter. A 1994 magazine profile of the president of a leading national airline, ACES, was typical of the selective reporting. Juan Emilio Posada Echaverry was described as a first cousin of a potential presidential candidate, Noemí Sanín, the recently appointed ambassador to Britain. No mention, however, was made of Posada Echaverry's brother-in-law – Jorge Luis Ochoa, Pablo Escobar's principal partner in crime.

In such a climate, I am therefore all the more grateful to those Colombians who have shared with me their time and confidence in helping to piece together the story of how cocaine wealth has corroded their country on so many levels. It is these direct sources who are not so easy to acknowledge. Whether journalists, lawyers, taxi drivers, shopkeepers, policemen, bankers, academics, public officials, politicians or businessmen, their mention here by name might prejudice both their lives and their jobs, as well as their families. Hence, the identities of my interviewees – about three hundred and fifty – are given only where appropriate in the text.

Similarly, I believe it preferable not to mention those who collaborated with me on a personal and professional basis with the writing, reading, editing and production of the book itself. They know who they are and the very deep gratitude I bear them.

Among foreigners who have generously provided me with their information and professional insight, however, I should like to declare my special thanks to Joe Toft, the courageous and embattled head of the DEA's Colombia office for six and a half years until 1994.

Simon Strong
January, 1995

Every society has the quantity of criminals it deserves

Colombian National Police

I have the blood of the people

Pablo Escobar

PREFACE

The pine needles crunched under foot. A clap of thunder burst tiredly through the treetops. Somewhere below us, the drone of a chain-saw died away in the dusk. One by one, ten police commandos emerged above the tree line, stepping out on to a ridge that fell away into rough mountain pasture. A short-wave radio crackled. 'Zero-Three, Zero-Three, what is your position?' The major described it, was told to stay put, and sat down. His men followed suit. Hundreds of metres below, the city of Medellín started to flicker with yellow dots as the street lights came on, its lush daytime exuberance fading into a nervous, nocturnal pitter-patter. Its proudest landmarks were snuffed out by cloud.

The commandos laid aside their Galil rifles, tore the wraps off their toffees and chewed in silence. With the exception of the major, they were all in their twenties, policemen summoned from all over Colombia to participate in the biggest manhunt in the western hemisphere. They were tired, they were scared, and they only wanted to succeed because they wanted to go home. Right now, they faced a chilly night on a hilltop. '*Hijo de puta, HIJO de puta,*' muttered the major, grinding his front teeth into a tortured snarl of frustration, his body coursing with rage.

It was Monday, 11 October 1993. The target had been located

in the next valley. Two hours earlier, police intelligence had picked him up speaking on a short-wave radio. It was the first intercept for more than a year. He was isolated, tired. Since he had walked out of prison in July 1992, the 600-strong task force that had been set up to hunt him down had carried out more than 10,000 raids; his most trusted colleagues, friends and bodyguards had either deserted him, were back in jail or were under the ground. The previous week, his wife and children had come under gunfire and grenade attack and the last of his former henchmen, 'Angelito', had been cornered and shot. Time was running out for Pablo Escobar.

Minutes after the radio intercept, hundreds of police and soldiers had been bundled into trucks and sent up into the hills and forests above Medellín. For more than a decade the city had been the epicentre of the world's cocaine industry. It was Pablo's kingdom. From there, he had fuelled economic growth and bankrolled presidents. From there – betrayed by the very politicians he had supported – the master of kidnap, bribery, extortion and terror had unleashed a war upon the state in which thousands of police, judges, civilians and politicians had perished.

All in the name of cocaine. Or rather, in the name of the illicit trade of a psychologically addictive, luxury commodity satanized in the countries of the First World that bought it and converted it into the far more lethal version, crack: a trade that was impossible to stamp out and whose illicit nature generated terrorist monopolies, gigantic profits and deeply corrosive national and international corruption.

After trudging up a muddy mule track, with helicopters dropping off other police patrols on the peaks, we reached the edge of a pine forest. My patrol started to bed down for the night, anticipating a long wait. We were one of several patrols covering the south-west flank to block Escobar's eventual escape from the valley of Aguas Frías. The operation had been sudden and nobody had brought extra clothing; the only sources of warmth were the major's sleeping bag and a German shepherd dog. He got the bag, we got the dog. As the radio crackled away in the major's ear, the thunder moved further off. Thick mists swept up the slope. We dozed.

'The target is wearing a red shirt, black jeans and tennis shoes. His hair is short, he has a light beard and no moustache.' It was 11 p.m. The voice of Colonel Hugo Martínez Póveda, the Search Force leader, calmly issued Escobar's description over the radio.

Escobar had almost been nailed. A small farm at the very head of the Aguas Frias valley had been raided by police and a pair of floppy black suitcases had been found containing his belongings and more than $7,000 in local currency. Two women, one of them a seventeen-year-old girl, had been arrested. They claimed a stranger had arrived the day before with bodyguards and that they had been forced to keep house for them. The men had just left, they said.

Escobar would have been tipped off the moment the task force entered the valley. There was only one road leading up into it and word would have reached him in an instant. His escape route would have been pre-planned, and a fully equipped, sophisticated *caleta* or hideout – probably underground – awaiting him in the forest. The refuge was likely to be on the land he had given to his wily, if ga-ga, puppet priest, Father Rafael García Herreros, who had acted as a go-between in his surrender in 1991; several patrols, including mine, were positioned there.

Whatever the warning, Escobar had left in a hurry. Not only had he abandoned his clothes and toiletries, a dark wig, four walkie-talkies and two automatic rifles, but his personal letters were still on a table. Among them were obsequious missives from prisoners offering their services to '*El Patron*'; others were from his old henchmen, also in jail; and two were from his children. Most telling of all was a letter written by Escobar himself, to his mother, in which he told of his weariness and his desire to surrender again. He was despairing of the government's willingness – never mind that of the security forces – to allow it to happen.

There were also some cassettes. One of them was a discourse on panic and tranquillity. The rest included tangos, salsa, muzak and Bach fugues. Tango is a strong cultural tradition in Medellín. It celebrates low life, tragic love and solitude; it often intimates death. Among Escobar's selection was 'Cambalache', a famously gritty tango asserting immorality to be the soul of existence. Perhaps it provided Escobar with moral solace:

> *Today it seems it's the same*
> *To be upright or a villain . . .*
> *And he who doesn't go to any lengths is a fool,*
> *Go for it . . .*
> *Nobody cares if you were born honest,*
> *If he who works night and day*
> *Like an ox is the same . . .*
> *As he who kills . . .*
> *Or he who is outside the law.*

Since the task force had been set up a year earlier, Escobar had never come as close to capture as he did that night. The following day, which was hot and sunny, hundreds more soldiers were flown in to strengthen the security cordon, helicopters hovered and swept low over the hills, and generals arrived from the capital, Bogotá, to take over the operation. Apart from the arrest of a taxi driver allegedly summoned to help Escobar escape, nothing happened. The man with $12 million of reward money riding on his head – making him the world's most wanted criminal – had disappeared.

On Wednesday the frustration of Colombia's security forces finally boiled over. Raw from public mockery at their continued failure to catch Escobar, and furious as ever that the government had allowed him to hand himself in and then to escape in the first place, the task force showed that Escobar's fears about not letting him surrender were fully founded. They did indeed want him dead, not alive. Army Colonel Gustavo Bermúdez, a leader of the task force, said so. And at midday, when intelligence sources claimed Escobar had slipped the net and handed himself in at the mayor's office in the nearby town of Envigado, 160 police and soldiers abandoned Aguas Frías and raided the Envigado building with a diligence that went far beyond the provision of security for a penitent delinquent. However, Escobar was not there. It was disinformation.

Late that afternoon, back at the task force base, I spoke to a truck full of soldiers who had just returned from the hills. They were jubilant, laughing and joking as if a war had just ended. In a supposed attempt to flush out Escobar, helicopters had blindly loosed off volley after volley of machine-gun fire into the pine trees and bombarded the forest with tear-gas canisters and grenades. But it was more like an act of despair: a wild venting of frustration, a way of exorcizing tensions and the demons of failure. It was not seriously expected to work. It just made everybody happier.

The bombardment embodied something far deeper in Colombia. It symbolized the determination to obliterate Escobar from the national consciousness; and with him, to pulverize memories of a decade dominated by the drugs trade. In the 1980s, Colombia's historic tradition of violence reflowered. By its close, drug-related crime, common delinquency, guerrilla terrorism and the military and paramilitary response to it were killing nearly 30,000 people every year. Nobody came through the decade untouched. Large sectors of society were traumatized. The collective amnesia that developed, which stemmed partly from a sense of collective guilt, was reflected by the muteness of the national press and media.

Meanwhile, Colombia's most famous villain had to be finished off. Heavily corrupted by drug-trafficking money – at all levels, directly and indirectly – the state, business sectors and civilian population as a whole were again anxious to turn their backs on a trade that they had overlooked until it became irrevocably associated with violence and terrorism. Escobar's jail escape made the country into an international joke. Thereafter, as if by consensus, all the sins of the past were heaped upon the most

5

conspicuous devil around. He became a redemptive figure whose death would wipe the slate clean – as well as save many corrupted public personalities from the risk of exposure. Telling tales was Escobar's last card. Nobody planned to let him play it. And he never did.

CHAPTER ONE

BIRTH OF A
DELINQUENT (1948–72)

Three bullets from a cheap imitation Smith and Wesson struck the politician, perforating the skull and liver. It was 1.10 p.m., Friday, 9 April 1948. Jorge Eliécer Gaitán, the charismatic leader of Colombia's Liberal Party, upon whom millions of people were pinning their hopes for radical reform, collapsed. He died half an hour later. By then his assassin had already been lynched by a mob outside a pharmacy, and his naked corpse dumped accusingly on the steps of the presidential palace.

Bogotá erupted in fury. The Colombian capital was engulfed in flames as tens of thousands of people went on a three-day rampage. Shops were looted; government ministries and buildings and Catholic palaces and monasteries were burned and their windows smashed; cars and trams were turned over; whole neighbourhoods went up in smoke. Nuns were raped in convents. Police and radio stations were seized. So great was the rage, so dashed were the hopes, that factory workers, small traders and the emerging middle classes rose up in a blind and anarchic frenzy. There was collective hysteria. People screamed, tore at their clothes and threw themselves to the ground; they drank themselves into oblivion, killed each other in futile quarrels and left the wounded to burn among debris.

The *Bogotazo* riots triggered off an open civil war between the Liberal and Conservative parties that by its conclusion in 1965

7

had cost anything between 200,000 and 300,000 lives. It sowed the seeds of Communist guerrilla insurgencies, too. Indeed, that day a twenty-one-year-old Cuban, Fidel Castro, was in Bogotá for a Latin American Communist student conference timed to co-incide with an anti-Communist Pan-American one under the aegis of the United States. Castro, who had met Gaitán, later admitted to firing four bullets from a Mauser rifle at the Ministry of War; he also had his wallet stolen.

The immediate challenge facing the Conservative Colombian president, Mariano Ospina Pérez, was to bury Gaitán's corpse, the presence of which incited revolt. In exchange, the widow was insisting on the president's resignation. Eventually, it was agreed the government should buy her house, bury Gaitán under the dining-room floor and make the place a national monument. Ospina – whose own grandfather had conspired to kill Simón Bolívar, the hero of Latin American independence – was, at heart, a conciliator.

Ospina next had to convince public opinion that it was not the Conservative Party that had assassinated the man who other-wise would have been destined for the presidency. Who had done it? The Communists, who mainly viewed Gaitán as a populist traitor who had sold out the masses? The traditional wing of the Liberal Party, which was beginning to come under the sway of a future president, Julio César Turbay, supported by Darío Samper, the uncle of another future president, and which viewed Gaitán as a loose cannon inside its ranks? The other Liberal wing under Alfonso López Pumarejo, a former president whose son would follow in his footsteps too? The Conservative Party, whose members had openly been calling for Gaitán's murder and which under the next president, Laureano Gómez, and his son Alvaro would endorse paramilitary action of one kind or another for most of the second half of the century? Or was it a rogue police unit inspired by the Conservatives? Or simply a solitary madman?

It was left to Scotland Yard to find out.

In June, at the request of the Colombian government, Sir Norman Smith, Peter Beveridge and Albert Tamsill arrived in an attempt to throw fresh light on the murder (their ostensible mission was to advise on the reorganization of the police force). They were not successful. Meanwhile, Tamsill suffered the same misfortune as Fidel Castro. He had his wallet stolen.

On the eve of their departure the following month they wrote somewhat elliptically to the special investigator assigned to the case: 'If your conclusions are in any way wide of the mark, then we are mistaken to the same degree, since, as we have said before, we agree with you entirely.' The special investigator, Ricardo Jordán Jiménez, confirmed that the detectives had endorsed his own view that Gaitán's killer, Juan Roa Sierra, was simply a motiveless assassin. The confirmation accompanied the official closure of the case – thirty years later.

Gaitán's murder was like the lancing of a boil, whose poison would continue to flow for decades. The same political forces and the same personalities caught up in his killing would bedevil Colombian life into the closing years of the millennium. Not only unable to digest its history, Colombia was determined to forget it, and therefore condemned to repeat it in innumerable incarnations. The waves of violence that struck the country, first in the form of civil war, then guerrilla war and finally a drugs war, scarred the national consciousness. No family was left unbloodied. Quite apart from social justice, criminal justice almost ceased to exist. The state, historically undermined by Colombian regionalism, lost its power to impose the law; it lost its status.

The absence of retribution aggravated the collapse in Christian ethics. In a country where the forces of money and power ran wild, common banditry and top-level corruption thrived. Indeed, they walked hand in hand like Castor and Pollux through the Colombian firmament. While the state tried to cover up its judicial impotence under stacks of laws and regulations that tended to enable indefinite legal procrastination, society ceased to care about what was right and wrong. Instead, people's central criterion was what they could get away with. Where a penal sanction was applied, it was rarely accompanied by social stigma. Who would dare to throw the first stone? Only when there emerged a figure who not only went too far and reflected their guilt before the eyes of the world, but in whose downfall they could also bury the past, would public hypocrisy rise up and destroy him.

The civil war, which came to be called *La Violencia*, had been foreshadowed by bitter struggles ever since the inception of Liberal Party rule in 1930. It was the reforms of Alfonso López Pumarejo, who became president in 1934, that triggered the tension. Independent unions were given their head, ragged attempts were made at land reform and the Church's grip over the state was eased. Industrialists, coffee producers, landowners and bishops fought back. Paramilitary associations linked to the Conservative Party were formed, just when its more radical faction was being influenced by the fascism of Franco and Hitler. By 1948, street protests and strikes were not only breaking out with ever greater intensity across the country, but killings and massacres on all sides were growing more common. The failure of state regulation in social conflicts gravely accentuated party polarization, especially outside the cities. The murder of Jorge Eliécer Gaitán, whose mass appeal threatened the economic élite as well as the traditional party power structures, detonated the fuse.

Although the nature of the conflict varied regionally, it mostly revolved around local, rural party bosses. The Conservative government's police, soldiers and paramilitary forces, backed by the Church, took on peasant guerrillas organized by the Liberals; the Conservatives were also fought by Communist guerrillas, who later turned on the Liberals too. The internecine struggle, which lacked any significant racial or ethnic element in a country whose population is more than 90 per cent mixed Spanish/European and Indian, reached barbaric levels of bloodthirstiness and cruelty. It was a war of attrition and revenge, revenge and attrition.

Most affected were the departments of Tolima, Boyacá, Santander, Valle del Cauca and Antioquia, as well as the Llanos Orientales or eastern plains. The atrocities were widely chronicled. Bodies were quartered, chopped up into bits and decapitated, the heads kicked around like footballs in village squares. Fingers and hands were cut off until a victim 'sang' on his peers. Fathers were made to witness the multiple rape of their wives and daughters. Men were castrated and their testicles stuffed into their mouths. Pregnant women had their foetuses removed and replaced by cockerels in accordance with the dictum *'No dejar ni la semilla'* or 'Don't even leave the seed'. ('You've got to get your enemy where it hurts the most . . . the mother and the fucking children', one torturer was recorded as saying.) Corpses were hideously maimed through a variety of 'cuts'. People were thrown from airplanes or into abysses or burned alive. Colombia's rivers literally ran with blood.

It was during these years that Colombia gave birth to a culture of violence. Life lost its value. The country's language, psychology, customs and behaviour were moulded for generations to come. The word *sicario* (meaning hired assassin) emerged for the first time, not only in connection with the killing of Gaitán but also with gangs in the departments of Caldas and Valle del Cauca. Other words and idioms, such as *sapo* (informant) and *hacer un trabajo* (carry out a job, i.e. kill) were also to remain in vogue. The use of aliases to confuse the enemy and to protect families became generalized. Extortion, land piracy and kidnapping developed as means of raising money and supplies for local guerrilla groups, later becoming ends in themselves. Meanwhile, bandits in western Caldas and Valle del Cauca became notorious for smoking marijuana as a 'job' stimulant.

As the family unit and that of the village community broke down, leadership in general vanished from the elders' grip. It fell to younger men, to the most violent, to those who were scared of nothing and made others who identified with their fatalistic audacity feel strong and protected. It fell to those whose contempt for life derived from seeing their homes destroyed, their parents killed, their mothers and sisters raped. The absolute loyalty demanded was that of an abominable child warped by a lack of affection; any hint of betrayal or even unauthorized departure, by men or women, was liable to be met with execution.

Meanwhile, coffee exports flourished. Coffee, which was

grown mainly in the valleys of the central Andes, was the traditional life-blood of the Colombian economy. As cocaine would one day become, coffee was a magnet for the violence; its harvest was the bloodiest time of the year. Crops and lands were stolen and instant fortunes earned by the thieving bands, who sold the coffee cheaply to the bold and unscrupulous traders who were prepared to run the risk of transporting it out of the region. Coffee was also traded for foreign weapons.

Although the inter-party conflict ended in 1958 with the setting up of the National Front, whereby power was shared between the two parties, the banditry and the struggles by Communist guerrillas continued. However, by 1965 many of the chief bandits had been killed and the Revolutionary Liberal Movement, under Alfonso López Michelsen, had emerged as a powerful faction within the Liberal Party that offered a political outlet for the remaining dissidents opposed to the National Front. Meanwhile, the stage was being set for the following act. While the Colombian army was being pumped with cash by the United States to counter Communist subversion, in 1966 the Communist guerrillas officially launched the Revolutionary Armed Forces of Colombia (FARC). Other Communist guerrilla groups soon materialized.

The war had created massive migration from the countryside to the towns and cities, particularly to Bogotá, Cali and Medellín. By 1965, the predominantly rural population of twenty years earlier had converted into a 70 per cent urban one. The cities were unable to cope. The refugees found neither housing, jobs nor schools. Amid the rich manure of poverty, nightmarish memories, broken families and lost identity, the seeds of urban criminality took root. They would boast a terrible flowering.

An obscure composer, Ismael Díaz, summed up the sadness and desolation of *La Violencia*'s refugees in a tango:

> *In the village one can no longer live*
> *And in the fields one cannot work,*
> *The seven children left from my wife*

> *Will in time die of hunger . . .*
> *The violence ended my family,*
> *They burned my farm and destroyed my home . . .*
> *Seeing that my life was in danger I left*
> *For the hills. I latched on to the guerrillas,*
> *From a rifle I received a shot in my body*
> *And from then on I was an invalid,*
> *Exiled from my village I went away*
> *In search of new surroundings in the city,*
> *I am a poor, suffering invalid*
> *Who begs in the streets for charity.*

Tango was the favoured music in the department of Antioquia, one of the most affected by *La Violencia*. The capital, Medellín, was the industrial and financial powerhouse of Colombia. Gold and coffee had funded the emergence of a powerful manufacturing sector under the rigid control of the Conservative Party and the Catholic Church – which by the time of Gaitán's death controlled several unions, particularly in Antioquia. Bordering the Caribbean to the north, into which its rivers flow, Antioquia is a geographical paradox: womb-shaped, it is at the strategic heart of Colombia as well as being physically isolated by mountains and sub-tropical jungle. It possesses a fierce regional identity and is somewhat envied by the capital, with which it has traditionally battled for autonomy. It is proud of its capacity to trade, to colonize, to break new barriers. Mining bonded it to money, agriculture to land. Most of all, it loved money.

The beginning of *La Violencia* coincided with dynamic growth in Medellín, sucking resources from the countryside and marking the long-term downfall of nineteenth-century Antioquia; a mythical land of promise in which the family was the paradigm of the social order. On the one hand, disobedient daughters were whipped, and prostitution and single mothers were treated brutally by the law. But on the other, virtues such as honesty, hard work, frugality and simplicity were revered in a God-fearing and relatively democratic region of small and middle-sized coffee estates whose cultural totems were the machete, poncho, *aguardiente* and *fríjoles* (cane liquor and beans), mule trains and scapularies of the Virgin Mary.

Yet this myth of the *paisa* (an inhabitant of Antioquia) responded only to the south. And it was a later, white man's myth. The northern valleys of the great rivers Cauca and Magdalena, and the western gateway towards the Gulf of Urabá on the Caribbean coast, were the first and last frontiers. They were either sparsely inhabited or home mainly to indigenous Indians, or the descendants of African slaves shipped to Colombia to work in the old gold mines, which had wound down at the end of the eighteenth century. They were zones of refuge and chaotic colonization. They were mostly poor, heterogenous, conflictive and lawless. Honesty meant keeping your word, it did not mean keeping the law. The law was to be broken in the name of profit if its sanction could be avoided. The *paisas* here were miners. They were gamblers, dice players. And, resentful of an absent state to which they felt they owed little allegiance, they were quickly swallowed up by sectarianism, of any kind. These zones suffered the worst of *La Violencia*.

Police atrocities in February 1952, in the village of Urama, about 200 kilometres north west of Medellín, were typical of the period. A sergeant had been shot, the guerrillas were nowhere to be found. The police, wrote one chronicler, 'went to the house of Don Luis Manso and killed his wife, one married daughter and raped two others, leaving them hanging by their necks. Then they burned everything'. The village was sealed off, the men brought into the square and split into three groups. The first group was led off, robbed and knifed to death 'with machetes, bayonets and daggers'; nineteen bodies were found. The second group was massacred somewhere else. 'The rest were obliged to carry the sergeant's body towards Uramita ... those who collapsed were killed. The police threw sixteen bodies into the irrigation channel of the Uramita aqueduct and, days later, the water swam with human scraps.'

Murder was often sadistic and slow. One bishop told of how

14

a woman in Santa Rosa de Osos, hysterical after witnessing the dismembering of her husband and three eldest sons, injured one of the bandits. 'The eleven bandits . . . then flayed her from head to foot and left her alive and bleeding among her vegetables, under the sun, flies and carnivorous animals, until she died.' When the registrar in the town of Caucasia had his hands and feet cut off in small pieces, and begged to be killed quickly, he was told: 'We want you to suffer.'

In the south, a Liberal guerrilla wrote: 'I have seen arriving in the towns mutilated men, raped women, thrashed and wounded children. I have seen a man whose tongue was cut out while tied to a tree, and some who have had their genitals amputated so they do not procreate more Liberals; others who have had their legs and arms amputated and were made to walk on their bleeding knees. I also heard of the burning of . . . the town of Rionegro for being the mecca of liberalism in Antioquia. These atrocities were cloaked in impunity and incited by high government functionaries. And all this was committed in the false name of God, with scapularies in the pocket and without remorse.'

God's aid was invoked on all sides and in all forms. The Church, which was virtually a parallel form of government, officially supported the Conservatives' violence. In the coffee-growing areas, the alliance was symbolized by the hiding of weapons inside statues of the Virgin of Fátima as she was carried on her inter-village pilgrimages. The Virgin was named after her reported apparitions in Fátima, central Portugal, in 1917. By the mid 1960s, the boot was on the other foot. A group of about twenty Catholic priests in Antioquia were sowing the seeds of liberation theology: a Marxist-driven movement within the Church that sought to address poverty and the perceived oppressive systems that maintained it by empowering people to defend themselves and to initiate change. The movement was part of a national and Pan-Latin American one that, at its extreme, saw one Colombian priest, Camilo Torres, reconcile violent rebellion with Christian ethics and become a leader of the National Liberation Army (ELN). Two years after he was killed, Medellín played host in 1968 to the Latin-American bishops' conference, which laid the groundwork for what was later called the 'preferential option for the poor'.

The city of Medellín, and Antioquia, became a battleground between the traditional and reformist sectors of the Church. The latter was prospering amid the slums that were shooting up around Medellín – particularly *las comunas* on the hills north of the city centre – where migrants were pouring in from the countryside. By 1964 the population had more than doubled since Gaitán's death, to about 750,000; bordering towns such as Bello, Itagüí and Envigado were also bursting at the seams. The valley started to choke. Meanwhile, as the refugees invaded the north of Medellín, city planners moved it to the south: local government and building projects were re-focused down the valley. Not only did the new arrivals come upon a drastic shortage of housing, schools, hospitals and employment, but the authorities were looking the other way. The city split in two.

At the same time, there were the beginnings of an industrial crisis. The old working-class areas near the city centre fell into decline. Factory hands found themselves tossed into the streets alongside the migrants already hawking their wares in the informal market. Money, which was the sole measure of success and social status for the white, pioneering *paisa* – his frugality and insatiable hunger for riches ascribed to his Spanish-Jewish forebears – became even more of a generalized obsession. The mixed-blood, multi-cultured migrants now wanted their share, too. Medellín, which itself had largely escaped the bloodiness of *La Violencia*, started to turn dangerous. Gang leaders emerged: slick, charismatic thieves who would as soon stick a knife in an abdomen as dance a tango.

About this time, too, fortunes were beginning to be made in the nascent marijuana trade. The drug was initially exported mostly in banana boats from the Gulf of Urabá, an area historically notorious for contraband. The trade came to be handled by traffickers from Medellín's Antioquia district, an area near the old airport famed for crime and prostitution. Nearby, in the small town of Envigado, a teenager, Pablo Escobar, was just starting his own career as a petty gangster. He would be successful beyond his wildest dreams. Developing a limitless appetite for violence, he would not only take on Colombia. One day he would even, briefly, plot the assassination of the President of the United States.

Pablo Emilio Escobar Gaviria was born on 1 December 1949, one year after *La Violencia* began. His parents, Abel de Jesús and Hermilda, lived in a hut with an earth floor and mud-and-dung walls, high up a hill south-east of Medellín in the cattle farming district of Rionegro. There was no electricity, but there was running water – a small stream ran outside the front door. Escobar's father owned about half a dozen hectares and half a dozen cows; he also tended the nearby farm of a Conservative politician, Joaquín Vallejo, to whom he had recently sold the land. Twenty years later Vallejo would be Colombia's ambassador to the United Nations. It was upon Vallejo's farm, La Fátima, in the village of El Tablazo, that Escobar was actually born. Being the patrón, Vallejo was made his godfather; the baptism was held in the church of the Virgin of Chiquinquirá.

'Abel is a very good man, a peasant, simple and honest,' recalled Vallejo. 'They were quite poor and lived off Hermilda's salary as a primary school teacher.' Seated beside her son's coffin forty-four years later, Hermilda had no doubts as to which parent he had shared most in common with. Red-eyed and trenchant in the midst of her tragedy, Pablo Escobar having died rather than be recaptured, she insisted with unabashed pride: 'Abel is as honest as a saint; I'm the one with intelligence. Pablo took after me.' At the time of Pablo's birth, she already had one son, Roberto, and a daughter, Gloria Inés; later, she would bear another son and three more daughters.

The family moved to Medellín two years later, before travelling to a series of villages where Hermilda worked as a teacher. By the mid 1950s they were back in the city, living downtown near the railway station. While Pablo finished at the José Celestino

Mutis primary school in the old, Buenos Aires district, Roberto became a sports cyclist at the Semillero Club and began to study electronics. Meanwhile, according to a family friend, the ever-enterprising Hermilda was using ants to illustrate basic mathematics.

However, Abel's career as a farmer had ploughed to a halt. It was with Hermilda's earnings that, after renting a house for a few years in the town of Envigado, bordering the city to the south, they bought their own house there. While Hermilda helped to found the Leticia Avendaño school in their district, La Paz, Abel came in from the countryside to take up the post of neighbour-hood watchman.

La Paz was a new, working-class area of Envigado which had been built to absorb migrants; the one-level houses were offered cheaply on government credit. Its development, along with that of others, was a dramatic break from the past for a town of 32,000 people that considered itself the cultural and intellectual nerve-centre of Antioquia, never mind Colombia, was headquarters to some of Medellín's biggest companies, and was home or weekend and holiday home to many of the city's most prestigious families. Per capita, Envigado was one of the richest municipalities in the country. It regarded itself as a cleverly budgeted, civic and spiritual paradise.

The town's official history began in 1775 after it obtained episcopal independence and any remaining Indians were expelled. Its official forefathers bore names from the regions of Asturia, Aragon and Navarra in northern Spain. Yet local legend kept vivid memories of an older time; of when Indians known as the Anaconas came up from the south and took control over the warring Chibchas and Caribs. The Anaconas were said to be from the slave caste of the Peruvian Incas; allegedly taken prisoner by a *conquistador* anxious to ship them off to Spain for the benefit of human science, they had been abandoned after a long trek in the valley of the river Cauca. Some had continued northwards, beating the Spanish to the valley of Aburrá and settling near deposits of fluvial gold. The Chibchas, Colombia's dominant but unsophisticated pre-Hispanic civilization, which had pushed westwards and had already seen off the wild and primitive Caribs coming down from the coast, were impressed by the Anaconas' intelligence. The two groups interbred, only to be dominated and gradually 'relocated' by the Spaniards; because of its thick woods, which boasted massive trees that were cut down to make beams or *vigas*, the land became known as Envigado.

Occupying 50 square kilometres, from the banks of the river Medellín to the crest of the Cordillera Central, capable of producing everything from sugar cane to potatoes, Envigado became a vital food and wood dispensary to Medellín. Sustained growth in its agriculture and commerce, combined with tight municipal budgetary control and a dominating, wealthy landed gentry, granted Envigado a social and political stability that enabled it to keep its head above the civil wars. At the same time, it produced a series of eminent leaders and intellectuals and became an important centre of learning. The élitist nature of Envigado society was characterized by the relatively cosy and pragmatic mingling of Liberals and Conservatives. At the height of *La Violencia*, although Liberals were chased out, they were not, at least, massacred.

Envigado was also famous for its mules. Between the late nineteenth century and the 1930s – by which time rail transport had rendered them obsolete – mule trains had been the life blood of trade and industry in the departments of Antioquia and Valle del Cauca. Goods were carried on the backs of mules to the river and coastal ports on both the Atlantic and Pacific coasts. Organizing mule trains was an art, and a discreet and dangerous one. Not only were they prone to attack and robbery, but weights, knots, formations and animal temperaments had to be perfectly gauged to minimize the risk of their cargo plunging down mountainsides. If one mule slipped, all did. Envigado's muleteers were famed for their courage and talent. Smuggling cocaine would be an opportunity to reinvent their skills; its carriers would be the 'mules' of the late twentieth century.

In 1966, a few years after settling into Envigado, Pablo Escobar abruptly abandoned his secondary school education. He was sixteen years old. He had attended the Lyceum de Antioquia, a respected state college nestling in the hills above western Medellín that would fall into decline and finally close down twenty years later after its director was shot dead in a classroom. Escobar's grade cards showed him to be a good student. Apart from the odd failure in mathematics or geography, and an increasing tendency not to turn up, his behaviour was exemplary. However, he completed only three out of the six years required. In September 1966, two months short of finishing his fourth grade, he dropped out of school because of what Hermilda claimed at the time was a 'domestic calamity'.

A domestic calamity it might well have been, in the sense that Hermilda's great hopes for her son were dashed because his growing absenteeism had triggered what amounted to expulsion. Escobar's nocturnal activities were leaving him too exhausted to get up in time for his classes. He was also trying to dodge the police.

Escobar had quickly won a reputation for keeping bad company. While still at school, he was known for hanging out at the Dos Tortugas bar in Medellín's Jesús de Nazareno district, a fashionable haunt of petty extortionists, car thieves and bank robbers. The sixteen-year-old boy with the serious look in his eyes, whom childhood friends remembered chasing balloons, was starting to give vent to his sky-high ambitions. Even while still earning the odd peso washing cars and running errands, Escobar used to tell his mother he wanted to be 'big' – to be rich – in order for her 'to get ahead'. His heroes were the textile pioneers of Antioquia. Soccer was his passion.

Legend had it that tombstones were the cornerstone of Escobar's career. Allegedly, he stole them from cemeteries at night, polished off their engravings and resold them to the newly bereaved. He was also reported to sell them for export. Yet his mother, with all the vehemence of one whose son may have been guilty of many crimes but at least was not guilty of that, denied it. And, perhaps more tellingly, Escobar was deeply superstitious. Taking after his mother, and typical of rural Antioquia, his professed Catholicism was nothing more than a very pagan belief in appeasing whatever spirit was around him. However, it was no less intense for that. Although Escobar would never respect the dead themselves, his own sense of self-preservation might conceivably have ensured that he respected the deity in whose honour they were buried.

For Abel, on the other hand, the dead were indeed an object of profit. Goaded on by a friend amused by his greed and gullibility, he began to spend his Good Fridays hunting for nocturnal, other-worldly lights that would guide him to Indian graves whose riches he could then proceed to plunder; in order to scare off evil spirits, he would make the sign of the cross over his bullets and machete. His efforts were reportedly fruitless.

By the late 1960s, Escobar had formed his first gang. Operating outside Envigado, they pulled small-time moves such as *el paquete chileno, el gavilán* and *la lotería*: huckstering people out of their cash as they left banks, mugging them and selling fake lottery tickets. Although Escobar had gone back to school for two years at an evening college opened by the Lyceum de Antioquia, where he won a reputation as a trouble-maker, he had failed his sixth and final year. (He officially graduated eleven years later, finally passing chemistry and calculus; already a millionaire at the time, the grades were almost certainly purchased with bribes.)

Under the influence of a notorious, pot-smoking Envigado crook called Mario 'Cacharrero' Garcés, Escobar also learned about more lucrative trades: selling off the parts of stolen cars and dealing in drugs. Another of his role models was Gilberto Saldarriaga, nicknamed '*El Zapatero*' or the shoemaker, an emerald smuggler from the next-door neighbourhood of El Dorado who made his name carrying cocaine to the United States in the heels of his shoes. But for the time being Escobar concentrated on the car business.

Car theft became an art form under Escobar. Under his leadership, what had once been an occasional and discreet one-man, break-in-and-jump-the-motor-at-a-car-park affair matured into a flourishing industry run by professional gangs in which vehicles were hijacked in the midday traffic, their owners thrown on to the pavement and their parts unbundled and distributed through crooked shops within a matter of hours. The gangs were at Escobar's service. Years later, he was famed to have expanded into car insurance. Nobody would touch vehicle parts embossed with his code; so the only way to guarantee not having a car stolen was to pay insurance to the city's biggest car thief.

Escobar's delinquency continued with his return to school at the Lyceum Lucrecio Jaramillo in 1967. He resumed his studies alongside his cousin, Gustavo Gaviria, who was two years older. Escobar became a class tyrant, fighting with teachers who refused to bend to his will. Although Escobar's grades were satisfactory at first, he became increasingly distracted by the pursuit of money. To his mother's chagrin, he failed his sixth grade in spite of cheating in his exams.

By 1970, Escobar had developed an operations base in Itagüí, a scrappy, dirty and disorganized industrial town next to Envigado teeming with migrants from rural Antioquia. By bribing people in the municipal transport office, Escobar obtained the requisite documents for vehicles that he stole. Hence, in the name of simplicity and cost-effectiveness, he was able to resell the cars in one piece. The man crucial to this adult version of car washing was a municipal clerk and future drug money launderer who became one of Escobar's closest colleagues.

Meanwhile, their mutual obsession with cars had already cemented Escobar's partnership with his cousin, Gustavo. With cars and spare parts that were mostly stolen, they started to race in local as well as national rallies. Gaviria proved an expert driver. According to neighbour gossip, it was while Escobar was still at school in the late 1960s that they moved their first small cocaine load in a car rally between the Ecuadorian border town of Tulcán and that of Cucutá on the Colombian frontier with Venezuela.

Escobar always remained closer to his cousin than to his older brother, Roberto, who only became involved in Pablo's criminal business much later. A talented cyclist, Roberto rode in national and international rallies and set up a bicycle shop in the city of Manizales six hours away from Medellín. Cast into the shade by Pablo, even the Colombian state security police, DAS, described him as initially 'morally solvent'. Gaviria became Escobar's right-hand man – and his administrative brains.

It was June 1971. Tens of thousands of hippies from all over the country were descending on Medellín for the biggest open-air rock concert in Latin America. One by one they crossed a little wooden bridge into the park of Ancón, a few kilometres south of the city. Heavy rain had turned the hills and fields into muddy bogs, but Colombia's middle-class rebels poured into the park for a three-day festival that marked a turning point in Medellín's history.

The city that had long since adopted as its musical patriarch Carlos Gardel, the legendary, low-life Argentinian tango artist killed at Medellín's airport in a plane crash in 1935, was in the grip of sex, drugs and rock 'n roll. The hippy culture had been imported from the United States by the sons and daughters of wealthy farmers and industrialists returning home from their school and university studies. Marijuana, which since the age of *La Violencia* had been viewed as a vice of beggars, bandits and brothel creepers, suddenly became fashionable among artists, students and intellectuals. Smoking the weed symbolized social and political rebellion.

The week before the Ancón festival – which coincided in the United States with the countdown for the launch of Apollo 15 – riots broke out at Medellín's biggest university and spread to the streets. The mayor, Alvaro Villegas, said he hoped a few days of music, love and peace would defuse the violence by 'bridging the generation gap'.

As the crowds squeezed into the park to listen in torrential rain to one-night bands such as Hidra, Free Stone de Medellín and – from the USA – Kansas City, the first thing to give way was the bridge. Several people, drugged to their eyeballs, were swept under by the swollen river. Although dozens of witnesses swore they had seen the bodies washed away – and filmed them – the deaths were officially denied.

The party went on. Not only was there masses of pot available – 'You couldn't breathe without getting stoned. I left,' sniffed one girl studying in a convent at the time – but several varieties of hallucinogenic mushrooms too. Nobody recalled cocaine. And nobody recalled much food or drink. Nor lavatories. Just music, mud, sex, pot and mushrooms.

The authorities were unable even to recall the drugs. Although the mayor was forced to resign – along with the rector of the University of Antioquia because of the rioting there – an investigation by the district attorney's office into whether drugs had been consumed at the festival was closed for lack of evidence.

The festival popularized marijuana in Antioquia. Pot smokers came out of the closet. In Medellín itself, it coincided with an anti-establishment but mostly upper-middle-class movement called Nadaismo. The Nadaistas delighted in ferociously profaning all traditional norms; their anarchic irreverence had a mystical edge, too. A local philosopher, Fernando González, was their principal guru. González, who had died in 1964, was a brilliant, rebellious and idiosyncratic intellectual whose works had been banned by one of his most cherished targets, the Church, and who had been proposed for a Nobel Prize by Jean Paul Sartre (who, at the time of the Ancón festival, was facing arrest for defamation of the French police). González' university thesis was entitled 'The Right to Disobey' and he had lived in Envigado, where his house had been converted into a museum.

The explosion in the local pot market was accompanied by an epidemic of pharmaceutical drug abuse in the prisons, of which

Escobar had already enjoyed his first experience in the late 1960s when he was jailed briefly in the La Ladera prison for presenting false documents. Barbiturates and tranquillizers were mixed with everything from cough mixture to spider webs. Medellín's prisons, whose populations were multiplying as the pressures of rural migration triggered a rise in crime, suffered a frenzy of violence. Dozens of prisoners were killed every month, along with the guards who were bribed to let the drugs be smuggled in. The violence went unreported but Escobar took note: those who proved themselves the most able, dogged and vicious of the villains would become the heart of his organization. Similarly, the lawyers who specialized in defending the illicit importers of pharmaceutical drugs would later become his own legal backbone in the export of cocaine.

Meanwhile, American hippies and dealers were looking for pot, too. Supplies from Mexico and Jamaica were drying up following the destruction of plantations in line with the tough anti-drugs policy of the US president, Richard Nixon. The Colombians were quick to oblige. The local pot market swelled in Urabá in northern Antioquia, where a 450-kilometre road connected Medellín to the Caribbean near Panama. Marijuana grown in southern Colombia was shipped out of the gulf hidden in banana boats. From there, by a succession of boat and land transfers, it found its way to California or the Florida keys.

The Gulf of Urabá had been a passage for stolen goods and a smuggling route ever since the Spaniards arrived in South America. Indeed, it was in a ring of low hills on the north-eastern edge of the gulf that the Spanish built their first settlement on the continent, San Sebastián. In 1509, after earlier Spanish visits had encountered passive Indians boasting impressive quantities of gold artefacts, Alonso de Hojeda disembarked there with 200 men. After their previous experiences of rape and pillage, the Indians were no longer so passive. Several months later, suffering from hunger, disease and tireless attack from poisoned arrows, the Spaniards abandoned the settlement. While Hojeda died of his arrow wounds, two other Spaniards who had been with him,

Vasco Núñez de Balboa and Francisco Pizarro, went on respectively to discover the Pacific Ocean and to conquer the Incas in Peru.

Other and more substantial Spanish settlements around and north of the gulf were the bases for tomb-looting raids of the Indians in the Urabá valley. It was down through the valley that Jorge Robledo travelled to found what became the colonial capital of Antioquia, Santa Fe, in 1541; its wealth was centred on mining. The Spaniards were even reputed to have shipped treasure up from the Pacific Ocean into the river Atrato, whose many deltas disgorge into the Urabá gulf. With the abandoning of the Urabá routes because of easier and safer ones elsewhere – the Panama isthmus and the river Magdalena – the gulf became a home for English, Dutch and French pirates. In return for guns, gunpowder and brandy, the Indians offered them succour for their attacks upon the hated Spaniards in the Caribbean. The pirates hid in the mangrove forests of the gulf and up the river Atrato itself.

Contraband thrived. Since trade with any country other than Spain was banned in the colonial period, foreign ships sold their goods in the gulf, whence they were smuggled south up-river. Similarly, in order to avoid taxes, the gulf was used to smuggle out gold. When Spain ordered the river Atrato to be sealed off from trade, prices were simply boosted: of outgoing gold as well as incoming textiles and ironmongery. Not only were the authorities incompetent and corrupt, but the number of available routes rendered the task impossible. By the time trade was freed up in the nineteenth century, the Cuna Indians were so accustomed to taking their cut of the illicit shipments that they turned to straight extortion instead.

By the middle of the 1960s the Urabá valley had developed into a dynamic centre of growth following the building of roads and a huge banana boom. It was rough, disease-ridden, frontier territory. And once again it was a centre of contraband. Soaring world coffee prices were higher than in Colombia, hence coffee was smuggled out. Cheap Chinese domestic goods flowed in from Panama, as did weapons for the Communist guerrillas. The US marijuana demand could not have been more opportune. It occurred just when the banana producers were switching from transparent plastic bags to cartons. The marijuana became easy to hide: it was loaded directly on to banana boats in the Atrato deltas after being shipped downriver. In a culture where risky and illicit business was the norm, and where police, customs and boat captains made a living out of bribery and extortion, marijuana smuggling was just another venture. It was contraband, not drugs, that initially attracted most of Pablo Escobar's attention.

Three months after the 1971 festival of Ancón, on the day that the astronauts of Apollo 15 popped out of space into the Pacific Ocean, another epoch-making event shook Medellín. The beaten and strangled body of a leading and much respected industrialist, Diego Echavarría, was discovered in a hole in the ground 14 kilometres east of the city in the hills of Rionegro. He had been kidnapped six weeks earlier outside his mock-medieval castle in the lush, luxury neighbourhood of El Poblado, on the edge of Envigado. According to police at the time, the ransom was initially set at 20 million pesos; when negotiations with the family reached an agreed price of one million pesos, it was reported that Echavarría refused to sign the note and was murdered.

However, two decades later the police hunting Pablo Escobar claimed not only that he had been behind the Echavarría kidnapping, but that he had also collected the 1 million pesos (about $50,000). The accusation may have been part of the overall demonizing of Escobar, but in the underground world of Medellín in the early 1970s Escobar was proud to wallow in the credit. He was dubbed Doctor Echavarría, later shortened simply to 'The Doctor'. 'It was common knowledge that Pablo was one of the people behind it,' murmured a man who had worked for the family as a driver and clerk. 'Pedro', a rough, acne-pitted mechanic, was talking in one of Escobar's favourite haunts of the period, El Perro Negro or the Black Dog in the run-down, downtown district of Guayaquil. Dogs nosed around in rotting vegetables outside, and a group of middle-aged killers conversed over tiny cups of steaming black coffee near the bar. A tango played. An old man hawked 6-inch pocket knives and a woman with massive and mostly exposed breasts prostituted herself below the low wooden arches giving on to the street. 'Diego Echavarría symbolized old Antioquia,' said my friend. 'He was seen as an oligarch and exploiter. His kidnapping was one of the first acts of popular justice. Pablo wished to identify with the poor – he saw himself as a Robin Hood figure.' A Robin Hood or not, a few years before the kidnap, Escobar had customarily cited Echavarría's wealth when giving the girth of his own financial ambitions.

Kidnapping became a speciality of Escobar's. As well as using it to exact his own direct financial or political gain, he offered it as part of a debt collection package for others. The capacity to seize people and their families, hide them from the police or other parties, and extract ransom was central to his power as an enforcer. Many of his kidnap victims would be people who either reneged on agreements or simply, in some way, betrayed a trust. And, as with his killings, he would delegate the work to others in such a way that those at the front end of the kidnap – who actually captured the victim – never knew for whom they were working. If they did, they were often executed afterwards.

Escobar continued to diversify. While orchestrating car thefts, bank robberies and the occasional, opportunistic middleman transport of small amounts of cocaine, he started to work in contraband, which had formed the hub of several old Antioquia family fortunes. Pot smuggling had swiftly concentrated in Colombia's remote peninsula of La Guajira, where it was even further out of the authorities' reach and much closer to the high-quality, high-altitude marijuana grown in the mountains of the Sierra Nevada. Instead, according to one former family confidant, Escobar spent much of the early 1970s developing contraband contacts around the Caribbean and in Central America. Escobar later claimed that his main criminal 'maestro' was a famous smuggler called Don Alberto. He maintained that his own reputation was forged during gangland wars to win control over the contraband of Marlboro cigarettes after market saturation depressed the price.

In that struggle, he had acquired fame as a gunman shooting from a Lambretta scooter that he had originally used in car thefts. He was one of Colombia's first motorcycle hitmen.

As Escobar's criminal organization grew, so did the need for discipline within his own ranks. An iron hand was required because he was unable to resort to the courts. Treachery was met with execution. Escobar told a journalist friend, Germán Castro Caycedo: 'That is the problem with drugs and contraband – that they go hand in hand with guns. It's that, in this thing, the decent guy, or rather the idiot, either goes bust, ends up in jail, or dies.'

His first serious clash with official justice occurred in September 1974. The state's justice proved far less efficient than Escobar's. Caught red-handed in a stolen Renault 6, he found himself back in the La Ladera jail. Not only had the stolen car been spotted during the theft of another Renault, but both witnesses cited by Escobar denied his version of events. The two men, Francisco Pizano and José Dolores Galeano, who had been paid by Escobar to carry out work disguising the Renault's identity, claimed total ignorance of the matter. However, Escobar bought his way out of prison. Two years later, on 30 May 1976, the witnesses paid the penalty for letting Escobar down. They were murdered: one was shot in the head and the other had his head smashed by an iron bar. A few years later still, on 11 June 1983, the entire archives in the corresponding court were burned by five armed men. The case against Escobar had gone up in smoke.

Since the kidnap of Diego Echavarría, Escobar had won a reputation in the Medellín underworld not only as a cold-blooded killer but also as a master schemer and evader of justice. Yet he was an unlikely figure. Physically, he was rather fat, inclined to an obesity common not only to his family but to the families of the other traffickers with whom he would eventually team up. It would not be long before his neck puffed out to form a wide and sizeable double chin. His dark, coffee eyes wore a distant, contemplative look that scarcely registered emotion. He watched and listened and when he spoke others obeyed. Escobar led from the midfield.

In spite of his plumpness, and despite being an habitual late riser – he rarely went to bed before 3 a.m. – he was by no means slothful. He moved fast and with stealth and he enjoyed speed. Escobar graduated from bicycles to motorbikes, from rally cars to Porsches. Along with other traffickers, he also developed a taste for water sports: not swimming or ski-ing, but comfortably sitting astride water scooters or piloting motorboats. However, his Olympian ability to elude the Colombian police and army would later owe more than a little to Escobar's capacity to take evasive physical action.

A bristling, black moustache was Escobar's most notable facial feature. It came to symbolize Escobar's identification with one of his biggest heroes: Pancho Villa, the Mexican bandit and bloodthirsty darling of the 1919–20 revolution. According to local legend, Pancho Villa was born in Envigado. The real name of the rebel who killed his captives by stretching them out over fast-growing cacti is recorded in Mexico as Doroteo Arango. When Arango's original gang leader was killed, Arango threw himself upon the corpse, swore to follow in his footsteps and assumed his name, Pancho Villa. The name Arango, which is almost unheard of in Mexico, is native to Antioquia. Meanwhile, an Envigado birth certificate dated 1875 documents a Teodoro Arango, who, aged twenty, was said to have fled the village after killing a man who had slept with his sister. Oral tradition recounts how the man who became Pancho Villa passed through villages to the south before catching a boat to Mexico from the Pacific port of Buenaventura.

On the edge of a lily-strewn lake in Medellín's botanical gardens, a former errand boy of Escobar's organization described his boss's fixation for the bandit: 'Pablo idolized Villa, he made a cult of him, buying hats, boots, weapons and costumes he was supposed to have worn, especially hats, and bibliographical material. For Pablo, Villa was the prototype of someone who'd

30

fought to unmask the oppressors who'd treated the poor badly.' The version was reinforced by a famous photograph later discovered in which Escobar was proudly dressed up as the Mexican bandit.

Cool and calculating that he was – Escobar rarely lost his self-control and frowned on cocaine use – he enjoyed marijuana. However, unlike his fellow *paisas* of Antioquia, Escobar was not a big drinker. He smoked marijuana at parties and for late-night relaxation, as well as to quicken his pleasure in driving a fast car or having sex. But he never went over the top and even had a fondness for alcohol-free beer. Although frugal and even mean in their other habits, *paisas* love to get intoxicated. Antioquia is the most alcoholic department in Colombia, consuming nearly twice as much *aguardiente* per person as the rival Valle del Cauca department to the south.

Sales of rum and *aguardiente*, a departmental monopoly, contribute 80 per cent of Antioquia's budget. They pay for its education. 'We're self-financing,' joked one university professor in an after-work, drink-soaked *tertulia* – an informal get-together – in Medellín. In bars, restaurants and in private homes, women top up the glasses of their menfolk until their heads topple successfully on to the table. Visitors to the city's mayor are even served a delicious, creamy liqueur in their early morning coffee.

By 1975, the city of eternal spring – Medellín enjoys an average temperature of 23 degrees centigrade – was on the brink of traumatic change. Migration was boosting its population by several per cent a year. Birth-rates were high and people were fleeing from the struggles between the Communist guerrillas and the army in the Urabá and the Magdalena valley, where peasant colonists were being forced off their land by big landowners arriving with the law in their pocket. At the time, Medellín was hopelessly unable to cope. The densely packed slums or *comunas* scrambling up the sides of the Aburrá valley not only lacked basic services, they lacked space in which people could move. The city

itself had been dehumanized by a soulless modernization programme. Even the river was starting to die.

Medellín was also suffering from an industrial crisis. Between
1970 and 1971, gross output collapsed by 15 per cent. Manufacturing as a whole, which looked to substitute imports, and the
vanguard sector of textiles in particular, had been faltering since
a few years back. The domestic market was too small, and Asian
textiles were not only seizing Antioquia's textile markets abroad,
but also coming in as contraband – through the Urabá as well as
elsewhere – to beat them on their own ground. The growth areas
focused on by the traditional business sector were the city's
infrastructure, the banana industry and intensive cattle farming.
'The new industrial model was more closed, more monopolistic
and more inaccessable to the average person,' said María Teresa
Uribe, of the University of Antioquia. 'The horizon for the [licit]
accumulation [of capital] was no longer open to the most able
and daring. These requisites now had to be associated with
money.'

Unemployment in Medellín raced to around 15 per cent by
1975, according to official figures, which was double the rate of
Colombia's other main cities. As well as there being little space in
which to move, there was little space in which to work. The state
entered a crisis of legitimacy, thereby opening the doors to the
left-wing guerrillas, whose anti-oligarchic, anti-imperialist message stoked up social unrest further. Absenteeism between 1974
and 1986 in presidential and congressional elections reached up
to 60 per cent. The Popular Liberation Army (EPL), the National
Liberation Army (ELN) and the 19 April Movement (M-19) were
all opening urban fronts in Medellín; the former were also active
in Urabá. The union movement which had once been reined in by
a conservative Church was now being given its head by Marxist
leaders. And the Church itself was focusing protest in the most
deprived neighbourhoods through priests who had adopted 'the
preferential option for the poor', reducing the emphasis on faith
and family.

The results were quick to follow. Crime rates soared. There

was not enough space in La Ladera jail either. Built for 800 prisoners, by the early 1970s it was holding more than 2,000. When a new jail for 2,000 was constructed, it was not long before the prison population doubled again. The jails became criminal training schools in which only the toughest and richest survived; if not, they were robbed, raped or killed. Between 1973 and 1975, murder in Antioquia increased by 10 per cent a year, several points higher than the national average.

Shrinking horizons were all the more dangerous because of the *paisa* obsession with money. 'The most characteristic desire of *paisas*,' said one Antioquia historian, Mario Arango, 'is to make a deal, of what ever kind, even if just a simple *cambalache* [swap], but always with an eye on obtaining an excessive profit, even if it means knocking out the other party. That is why when he offers a mortgage he is not interested so much in getting back his money and interest, but in getting hold of the property.' Disgusted by Medellín's conservative ethics and social hypocrisy, Gonzalo Arango, a leader of the *Nadaista* movement, was more contemptuous. He wrote: 'You do not admit change in your concrete soul. You are only impassioned by the passion for money.' An old *paisa* saying ran: 'Make money, my son; even if you don't make it honestly, make money, my son.'

Blocked on all sides, frantically ambitious, willing not only to run risks but also to break necks as their families had done and had been done to in *La Violencia*; re-inventing the colonial as well as republican traditions of contraband, of mule trains, of trading where no man had gone before; oblivious to everything but a good deal and convinced that God would not only forgive them but proffer a helping hand, Medellín's 1949-er generation of lower-middle-class migrants took up the gauntlet flung before them by the millions of North American and European hippies who had climbed aboard the big dipper of psychotropic greed. They might not be able to give them all the dope they wanted, but they would give them all the dope they could.

CHAPTER TWO

GROWTH OF THE CARTEL (1972–78)

'**If you want** to hang out, you've got to take her out, cocaine/If you want to get down, down on the ground, cocaine/She's all right, she's all right, she's all right, cocaine/If you've got bad news and you want to kick the blues, cocaine/When the day is done and you want to ride on, cocaine.' Eric Clapton covering a J. J. Cale song, 1977: a hit from Clapton's *Slowhand* album that caught the mood of a generation in North America and Europe. It was the year that a Woody Allen sneeze scattered into the air a large pile of cocaine in the film *Annie Hall* – and provoked involuntary gasps of horror by Californian audiences intimately acquainted with the sparkling white dust that cost $100 a gram.

Yet cocaine was nothing new. It was merely fashionable again, this time on a massive scale. Forty-three years earlier, in 1934, Cole Porter sang about it in the musical *Anything Goes*: 'Cocaine doesn't give me a kick/I am sure that if I took it only one more time/It would bore me terrifically too/I get a kick – out of you.' The lyrics were only later altered to make it champagne instead of cocaine.

Half a century back again, in 1886 – when Sir Arthur Conan Doyle, the creator of cocaine-tooting Sherlock Holmes, was in his middle twenties – the future president of the Pharmaceutical Society of Great Britain, William Martindale, recommended it as a tonic to be taken instead of tea. The same year, the drink that was to become the world's most famous beverage, Coca-Cola, was launched; cocaine was the central ingredient. 'A valuable brain tonic and remedy for all nervous disorders,' said its creators. (The cocaine was removed in 1903, but the leaves were still used to give it the distinctive taste.)

Two years beforehand, Sigmund Freud – the father of psycho-analysis, which alongside cocaine and pot became so popular in the 1970s age of self-discovery – sang the praises of cocaine in his landmark essay, 'On Coca': 'The psychic effect of cocaine consists of exhilaration and lasting euphoria . . . One senses an increase of self-control and feels more vigorous and capable of work . . . Long-lasting mental or physical work can be performed without fatigue; it is as though the need for food and sleep . . . were completely banished.' In the same period, a Corsican chemist developed a cocaine wine whose contented consumers included the science fiction writers Jules Verne and H. G. Wells, the sculptor Auguste Rodin, the gramophone inventor Thomas Edison, and two popes.

The cocaine had first been extracted from the leaves of the South American coca plant, *Erythroxylum coca*, of which it was the principal alkaloid, a couple of decades earlier by European chemists. It sent one Italian neurologist, Paolo Mantegazza, into what he himself called a delirium: 'I laughed at the poor mortals condemned to live in this valley of tears, while I, carried away through the air on two coca leaves, was flying through the space of 77,438 worlds, each one more splendid than the last.'

Since at least 1,000 years earlier still, coca had been chewed by Indians in Peru, Bolivia, Ecuador and Colombia. Grown on the eastern slopes of the Andes, it became the sacred plant of the Incas, whose empire extended from central Chile to southern Colombia before they were crushed by the Spanish conquerors in the sixteenth century. According to Inca legend, coca was planted by the sun god with the help of the moon. It was the food of the gods.

However, at the time Pablo Escobar was expanding his illicit transport of cocaine in the middle 1970s, western governments did not agree. The coca leaves seemed harmless enough, but they were not the issue. Even Freud had relented of his initial rhapsodies about the cocaine extracted from them: one of his patients died of an overdose which he himself had prescribed. In some people, the drug generated immediate negative reactions. In others – particulary the weak-willed or those already inclined to self-destruction – regular use produced psychological, although not physical, addiction. In every case, tolerance increased.

Although its early, widespread public use had soon been restricted, cocaine had emerged slowly through the first half of the twentieth century as a drug for bohemians. Around 1915, cocaine was satanized for mainstream public opinion in articles such as one by the *New York Times*, which held cocaine responsible for mass killings by blacks whose gun aim it allegedly improved. The article claimed: 'Most of the attacks on white women in the South . . . are the direct result of a black brain driven crazy by coca.' Meanwhile, the United States had seized the global initiative against opium – also identified with a feared, minority group, Chinese immigrants – and in the Great Depression had gone on to adopt stiffer laws against marijuana – brought in and smoked mostly by Mexican immigrants – as well as cocaine.

However, in its tightening up of drug prohibition laws in 1970, cocaine was classified as a category two drug: allowable only in medically acceptable applications. One year later, the amount of cocaine impounded by US Customs was 197 kilograms. That was up from 29 kilograms in 1968 and just 3 kilograms in 1961. The customs were under no illusions: far from the increased seizures indicating that the customs were being more efficient, they indicated that more was coming in. Cocaine was replacing domestically produced amphetamines, which were going out of fashion: in the 'age of Aquarius' fluffy dust from the land of the Incas was more wholesome, more natural, more exotic, more *spiritual*.

In Colombia itself, reported crimes rose 25 per cent in 1970. The national police called it a 'criminal explosion' in their annual report. In Antioquia, there were twice as many killings as in Bogotá, although its population was only 10 per cent bigger. By 1972 – the first year that drug offences were officially collated – killings in Antioquia had shot up by a quarter and it hosted more than twice as many drug-trafficking crimes as any other department. By 1974, Antioquia's reported drug-trafficking related offences had doubled. That year, the police report blamed the crime rise on the sense of impunity felt by criminals who did not take the judicial system or its penalties seriously, on the decomposition of the family unit, and on a rejection of traditional moral values – as well as the desire to get rich quick.

'In the last few months,' said the report, 'it was shown that the export of cocaine to the markets of Europe and the United States, where there exists most demand for the product, was achieved through the use of women, who in the jargon are known as "mules" because they are people who, attracted by a good payment, render their services in moving drugs.' It was the age of the false-bottomed suitcase and the stuffing of cocaine into vaginas, rectums and bras; of walking on to a plane with a cargo worth $5000 and walking off it with a cargo worth $30,000 – wholesale. Foreigners, too, were coming to Colombia to spirit cocaine abroad for the first time: in 1973, dozens were caught attempting to smuggle it out at Bogotá airport.

The Colombian 'mule' movements had started in earnest following the 1973 *coup d'état* in Chile by General Augusto Pinochet. Chile had hitherto dominated the incipient US trade, obtaining the paste from Bolivia. Indeed, it was on a flight that landed at Bogotá airport from the Chilean capital of Santiago that Colombian police made their first seizure of cocaine. One kilogram of the drug had been hidden in the feet of some furniture, which broke open in the fuselage. The furniture belonged to a North American diplomat; although he allegedly turned out to be an innocent victim whose belongings had been hijacked by somebody else, the incident was never publicly revealed.

Within three months of seizing power and in order to ingratiate himself with the US government, Pinochet had deported twenty leading traffickers to the US and jailed dozens more. Many of the remaining chemists moved to Colombia, where, once their techniques had been mastered locally, they lost importance. By the middle of 1974, Colombians were beginning to cultivate and process the coca leaves themselves, instead of merely shipping on the finished product. That year, when US customs' seizures of cocaine reached just 320 kilograms, a survey by the US National Institute on Drug Abuse showed that 5 million North Americans had used cocaine at least once. By 1982, that figure was 22 million.

Pablo Escobar was only one of Colombia's many cocaine traffickers starting to expand his operations in the middle 1970s. His generation rapidly expelled the pioneers. The men who became the leaders and biggest allies of the Medellín cartel were, like Escobar, all born at the outbreak of *La Violencia* between 1947 and 1949: Jorge Luis Ochoa, the eldest son of a cattle dealer and horse breeder, José Gonzalo Rodríguez Gacha, the son of cheese-making peasants, and Carlos Lehder, an Adolf Hitler fanatic born to a German immigrant and a beauty queen.

In the department of Valle del Cauca, the men who assumed the leadership of what became known as the Cali cartel – which one day would become the instrument of Escobar's downfall as well as arguably the true, national bedrock of political power – were a similar age. José Santacruz Londoño and Miguel Angel Rodríguez Orejuela began their careers as members of a kidnapping gang, which was controlled mainly by the latter's older brother, Gilberto. Also from poor backgrounds, they started to import coca paste from Peru and refine it in laboratories in the early 1970s. Two months after Gilberto Rodríguez Orejuela, who became known as 'The Chess Player', appeared on a list of 113 names of people believed by Colombian customs to be drugs traffickers in 1975, he was captured in Peru with a plane containing 180 kilograms of coca paste. He was released shortly afterwards.

Jorge Luis Ochoa, who was initially known for being a second-hand car dealer, and his younger brothers Juan David and Fabio, were the great-grandchildren of a highly respected cattle farmer, Abelardo, who was famed for turning horses into a luxury hobby instead of mere instruments of labour. His son Tulio was credited with producing Antioquia's first *paso fino* or walking horse, Resorte. Tulio's son, Fabio, in turn became a horse breeder. In the middle 1960s, Fabio produced a remarkable stallion, Resorte III, which developed its own special walking step that became known as the *paso fino colombiano*. The family was not rich: they worked simultaneously in their restaurant, Las Margaritas, in Medellín.

When Fabio Ochoa went broke in the early 1970s – allegedly through dice gambling – the family moved to Cali, the capital of the Valle del Cauca, with nothing but Resorte III. The horse lived inside their house while Fabio's sons cut grass for it in the streets; his covering of mares covered their bills. During that time, Jorge Luis, who was alleged to have an uncle already leading one of the original cocaine-trafficking organizations in Antioquia, befriended Gilberto Rodríguez Orejuela. By the time the family returned to Medellín, the Ochoa brothers were trading cocaine.

Escobar's expansion as a cocaine trafficker occurred fast. Initially, he had emerged as just a middleman, obtaining small amounts of the drug from Ecuador and selling it on within Colombia or at the frontiers. Then, after buying it from the Colombian laboratories that were now springing up in the Amazon to convert imported coca paste into cocaine – a straight-forward, if delicate, process employing ether and acetone – he started both to employ 'mules' and to sell it on to his fellow contraband smugglers in Panama. In order to earn serious money Escobar had to make the business vertical: he needed enough money to buy bulk direct from Bolivia and Peru and he needed enough access to the consumer markets abroad. Mustering up the cash brought him into partnership with the Ochoa brothers, whose high-society links ensured a ready supply of investors.

Pot exports were mostly dominated by US dealers, who swept

in and out of the La Guajira peninsula in north-east Colombia by airplane or whose 'mother ships' collected the pot from smaller launches off shore. North Americans controlled the drug's distribution in their home country. The Indians who grew the crispy, red buds called Santa Marta gold and the pale, trippy Blond, parted company with their harvest in the Sierra Nevada mountains. Transportation down to airstrips and the water's edge cost money; so did organizing fuel supplies and boats; and, above all, so did protection. Although massive fortunes were made by families on the Atlantic coast, it was dealers from Antioquia who not only seized the initiative in co-ordinating the separate stages and in developing protection and intelligence structures, but also in baling the pot and dumping it in black plastic garbage bags off the Florida coast for their own networks to collect and distribute in the United States. At the same time, they initiated more sophisticated payment and money-laundering methods to avoid betrayal, theft and murder at the drug-collection points. Slowly, the US pot traffickers were pushed out.

With cocaine, the Americans never had a chance. They were too far away from its source and, aided by the sudden boost of Latin American migration during the 1970s, the Colombians were already developing their own US distribution networks. Escobar's first priority was to gather enough capital in order to import Bolivian and Peruvian coca paste himself – Colombian coca leaf was as yet of too low a quality – and to create cocaine in his own laboratories. By 1976, their contraband, kidnapping, car stealing and cocaine trafficking had yielded enough profits for him and his cousin Gustavo to make their biggest move yet.

It was a watershed year. In March – with special dispensation from a bishop – Escobar, twenty-six, married a fifteen-year-old girl, María Victoria Henao Vallejo. Discreet and devoted, she remained loyal to Escobar throughout his life and bore him two children, Juan Pablo – after the Pope – and Manuela. Although Escobar was a doting father, especially to Manuela, he was a dutiful husband only in so far as he heaped riches on his wife and had a deep concern for her physical well-being. His love was that of a fairly typical *paisa*: sexual fidelity was out of the question. And, as Escobar's empire grew and he began to indulge his every whim, he developed an ever more marked taste for young girls.

Escobar's brothers-in-law fell under his sway, too. Mario Henao, a university graduate in psychology and a disciple of a famous Marxist-Freudian who had been a good friend of the Envigado philosopher Fernando González, became one of Escobar's closest confidants, and even his intellectual counsellor. Huddled in a bar over a bottle of *aguardiente* as the rain billowed in through the entrance near Envigado's main square, a tango singer whose lush, mother-earth beauty was all the riper for middle age, recalled Mario Henao's ideas. 'Mario used to say they wanted power and government in order to use drugs to weaken North America's historic hold on Latin America,' she said. 'He said it was a way of fighting back, of bleeding North America of dollars and at the same time attacking its youth.'

In June 1976, Escobar and his family had their first full-blooded run-in with the police. Having collected 18 kilograms of cocaine from Ipiales, a small town on the Ecuadorian border, they stood to net half a million dollars once they shipped it to the United States. It was their most ambitious plan to date. The drug was hidden in the spare tyre of a pick-up truck. However, agents from the Administrative Security Department (DAS), the state security police, had already got wind of the move. The truck was tracked to Itagüí, the town beside Envigado. Escobar, his cousin Gustavo and Mario Henao were arrested upon their arrival at the rendezvous; bribery got them nowhere except deeper trouble still. It was Antioquia's biggest cocaine bust so far.

Shortly before his arrest, the witnesses against Escobar in the case of the stolen cars were killed. Shortly after it, the judge dealing with the cocaine charges learned that Escobar was planning to murder her as well as the regional director of DAS. During the ensuing months, the cocaine case was tied up in knots by objections placed by Escobar's lawyers. Such tactics thrived in a country where regulations are piled one above the other until they reach the point both of contradiction and no return, reminiscent of the circular and amnesic world of Macondo, the setting of the legendary novel *One Hundred Years of Solitude* by Gabriel García Márquez.

Escobar and the others were freed in September by a judge from a different area. Although the release orders were initially revoked, the case continued to bounce back and forth between courts until the investigation eventually shuddered to a standstill. Yet the two DAS agents who arrested them were murdered in 1977, their regional chief was murdered in 1981, and the judge who issued an arrest warrant against Escobar for the killing of the two DAS agents was gunned down in 1986. Escobar's clean-up would, nevertheless, return to haunt him once public attention focused on his past.

In the short term, however, Escobar's luck held. After leaving jail he is reported to have made his first trip to Bolivia, where he met the world's up-and-coming, major single supplier of coca paste, Roberto Suàrez. Bolivia, a land-locked and mostly Indian nation, is the poorest country in South America. With more than 190 *coups d'état* since winning its independence, its democracy was so feeble and its earnings from coca paste so high – by the 1980s they were estimated to match that of legal exports – that in 1980 Suárez helped to trigger a military coup. The man whom US intelligence accused of helping Suárez was Klaus Barbie, the former Gestapo officer in France known as the Butcher of Lyons.

Tragedy struck Escobar's family in Envigado on Christmas Day 1977. That night, in a solitary spot in the Zúniga neighbourhood, Pablo's younger brother was making love with his girlfriend in a car. A police vehicle passed by. Suspicious of the parked car, the police turned back and tried to draw alongside it. Pablo's brother, Luis Fernando, panicked. He switched on the engine, threw in the clutch and raced away. The police gave chase. Seconds later, Luis Fernando's car missed a curve and flew into the Ayurá canal. The car overturned and both lovers were killed; their bodies were pulled naked from the wreckage. Escobar was away at the time. However, weeping with rage as much as with grief, Doña Hermilda swore vengeance on the police over the coffin of her son. A funeral witness said: 'All the family blamed the police, who they said had killed the couple for nothing. They swore to get their own back.' Escobar was to more than fulfil the family vow.

On his return from Bolivia, from where Escobar planned to fly out coca paste provided by Suárez, Escobar met Carlos Lehder – the Adolf Hitler fanatic. Lehder, who had spent a year and a half in jail in Connecticut, USA, for possessing 107 kilograms of marijuana, was selling contraband luxury cars in Medellín. He also used women to smuggle out cocaine a few kilograms a time. A fluent English speaker, while in prison Lehder had befriended a North American pot dealer called George Jung, whose contacts were now buying all the cocaine he could supply from Lehder. Although a childhood friend of the Ochoa brothers – whom Escobar had also met through the car business – Lehder was too smooth, loud and unpredictable for Escobar's liking. Neither was he from Medellín. Nevertheless, when Escobar tested Lehder's boasts about his US contacts, he discovered he was as good as his word. During the next six months, Lehder regularly distributed shipments of 50 kilograms and more, collecting the cocaine in Miami, where it was sent by its owners Escobar, the Ochoas, Pablo Correa and Pablo Arroyave. The key US dealer, a friend of Jung's, was a hairdresser in Los Angeles who sold it on to Hollywood film stars. Suddenly, the Colombians were earning millions of dollars. By now, Escobar and the others had their own laboratories and airstrips in the Urabá region and the valleys of the river Magdalena to the east; they were able to import the coca paste directly from Suárez. The next stage was the fulfilment of Lehder's dream to fly the finished product to the United States in bulk.

Meanwhile, the criminals from Medellín and Cali were by no means the only people opening up supply and export routes for cocaine. Neither were they only selling it abroad. And nor was it only the traffickers who were profiting from the trade. Colombia's top politicians were already snorting up their share of the profits, as well as the drugs. Some were trafficking cocaine themselves.

The drug smugglers were simply another, albeit major, source of revenue for politicians who sought electoral funds through alliances with business leaders, or who often depended on the direct buying of votes by regional strongmen. The fact that the cash was illicitly gained troubled few politicians, especially when in refusing it they ran the risk of bolstering opponents who were less fastidious. Colombian politics had always been rough and most politicians had historically sought to use their power for their own economic advantage, legally or otherwise.

In 1974, Alfonso López Michelsen, the son of the last elected president preceding Mariano Ospina Pérez, who was president at the outbreak of *La Violencia*, was elected president in turn. A financial scandal involving López Michelsen had been partly responsible for his father's resignation in 1945. Years later, Lehder told a US court that López Michelsen was 'the cartel's protector' whom Escobar had made his 'political godfather'. Lehder claimed that he was personally aware of two payments received in 1982 by López Michelsen from the Medellín drug traffickers, for $520,000 and $400,000. Evidence of President López Michelsen's links with the Ochoas at a time when they were already becoming notorious as drug traffickers in Medellín was provided by a young lawyer who saw them together. 'López Michelsen arrived at Las Margaritas [the Ochoas' restaurant] for lunch,' she said. 'He came by helicopter as if it were the most normal thing in the world.'

In return for their help in getting him into office, Alberto Santofimio, the leader of the Liberal Party in the department of Tolima, and Julio César Turbay Ayala, López Michelsen's campaign leader, were suitably rewarded. The former was appointed minister of justice and the latter ambassador in Washington. Eleven months after swearing that he would 'fight corruption', Santofimio resigned following corruption allegations that led to him spending six months in jail in 1978. Santofimio was claimed to have created 'one of the biggest armies of functionaries' that any minister had ever put in power. However, he refused to introduce new, and tighter, penal codes; perhaps as a reflection of the government's laxer attitude, the annual police report also ceased to give a breakdown of drugs crimes. After Santofimio's resignation – and while in jail – he was elected a senator; he even felt confident enough to declare himself a future presidential candidate.

According to a police colonel, Santofimio, a slick and brilliant politician, was involved with cocaine traffickers in the capital of Tolima, Ibagué. In February 1976 a leading Liberal Party colleague in Tolima, José Ignacio Aguirre, was captured in a shoot-out with police at Bogotá's airport following a meeting of drugs traffickers. Aguirre's bodyguard was killed. When the two other leaders were caught in their aircraft, the patrol taking them to jail was attacked. Within a month, Aguirre, the other leaders and those who attacked the patrol had been released. However, the arresting officer had been charged with homicide; two countries offered him asylum because he feared Santofimio had put out a murder contract on him.

Turbay Ayala, the ambassador in Washington, was a veteran, Bogotá-based politician from the Lebanese community, which dominates the contraband in the La Guajira department. While ambassador, Turbay Ayala was accused by an arrested cocaine dealer in the US, Karl Hans Schmidt, of being his 'financial chief'. In a 1976 statement to the US Drug Enforcement Administration, Schmidt accused Turbay Ayala's embassy of providing 'the diplomatic bag to send money [from cocaine sales] back to Bogotá to pay for the purchases [of more cocaine]'. When the DEA illegally opened the bag on its way to Colombia's New York consulate, they discovered twelve leather-bound volumes of Colombian Congress journals sent from the Ministry of Foreign Affairs; each contained 1 kilogram of cocaine. However, the bag had to be resealed.

The grandsons of President Mariano Ospina Pérez himself (who was in turn the grandson and nephew of two other presidents), the brothers Rodolfo and Mariano Ospina Baraya, were also trafficking in cocaine. It was reported that they shipped it out in the boxes of flowers exported from their grandparents' estate.

By February 1976, they were already involved in drug vendettas: that month nineteen-year-old Rodolfo survived a carefully planned sub-machine-gun attack in the district of La Estrella near Medellín. In August 1984, Mariano was arrested in Miami for laundering $1.3 million of drug money; he was jailed for ten years. His brother Rodolfo was implicated too, but escaped to Colombia, although he already faced a jail sentence in Medellín for contraband cars licensed in Envigado.

Three years later, on the run from US as well as Colombian justice, Rodolfo Ospina Baraya was wounded in an attack in a restaurant outside Bogotá, during a family meal presided over by their widowed grandmother, a former senator herself, Bertha Hernández de Ospina Pérez, and in the presence of Colombia's actual consul in Boston, Rodolfo's first cousin, Bertha Olga Ospina. The hitmen shouted: 'Keep to your deal.' Initially, the presence of Rodolfo, who defended himself with a machine-gun, was hushed up and Bertha Hernández was made out to be the target. Amid much public, chest-puffing indignation by Colombia's political worthies – the former senator was described as a 'symbol of democracy' by Alvaro Gómez, the son of a president who had done his best to subvert it – the truth leaked out. *El Espectador*, the only newspaper ever to combat the drugs trade, revealed that the fight had broken out because of 'an operation between members of the Medellín cartel and the Ospina Barayas . . . whose terms [were] unfulfilled or broken'. However, the story was not followed up. Like all sensitive revelations touching the rich and powerful in Colombia, it not only sank like a stone but created no ripples. (Escobar eventually enforced his revenge: he kidnapped a younger, innocent brother. In return for his brother's release, Rodolfo Ospina Baraya signed assets over to Escobar and withdrew declarations he had made against him before the Colombian authorities.)

The fortunes of Escobar and his partners in Medellín were founded on an idyllic Caribbean island. Norman's Cay was at the tip of the Bahamas archipelago, about 55 kilometres south of the capital, Nassau. It was named after an English pirate and boasted about a dozen cottages, an old yacht club and hotel, white beaches and a 3,000-foot airstrip. Electricity came from diesel-fuelled generators. There was one telephone. In May 1978, Carlos Lehder bought the biggest house on the island for $190,000. The other inhabitants were quickly pushed out and forced to rent their properties to Lehder's employees. Neighbours that complained were threatened; when help was sought from the Nassau police, nothing happened. Casual visitors were prohibited.

Lehder was installing a transport base for cocaine shipments. By now he had not only proved himself to Escobar for his ability to distribute cocaine fast in the United States; he had also organized the mafia's first 250-kilogram move by airplane. This had been flown by a North American pilot, Barry Kane, from a property of Escobar's in La Estrella, Medellín, via Nassau for a fuel stop, to Florida. The shipment, in August 1977, had been snapped up in Hollywood and grossed more than $10 million for its suppliers. Lehder and his American partner, George Jung, took a 10 per cent commission.

Norman's Cay was converted by Lehder into a sinister island empire. Equipped with sophisticated communications equipment and navigational aids, manned by German security guards with Dobermann pinschers, offering pilots, planes and mechanics, and protected by the Bahamian government, it was a paradise for the big traffickers – even if was run by an increasingly cocaine-stoked, paranoid autocrat. Escobar and his partners started to fly in loads of 400 kilograms a time. Often they would use a different aircraft for the run-in to Florida, where Escobar's shipments would be dropped into the Everglades, picked up by launches and taken to Miami. Other onward routes quickly developed.

A police raid in September 1979 served merely to cement Lehder's relationship with the government. The Bahamas, which after the revolution in nearby Cuba succeeded it as a centre for gambling and money laundering for the US mafia, was being run by the Progressive Liberal Party of Lynden Pindling, inspired by the Black Power movements in the Caribbean and United States. The islands had been a transit point for pot and cocaine shipments since the late 1960s; with the Nassau airport congested by drug flights and under the scrutiny of US law enforcement authorities, the business had spread to at least a dozen other islands. A British Royal Commission of Inquiry later declared that a Cabinet minister, George Smith, had received a pay-off from Lehder. The prime minister himself, Pindling, was alleged in an American trial to receive drugs money too.

The Bahamian banking secrecy laws were also convenient for the traffickers. Accounts were opened by Escobar and Jorge Luis Ochoa for Lehder to deposit the cash proceeds from the cocaine, with the money then being transferred by wire to bank accounts in Panama.

Although there were two more police raids in 1980 and 1981, Lehder was tipped off. However, after a drug-smuggling indictment in Jacksonville, Florida, in January 1981, and the building up of pressure on him within the Bahamas – where his men were suspected of killing an elderly yachting couple who had come too close to the island – Lehder returned to Colombia. But Lehder's transport service, which by then was only part of one of many routes and networks used by Escobar and other traffickers, continued. At the same time, as the quantities of cocaine being imported into the United States multiplied, the distribution networks inside the country expanded accordingly. Extra tiers developed, although the dealing stayed mostly in the hands of Hispanic immigrants. As the cocaine was sold and resold on to the street, it was increasingly adulterated or 'cut' with other substances in order to maximize profits by making it go further. At the top of the chain were the Colombians. They always boasted they sold it pure.

By 1978, Escobar was becoming a public figure both in Envigado and Medellín. Envigado was no longer the exclusive, genteel place of the previous decade. Migration had roughened it up. In order not only to win popular support but also apparently out of a genuine desire to help his neighbours as well as to show off his wealth, Escobar donated money for roads, electrically lit football pitches and other local works. He was also providing employment for young male teenagers, particularly from his own area – the districts of La Paz and El Dorado. After working in Escobar's cocaine laboratories for a year or two, they would return rich enough to buy a house and car. According to one neighbour, by the middle of the next decade most of Envigado's male teenagers were working for him. They were mostly sweating in Escobar's laboratories or else operating within his US distribution networks; Escobar's killers tended to come from the tougher parts of the Aburrá valley around Medellín.

Although Escobar's initial political mentor in Envigado was a much-respected doctor and future senator, René Mesa, Escobar did not make his own challenge for power until the municipal elections in 1980, when he backed another Liberal, William Vélez. 'Everybody already knew that Pablo's money came from drugs,' said one local economist. 'But they just looked the other way.' Although Escobar poured money into Vélez's campaign to take over the council, at first he failed. Nevertheless, Escobar exerted influence as Vélez's council substitute.

However, Escobar was already politically active at a regional as well as a national level. In 1978 he met Diego Londoño White, a property dealer and politician from a leading Antioquia family, through whom Escobar sought to invest his profits in land. Londoño White, who was already a friend of the Ochoa brothers through their mutual interest in horses, was the Antioquia co-ordinator of the presidential campaign for the Conservative Party's candidate, Belisario Betancur. 'Political campaigns need a lot of finance and politicians look for money wherever they can get it,' he told me while under police custody accused of conspiracy to kidnap. With complete candour, he added: 'Everybody knew Pablo and the others were traffickers, although it wasn't openly said. They offered to collaborate, lending helicopters and small planes, and contributed about one third of the committee's resources.' A close colleague of Londoño White's went further, but insisted on remaining anonymous: 'Belisario himself attended campaign auctions of art, horses and cattle, knowing that the traffickers were the main vendors.'

According to a former Liberal senator for Antioquia, the traffickers simultaneously financed the campaign of Julio César Turbay Ayala, who won the election in 1978. Backing both sides is traditional practice among Colombian businessmen anxious to cover their bets. However, it was with the Liberals that Escobar later placed his own personal, political future in a move that sowed the seeds of his downfall.

Like other Colombian traffickers, Escobar poured his money into land and buildings. Central Bank figures indicated that construction in Medellín quadrupled between 1975 and 1981, when it accounted for 28 per cent of the national total. At least half the finance was estimated to come from the mafia. Luxury apartment blocks sprang up in the hills around El Poblado and Envigado; one even had a swimming-pool on every floor. Mafia money was largely behind the development of the big shopping centres. The traffickers also bought up the prettiest weekend farms. They offered up to twice or three times the normal value and paid in cash – sometimes turning up out of the blue and demanding the owners left the same day, abandoning their furniture. Most vendors were only too happy to take the money. Others sold against their will knowing that, if they did not, they would take a bullet instead.

Similarly, the traffickers bought up hundreds of thousands of hectares of land: particularly in the valley of the river Magdalena, the Urabá and along the south-west Caribbean coast, and the savannahs east of the Andes. Throughout the 1980s, their territorial expansion continued, mainly southwards, until the traffickers had a hold in every department. Often, their land was either virgin and inaccessible except by aircraft, or it was simply remote enough to act as a refuge, laboratory base and airport untroubled by the police. However, it did bring them into contact with the guerrillas, for whom, now that they had joined Colombia's landowning and business élite, they soon became a target for kidnapping and extortion.

Escobar's pride and joy was a 3,000-hectare ranch he began to build in 1979 near Puerto Triunfo on the river Magdalena. About half-way between Medellín and Bogotá on what became the major highway between the two cities, at the time of its purchase the ranch was a 23-hour, dirt-track drive from Medellín in barely colonized light jungle. Escobar bought a corridor of land connecting the ranch to his properties in Envigado, more than 170 kilometres away. In homage to the Italian mafia with whom he identified and was starting to do business, he christened the ranch Nápoles.

One visitor there in the early days related his experience: 'We were camping nearby when two men on motorbikes came up and joined us, Pablo and his cousin, although we had not yet heard of them. We drank *aguardiente* and smoked marijuana together. They were very courteous and friendly and invited us to their ranch the next day. It was obvious they were *mafiosos* the moment we arrived. There was a huge board by the entrance gate saying that because they were nature lovers they protected flowers and animals, and hunting was prohibited. But instead of cutting down trees in a civilized manner, they had just burned them to their stumps. A waiter showed us to a table by a gigantic swimming-pool. Around us it was like a motel, and although there were two or three other groups, they didn't appear for lunch. It was very eerie. When we were invited in, Pablo materialized at the other end of a huge table with a woman and a waiter in a white hat. He didn't eat, he just greeted us dryly and invited us to play with his water scooters afterwards on the [man-made] lake. We were expecting a banquet but the food was horrible: a heavy meat stew in the middle of the jungle. Yuk! We couldn't wait to leave, water scooters or not.'

Soon, the swimming-pool was joined by five more. The lakes multiplied. A 1,000-foot runway was built. A hundred thousand fruit trees were planted. And then, two by two, the animals started to arrive. Elephants, buffaloes, lions, rhinoceroses, zebras, gazelles, hippopotamuses, camels and ostriches, as well as other species, arrived as contraband, mostly from Africa. The zoo, which was opened to the public, became famous in Medellín. However, the animals were more than just a personal extravagance. Escobar dunked his plastic bags of cocaine in their dung in order to fox the anti-drug dogs at US ports and airports. Put off by the smell of animals much stronger than themselves, the dogs steered clear of the shipments of cocaine. The Ochoa brothers also employed the method at their main shipment ranch, La Veracruz, near the Caribbean coast; their zoo boasted about 500 animals.

The Nápoles ranch symbolized the golden years of Escobar. Not only did he co-ordinate cocaine shipments and cartel killings from there, but he also used it for his own recreation and that of his employees, as well as for secretly flying in and entertaining important guests and clients, including a string of politicians. Among the most infamous of the visitors would be the Panamanian military strongman, Manuel Noriega, who was reported to have stayed at the Nápoles ranch in 1983. The traffickers paid Noriega to allow both their air shipments and cocaine cash deposits to go unmolested. Carlos Lehder later testified before a US court that the cartel paid Noriega $1,000 per kilogram in transit from Colombia. The cocaine was mainly sent on from Panama either to Costa Rica and Florida or through Mexico to Los Angeles.

Meanwhile, Escobar and Gustavo Gaviria built up a Renault 4 racing team, which competed successfully in rallies in Medellín and Bogotá. In 1979, Escobar himself was classified second in his category. The sport was heavily patronized by drug traffickers. Two racing circuits were said to be owned by the Rodríguez Orejuela brothers; the DEA was informed that cocaine was being dispatched inside racing cars when shipped to Miami for competitions there; and several drivers and a lawyer were murdered after Colombian police seized 30 kilograms of cocaine from a rally team.

Escobar soon retired from official races because he lacked the time for them, but it was to a racing magazine, *Auto y Pista*, that he gave his first public interview: 'I am a great friend and I do everything possible so that people appreciate me. What is worth most in life are friends, of that I am sure. Unfortunately, along life's paths one also meets people who are disloyal.' And woe betide the latter ... it was probably one of the most heartfelt declarations that Escobar ever made. However, its central premise was that Escobar had a divine right to buy up others – and an equally divine one to obliterate those who denied him.

Money was buying him everything. Already the centrifugal social force in Colombia, and particularly Antioquia, money was converted by Escobar and his fellow traffickers into an over-whelming moral force, too. It bought people as well as objects, beauty queens, priests, businessmen, lawyers and politicians as well as vintage cars, Ming vases, helicopters and rhinoceroses. The pillars of Colombian society were turning a blind eye to the rising number of killings in Medellín as well as nationally. According to the police, the national total of homicides doubled between 1970 and 1980; less than 2 per cent were attributable to guerrilla conflict. The killings increased alongside the cocaine industry and coincided geographically with its epicentres in Med-ellín, Cali and Bogotá. However, because almost all the victims were poor and publicly unknown, they were easy to ignore. Drug trafficking vendettas on the street as well as within the middle and upper echelons of the multi-headed mafia were noticed but dismissed with a shrug of the shoulders. The police, who at the start of the decade had complained of public apathy towards crime as well as of judicial impunity, were now swamped and demoralized and wide open to corruption. In a country that was prostituting itself before the mafia, Medellín was a city with its legs apart.

Gaining the support of Medellín's poor was comparatively cheap and easy, as well as appealing to Escobar's ostentatious, philanthropic streak – which was a characteristic common to the other leaders of the cartel, with the exception of the more upper-crust Ochoas. He provided floodlit soccer pitches and team uniforms, sent food, doctors and dentists into the *comunas*, and offered employment to the toughest villains who came to his attention. Escobar rapidly became a role model and hero for tens of thousands of people. His authority and codes of honour were readily accepted by a rudderless and marginalized population, which latched on to a strong and bountiful leader who had exploded from nowhere. In fact, Escobar's relationship with the poorer districts of Medellín was not very different from that of the rough, lower-middle-class, I'll-scratch-your-back-if-you-scratch-mine breed of politicians which was fast displacing the more staid, élitist and autocratic breed of the past.

The Church also jumped into bed with Escobar. The key figure in public was Father Elías Lopera, a member of the ecclesiastical tribune of Medellín and a close adviser of the archbishop, Alfonso López Trujillo. The nomination of López Trujillo, considered by some a proud and arrogant despot, was so bitterly opposed by the Church's progressive sector that a protest rally was staged outside the Cathedral when he was installed in June 1979. His hard-line, conservative theological beliefs were only part of the problem. A public communiqué by his opponents within the Church proclaimed: 'You are not a priest because you do not know your flock; you are a mercenary who seeks nothing but power and money.'

In 1980 Father Elías Lopera graduated in law from the University of Medellín, where since the mid 1970s members of the law faculty had developed a reputation for defending smugglers of and dealers in pharmaceutical drugs. It was here that Escobar formed the regional political base with which by 1980 he was seeking national political power. One former law student said: 'The faculty was famed for its speciality in penal law. There were no classes in ethics: the most talented and applauded lawyers were those who succeeded in freeing delinquents from prison. Most lecturers were practising lawyers and we knew which were bribable and that many were close to the smugglers.' By 1974 the faculty's substance analysis laboratory was already corrupted, according to the former student. 'Even when it told the truth, the documents were switched by court employees with the lawyers' – that is the lecturers' – connivance,' he added. As the cocaine business soared, fierce struggles broke out within the university to secure important posts with power to nominate judges and magistrates and thereby extract a cut of the traffickers' bribe money. The battle for quotas of 'nominative' power within the faculty was also political: it was waged by different factions of the Liberal Party.

The University of Medellín, which was one of the city's four main universities, later acted as Escobar's springboard into national politics. In August 1980, the former justice minister, Alberto Santofimio, launched the Liberal Renovation Front. A Liberal Party faction, it invoked the memory of the assassinated Gaitán and was described by Santofimio as a 'party of the masses'. Its Antioquia branch – whose headquarters was inaugurated by Santofimio – was led by a former law faculty dean of the University of Medellín, Jairo Ortega, and Pablo Escobar. Three other candidates on the group's electoral list in Antioquia for the 1982 congressional elections had held senior posts at the same university. Ortega, with Escobar as his 'substitute', headed its local list of candidates for the House of Representatives.

Below the pair's campaign billboards in the streets of Medellín, there figured the names of Elías Lopera and another priest, Father Hernán Cuartas, to indicate their electoral support. The priests had been collaborating with Escobar since the previous year on a charitable housing project called *Civismo en Marcha*, which was only formalized after the election. Lopera was made a committee member; Escobar was appointed president. Meanwhile, they, as well as Archbishop López Trujillo, were said by another priest to have visited Escobar at his ranch in Nápoles more than once. The relationship further exacerbated the division that already existed between López Trujillo and a left-wing section of the clergy. Father Pedro Nel Torres, who came to lead the underground opposition to the archbishop, said: 'López Trujillo proposed the housing project to Pablo Escobar and nominated the two priests; it was a social and religious façade for both sides. The archbishop was totally involved – he was just the right person for them.'

The rise of the drugs traffickers also coincided both with an industrial crisis in Colombia, which was felt most acutely in Medellín because of its heavier dependence on industry, and a financial revolution. Hard-pressed businessmen were soft targets for the dollar-rich traffickers; however, although their loans were welcomed, the traffickers preferred to invest in real estate. Industry was largely ignored, although businesses dealing in luxury goods and services thrived on the traffickers' custom and investment. Except for property, the mafia were most interested in a quick return on no-questions-asked deposits.

Their demands were conveniently met by the development of a more sophisticated financial system, which from the early 1970s was encouraged to expand, diversify and generally to be more audacious. In 1975, the López Michelsen government opened what became known as the 'side window' at the central bank, where unlimited quantities of dollars could be changed. This attempt to mop up black-market currency from drugs and other export contraband – there was a coffee price boom – was accompanied by the creation of speculative funds. These funds were poorly regulated in spite of being encouraged by the government. They competed for deposits by offering unsustainably high interest rates and investing the cash in their own businesses. Between 1976 and 1980 bank deposits in Colombia's four major cities more than doubled in real terms. The average growth of deposits in Medellín, Cali and Barranquilla – the cities mainly associated with cocaine and marijuana – outstripped that in Bogotá by nearly 90 per cent. The repatriated profits from cocaine were believed to be one of the principal sources of the extra cash.

Not only did exchange houses, real estate agencies and all manner of financial corporations come into existence offering high returns and tailor-made services to cocaine traffickers – and to other savers jumping on the bandwagon. Financial tycoons emerged, too. Among them was Jaime Michelsen Uribe, the trustee of his cousin, Alfonso López Michelsen. Michelsen Uribe was accused in the *El Espectador* newspaper of instigating a 'massive channelling of credits from the Panamanian branch [of Michelsen Uribe's banking conglomerate, the Grupo Grancolombiano] to take control of businesses' in Colombia. It later emerged that Michelsen Uribe had accepted deposits from Carlos Lehder. There was also Félix Correa Maya, whose Grupo Colombia empire bought a majority holding in one of Antioquia's flagship textile factories, Fabricato, which was in decline. A former departmental governor claimed that Michelsen Uribe had loaned Correa drugs money for the Fabricato deal. 'The mafia deposits allowed industry in Antioquia to borrow and renovate itself,' said one local economist, Jorge Lotero – although the textile industry continued to struggle.

However, having taken the mafia's cash for their land and properties, and having taken the mafia's cash for their industry, Medellín's business élite regrouped itself to resist further encroachment from all outsiders – supposedly respectable magnates included. The city's biggest financial and industrial groups bought into each other in such a way as to erect a common defence against external predators.

Correa Maya was shunned. 'It was presumed that his rise was propelled by money from the drugs trade,' wrote the local historian Mario Arango. 'But that situation was true for the whole Colombian financial system ... The moral rejection of so-called hot money is not so much that it comes from illicit activities but that it has enabled the rise of a new economic sector coming mainly from the lowest social levels.' Correa Maya's group was taken over by the banking regulators in June 1982, triggering financial panic and a run on deposits that spread to the whole of Colombia's banking system. To save the system from total collapse – the crisis continued for two years, with Jaime Michelsen Uribe's empire also crashing amid judicial investigations – most of the banks were taken over by the state. It was reported that on the night the operations of Correa Maya's Banco Nacional were paralysed, one of its executives received a death threat from

Gustavo Gaviria regarding a 400-million peso ($6.25 million) deposit. The money was returned.

United States law-enforcement efforts in Colombia were hardly graced with a fortuitous beginning. In December 1976, the year of the bicentennial celebration of North American independence, the head of the Drug Enforcement Administration in Bogotá was murdered in his office. Octavio González was hit by three bullets fired by a man from New York state who was claimed to be an informer, Thomas Cole. The killer was trapped and, according to the US government, committed suicide. However, his motives were never made clear and Colombian police were sceptical. Cole's body was found 18 feet from where he died, a rib was broken and the two bullets in his head were of a different calibre. There were indications that Cole had been sent to kill the DEA chief because of González's threats to expose both the CIA's abuse of DEA cover and its jeopardizing of anti-drug operations for political purposes.

The DEA's initial main objective in Colombia was the marijuana smugglers. The huge military campaigns it instigated against pot under President Turbay Ayala between 1978 and 1982 in La Guajira served to distract attention from the cocaine trade. Yet it was cocaine that was wreaking financial and homicidal havoc in Miami. While US customs' seizures of cocaine averaged only 1,300 kilograms a year during the Turbay Ayala government (that was, even so, four times the 1974 figure), bank deposits in Miami were bulging from the sales of the drug. By 1979, the Federal Reserve Bank of Miami was reporting a cash surplus of $5.5 billion – greater than the total surplus of all other Federal Reserve Bank branches in the United States. Property prices leaped. At the same time, between 1979 and 1981, the number of murders in Miami nearly doubled; up to 40 per cent were reported to be drug related.

If there were any single moment in the cocaine trade that signalled the sheer scale of US impotence and Colombian cynicism and audacity, it was the voyage of the Colombian navy's flagship, the yacht *Gloria*, in 1976. The yacht set sail from the Caribbean port of Cartagena in May in order to participate in the United States' bicentenary independence celebrations in New York. It was laden with cocaine.

The first arrests occurred upon its arrival in Miami. A sailor and a non-commissioned officer were detained aboard after 6 kilograms of cocaine were found in the ventilation system. The spectacular, square-rigged yacht – which enjoyed diplomatic immunity – came under US surveillance after the arrests in Mexico of four suspected Colombian drug traffickers. These included Gilberto Arboleta and Elizabeth Giraldo, from Envigado; Arboleta and another prisoner were accused of a quadruple killing in New York. Strangely – unless they were tortured – they admitted to collaborating in a cocaine shipment on the *Gloria*. The Mexican information had then been relayed to the boat captain and the discovery made near Miami. However, it was quickly claimed that the yacht carried vastly more cocaine. The world was now alerted.

A fortnight later, on 19 June, it was reported in Colombia that, after the finding of two more loads while the *Gloria* cruised off the North American coastline, a total of 30 kilograms of cocaine had been seized aboard her. Each time, the cocaine was reported to have been discovered by the crew; some of it was disguised as coffee. Another 10 kilograms was 'found' a month later – hidden under the deck – while the *Gloria* was anchored at Boston. Three days afterwards it was reported that 10 more kilograms had been seized and two more people arrested. 'I feel very proud of the *Gloria's* participation in this celebration,' said Colombia's former president and ambassador in the United States, Julio César Turbay Ayala, as the yacht sailed up New York's Hudson River for the bicentennial naval parade.

The man who became the initial scapegoat for the affair was a warrant officer, Genaro Arias Londoño, who had been named by the traffickers caught in Mexico and who openly insinuated that senior officers were involved. Other crew members told *El*

Espectador that cocaine had been discovered only because, in the first instance, the ventilation system had been specifically mentioned, and later, because of insistent US pressure. The newspaper also claimed to possess documents showing that the ship's captain, Rafael Martínez, had been warned of the existence of the cocaine cargo by the regional naval commander in Cartagena before its departure, and that the regional head of the state security police, DAS, had also been aware of it. Meanwhile, a US newspaper, *La Prensa*, claimed that US authorities had found as much as 150 kilograms of cocaine aboard and that the matter had been hushed up by all sides. Years later, Escobar himself claimed that only 30 per cent of the shipment was seized.

Gilberto Alboreta, who was freed soon after the scandal, was famed to be the main organizer. Alboreta had a reputation as a vulgar, womanizing killer who had fled to Envigado on the run from police in New York. Alboreta was directly linked with Pablo Escobar. His lover, Elizabeth Giraldo, was a beautiful, ambitious, middle-class girl, whose sister was the lover of a good friend of Escobar's, Jorge Tulio, who sold Escobar the Nápoles estate before dying in an aircrash. Furthermore, according to friends of Tulio, after Alboreta was shot dead in an Envigado bar called El Paraíso, Elizabeth had an affair with Escobar as well.

The *Gloria* incident highlighted the dilemma of the US State Department. Colombia's bluff could not be called. In a country where the cocaine trade penetrated the highest echelons of the government and armed forces, an all-out crusade against cocaine could not be waged without sacrificing bilateral relations. Yet Colombia, which was in a strategically vital geographical position in the Americas, had proved itself a staunch US ally in Pan-American affairs. Its strong anti-Communist stance was at its most valuable in bringing South American pressure to bear on the Cuban dictatorship of Fidel Castro, who supported Colombian guerrillas. Neither was Colombia a friend to the Sandinistas in Nicaragua, with whom it also had an historic dispute over some islands in the Caribbean. Hence, the United States' wider political considerations – principally its desire to stamp out Communism on its doorstep but also simply its unwillingness to risk a full-blown international confrontation over the issue – strangled the work of the Drug Enforcement Administration, which would never be allowed to expose the full ramifications of the cocaine trade within the Colombian government. It would only be able to chase targets that were non-politically sensitive.

The first compromise was apparently struck in September 1979. Allegedly in exchange for letting President Turbay Ayala off the hook, the United States secured an extradition treaty under which any Colombian who sent the country a cocaine shipment could be arrested and tried in the USA even though he had never set foot there. One Colombian journalist, Fabio Castillo, whose book *Los Jinetes de la Cocaine, The Cocaine Cowboys*, was the first and bravest exposé of the Colombian cocaine trade, wrote that 'according to diverse and very widely spread accounts' Turbay Ayala had endorsed the treaty in exchange for the concealment of evidence linking him with emerald smugglers as well as for the archiving of the so-called Bourne Memorandum. The latter document was a list of Colombian traffickers which had been drawn up in 1977 by the White House drugs adviser, Peter Bourne. The following year, Turbay Ayala, then a presidential candidate, along with two cabinet ministers, was implicated in drugs trafficking by a US television programme, *60 Minutes*.

The treaty was approved by the Colombian Congress in October 1980 in spite of a strong, mafia-inspired political opposition. However, President Turbay Ayala chose to leave its final promulgation to a presidental stand-in while he paid a three-day visit to the Dominican Republic. The lack of his signature was later to prove its death warrant when, bribed and threatened by the mafia as they were, the country's law lords debated the treaty's legitimacy. Under President Turbay Ayala, in the meantime, US extradition requests were simply ignored.

The inauguration of Ronald Reagan as US president in 1981 dramatically turned up the heat on Colombia's cocaine barons. However, in spite of all the money and manpower invested, the drugs war would always be more rhetorical than real. The war's demagogic, populist nature made it inevitable it would be sacrificed in favour of other, more traditional – if no less populist – priorities. On the one hand, it would be sacrificed in order to fight Communism in Central America or to protect US control of the Panama Canal. On the other hand, and with blissfully executed hypocrisy, drugs trafficking became coupled wherever possible with Communist guerrillas and governments in order to discredit them and justify some form of US intervention.

Alongside the growing political pressure from abroad, Colombia's cocaine traffickers were being confronted with a more immediate threat at home: left-wing and Communist guerrillas. By the late 1970s, the Revolutionary Armed Forces of Colombia (FARC), which had originally sprung up in the wake of *La Violencia* around peasant colonizers defending themselves from the predatory advances of rich landowners, had expanded into the vast fertile lands of the valley of the river Magdalena in the departments of Antioquia and Santander. Their expansion in the region coincided, and in some part was a response to, the bullying by the land-greedy cocaine mafia. As elsewhere, the FARC's eleventh front (by 1983 it had twenty-seven fronts nationally) endeavoured to protect the peasants and to extort money from the bigger landowners. Pablo Escobar's Nápoles ranch dominated one side of the river near Puerto Triunfo; José Gonzalo Rodríguez Gacha's lands dominated the other side near Puerto Boyacá. Neither man took kindly to the FARC.

At the same time, Colombia's youngest guerrilla group, M-19, whose roots were urban and middle class, was beginning to expand not only in Cali and Medellín but also into rural areas, including Antioquia. Its spectacular actions included stealing the sword of Simón Bolívar, the hero of independence; removing 5000 weapons from a Bogotá army barracks; and seizing the Dominican Republic embassy along with thirteen ambassadors and the Papal Nuncio. But M-19's speciality was ransom kidnapping to fill its war chest, and the cocaine traffickers were targets. Again, Colombia's drugs mafia suddenly discovered they had joined the ranks of the bourgeoisie.

Pablo Escobar had already built up a posse of personal enforcers whose own neighbourhood gangs carried out any contract murder he ordered. According to a police informant, among the group's rules and prohibitions were that nobody who received a murder contract could tell their colleagues or anybody else about it. Direct talks with the victim's relatives were also forbidden, as were contracts conducted for anybody outside the group and hits carried out for personal reasons if they risked damaging the organization. The rules derived from the Italian mafia, with which Escobar and other Colombian drug traffickers came to have a fixation. From being primarily concerned with the application of internal discipline within the traffickers' own, black-market world, it was only a short step to punishing those who encroached on it. As Escobar and the others grew ever richer, so did the need to defend themselves and so did their self-righteousness. Not inclined to remain on the defensive, they soon moved on to the attack and used exemplary violence to intimidate others. It was the guerrillas who took the brunt, at least initially.

Probably the first of the Medellín mafia to be subjected to a guerrilla robbery was Rodríguez Gacha, nicknamed 'The Mexican' because of his obsession with Mexican culture and successful launch of drug routes there. Rodríguez Gacha was held up by a FARC column in the department of Meta. He escaped. Carlos Lehder also escaped after catching a bullet in the back while running away from M-19. The so-called 'German–Colombian investor' was consequently treated like a hero in his home town of Armenia. Kidnappings of other traffickers from Cali and Bogotá proved more effective; several were forced to pay ransom. However, it was M-19's seizure of Jorge Luis Ochoa's youngest sister, Marta Nieves, in November 1981, that finally spurred the traffickers into concerted action.

At the invitation of the Ochoas, and at the instigation of the arch-kidnapper himself, Escobar, dozens of Colombia's top cocaine and marijuana traffickers – including those from Cali – were summoned for a landmark summit conference in Medellín.

Although kidnapping was at the top of the agenda, the meeting held much deeper significance. For the first time, contacts between the drug barons were cemented on a national scale. Not only was there an exchange of information but operational zones within Colombia were also carved up, along with routes and markets. Strategies and tactics were discussed – as well as the implications of the recently signed treaty of extradition.

Thirteen years later, in between packing his suitcases for Paraguay where he had recently been appointed Colombia's ambassador, the man who bore the full brunt of the traffickers' offensive against the state described the importance of that Medellín summit. General Miguel Antonio Gómez Padilla, the former director general of the national police, said: 'The conference consolidated the links between the traffickers and confirmed the leadership of Escobar and the others from Medellín. Their mutual struggle against kidnapping and extradition effectively unified Colombia's traffickers. It let them forget about the fight over markets, for a while.'

One Sunday in early December 1981, the drugs mafia bared their teeth. At the start of a soccer match in Cali between the local team, América, and Nacional, from Medellín – the former owned by the Rodríguez Orejuelas and the latter by Escobar and his cronies – leaflets fluttered down from a small aircraft into the stadium. The leaflet proclaimed the launch of an organization called *Muerte a Secuestradores*: Death to Kidnappers. It claimed that 223 top Colombian 'businessmen' had agreed to form a common defence group whose objective was 'the public and immediate execution of all those involved in kidnappings'. The victims would be 'hung from all the trees in public parks or shot and marked with the sign of our group – MAS'.

Although MAS did not observe the letter of its hyperbole, it more than matched its spirit. Within two months its assassins had killed dozens of M-19 leaders and militants in Antioquia as well as elsewhere. M-19's Antioquia chief was discovered stripped and bound in a Bogotá car-park, many guerrillas were turned over to the security forces and it was reported that the army itself accompanied MAS on some raids. In February 1982, the Ochoa sister was released, albeit allegedly for a small ransom and, apparently, after the mediation of Fidel Castro and Manuel Noriega. M-19 did not kidnap the traffickers again. On the contrary, the traffickers and M-19 were soon to form an alliance.

The creation of MAS, which, if its manifesto was to be believed, involved more than 2,200 men, was the mafia's first experience of running a jointly funded national paramilitary organization. Although its success left its original objectives quickly outmoded, it gave the traffickers a big boost in self-confidence as well as a public image of rather mythical invincibility. MAS also sowed the seeds of a much more sinister group in the valley of the river Magdalena: ACDEGAM, the acronym for a right-wing death squad based in Puerto Boyacá which systematically murdered left-wing leaders suspected of links with the FARC guerrillas. It was ACDEGAM (the Peasant Association of Farmers and Cattle Ranchers of the Middle Magdalena valley) that spawned the schools of hired assassins who by the end of the decade were plunging Colombia into a blood-bath and threatening the rule of central government.

CHAPTER THREE

IN PURSUIT OF POLITICAL POWER (1978–84)

They were convent girls, sixteen or seventeen years old. After saying goodbye to the nuns at the end of the school day, they would walk out of La Presentación, which was the most prestigious girls' school in Envigado, and make for the street corner. There, they were met by glossy, extra-large landrovers whose drivers' plans did not include assistance with their homework. Still in their pleated blue skirts, the girls were whisked out of town. Their destinations were the innumerable ranches of *los mafiosos,* men who in exchange for a few favours bathed them in gold, jewels, dollars and *perica* (cocaine). Not only was it profitable, but it was a lot more fun than double equations or the letters of St Paul. And it gave them status amongst their peers.

The girls were paid to satisfy the traffickers' every whim. Although they were sworn to secrecy, the mafia's orgies became the stuff of legend. Envigado's moral upper crust muttered darkly to itself about prostitution, sodomy and lesbianism. A mafia driver described one party with the school girls: 'They were made to strip at the top of the stairs then to slide naked down the rail. Everybody took it in turn to meet them at the bottom of the rail with their tongues.'

Envigado, the former model of old-fashioned Catholic values, the prosperous and historically élitist town whose vigorous democratic tradition had yielded some of Colombia's finest intellectuals, was sucked into a whirlpool of moral decline. Initially, in the late 1970s, Envigado had rejected the council candidates backed by Pablo Escobar because it knew where his money came from and, as one former councillor remarked, 'was not yet bought up'. By the early 1980s, however, several councillors were under his thumb. The most dangerous would prove to be an aggressive, unprepossessing man called Jorge Mesa, who initially rode on the back of his more charismatic political mentor, René Mesa (no relation), a former Escobar ally and congressman who was murdered in March 1987. During Mesa's mayorship a reign of terror was established. Between the municipal police – the Department of Security and Control – and the mafia's own hit men, outsiders were rapidly spotted and identified. Unwanted ones were simply shot dead; so, too, were beggars, thieves and, ironically, sellers of the deadly addictive *basuko* or cocaine paste.

Darting worried glances at the flat above as she spoke, one Envigado teacher recalled much later: 'No one spoke about the mafia. If you did you were dead. You still are! The atmosphere was very heavy. Big jeeps roamed the streets, men entered shops showing their weapons. They were often from poor families who had got rich overnight and killed you just because they did not like you, or held a grudge, or because you hooted at their driving. We literally hid. Envigado filled up with strange, vulgar people covered in gold chains, with women who were overdressed in exotic clothes. All the best cafés were choked by mafia bodyguards, the churches too. They just took over the place.'

Night-time was the worst. The formerly tranquil main square heaved with landrovers and motorcycles; its cafés and clubs roared with drunken *sicarios* and *mulas*, many from the bordering towns of Itagüí and La Estrella. Football games were regularly played until after midnight on the floodlit pitches donated by Escobar, especially in his homebase neighbourhoods of La Paz and El Dorado, where commentary was belted out over 1,200-watt loudspeakers for the benefit of those who were unable to watch the game because they were trying to go to sleep. 'The police would not do anything,' shrugged one nearby resident. 'And if you complained, they were more interested in knowing who you were, in order to have you lynched.'

The carnival bullying and abandon of ill-educated and cash-engorged delinquents was modelled on the mafia leaders. The same man who ordered convent girls to slip naked down his stair-rail had a famous Brazilian transvestite forcibly stripped of his underwear in the middle of his act. 'J M' and his guests wanted to check out the genitals. The wife of the congressman René Mesa, Cecilia, who was also suspected of murdering her husband and was eventually murdered herself and whose murderer, 'Berracol', was murdered in turn by José Gonzalo Rodríguez Gacha ('The Mexican') as a favour for her orphaned daughter, was famed for snorting cocaine, organizing orgies and appearing naked whenever and wherever she could. 'It was Bacchanalia,' said one woman. 'What had been a good Christian community was sodomized by the devil.'

Escobar himself liked his fun, too. At one of his birthday parties, it was reported that fourteen new Renault cars were lined up as prizes for girls who completed a series of dares. These included shaving their heads, eating a cockroach and wriggling up a palm tree in the nude. All the prizes were won.

'Money was all that mattered,' whispered one priest. 'Social, family, religious and civil values were simply cashed in. Boys and girls prostituted themselves and their parents didn't care where the money came from – they became very permissive. It had nothing to do with economic necessity, although there arose the idea that it was better to be rich for a short time than poorish for ever. The mafia was fashionable. Ostentation was fashionable. You were what you were worth so you flaunted it.'

While Escobar collected classic cars – particularly those associated with the Chicago gangster era of the 1920s and 1930s (in whose homage he riddled a vintage Chevrolet saloon with machine-gun bullets and parked it beside his Nápoles drive) – ancient Chinese vases and Old Masters, his average imitator was rather less discriminating. Original paintings, usually in bright, lurid colours depicting voluptuous women or seaside sunsets, were snapped up in the belief that anything original was intrinsically valuable; artistic merit as a concept was a complete enigma. Small, nondescript houses were suddenly caked with gold-plated taps and marble floors; crystal tables gleamed beside huge, shiny, chromium-framed chairs that were dwarfed in turn by immense televisions; stuffed deer heads peered out of the walls. Everything possible shone.

One Medellín artist said: 'Art prices went mad. The mafia were mostly ignorant people and liked to leave it up to their decorators to advise them. They wanted anything that was big and extravagant, which was the very opposite to the austerity typical of Antioquia.' The Ochoa brothers – Jorge Luis, Juan David and Fabio – whose main base was also in Envigado, came from respected family stock more attuned to regional traditions. But they were equally indulgent. When not running operations from the 120,000-hectare estate they had bought in northern Colombia, La Veracruz, they lived it up with champagne, caviar and orchestras outside Envigado. 'We all used to go to their parties,' said the artist. 'They were our friends, linked to us bohemians. And their women were upper class and beautiful. It all seemed so innocent.'

At the same time, there reigned a conspiracy of silence. 'Everybody knew who was who and doing what, and that if you spoke about it aloud you would be punished,' said the priest. He added: 'Don't use anybody's name in the town because you could be signing their death certificate.' By May 1989, when Envigado's municipal police force was dissolved, it was estimated to have murdered at least 450 people. Its downfall came with the revelations of a woman who was chopped up with an axe and survived to tell the tale. However, its involvement with Escobar, Bertha Inés Mejía – Escobar's main council ally – and Jorge Mesa remained judicially unproven. Nobody was prepared to bear witness to what everybody knew. Terror, money and complicity sealed their mouths. The triumvirate's power stayed intact.

Meanwhile, a curious alliance between Escobar, who was elected a local councillor in 1982, and a much respected Medellín industrialist, Diego Uribe, who was nominated mayor of Envigado a year later, revolutionized the town's finances. 'The municipality was broke when I arrived,' said Uribe. 'With the support of Escobar and at the cost of alienating my own party we raised all the taxes, paid all the debts and tripled the budget within ten months.' Drug-rich Envigado, which was already the base for important industrial and commercial groups whose presence it continued to attract, comfortably weathered the storm and even introduced unemployment subsidies. By 1986 Envigado had the highest budget per capita in Colombia. Nevertheless, according to one municipal administrator – who by the early 1990s had seen one third of his college class-mates become linked to and then killed by the mafia – Escobar himself was famed for not paying his taxes on time.

Escobar was now a national as well as a local celebrity. In April 1983, Colombia's main news magazine, *Semana,* had run a profile on Escobar dubbing the drugs lord a *paisa* Robin Hood. The alleged sources of his wealth – the lottery, car dealing and wise investments in real estate – went unquestioned. The word cocaine went unmentioned. And although the article asserted that 'since nearly three years ago many feel that almost nothing takes place in [Antioquia] without his direct or indirect participation', no reference was made to Escobar's massive, national, financial contributions in the 1982 presidential and congressional electoral campaigns. Perhaps this was not so surprising. The magazine's main owner was Felipe López, the son of the former president, Alfonso López Michelsen, who had stood again as presidential candidate for the Liberal Party.

López Michelsen had allegedly met privately the previous year with Escobar, Jorge Luis Ochoa and his brother Fabio, as well as with other drugs traffickers such as Lehder and the Mexican. In a suite at Medellín's Hotel Intercontinental, the Liberal heavyweight was rumoured to have personally received a campaign donation of 26 million pesos. The money, which was worth about

$400,000, represented more than a quarter of the Liberals' departmental campaign budget. If the rumours were true, it was accepted in the full knowledge of who the donors were; before allying himself with López Michelsen's former justice minister, Alberto Santofimio, Escobar had already been publicly expelled by the rival Liberal faction, New Liberalism, to which he had originally attached himself.

Also present, according to a Liberal Party activist close to López Michelsen, was Ernesto Samper, who was openly in favour of legalizing the marijuana trade and became president in 1994. Although López Michelsen's attendance lasted about ten minutes, Samper's discussions with the traffickers lasted for nearly half an hour. 'Ernesto wanted to know how big the drugs trade was in Colombia,' said the Liberal activist. 'Alfonso left because he was uncomfortable.' The meeting had been requested by Federico Estrada, a senator who was one of Antioquia's three Liberal leaders. Estrada was a lawyer from the University of Medellín, which Escobar had made the heart of his legal and political apparatus. The senator was murdered in May 1990, while acting as the campaign leader in Antioquia for the next president, César Gaviria. Estrada was an office partner of Jairo Ortega, the lawyer who was elected to the House of Representatives in March 1982, with Escobar as his substitute (and who was re-elected to Congress in 1986).

In the *Semana* article, a diamond Rolex-wristed Escobar was described as possessing ten airplanes, half a dozen helicopters and 200 apartments in the United States. To explain his wealth – cited at around $5 billion by the magazine – he said: 'At sixteen years old I was the owner of a bicycle rental business; I dedicated some years to the lottery, then I got into the buying and selling of cars, and, finally, I ended up dealing in property.' Escobar sold himself as a lifelong philanthropist. Of his schooldays, he declared: 'I didn't have any money but as a community action member of my *barrio*, I promoted the collective construction of a school and the creation of a fund for poor students.'

The week before the article was published Escobar had staged a forum on extradition. The transfer of Colombians to the United States to face trial for offences committed there was, he claimed, 'a violation of national sovereignty'. The forum was opened by none other than Father Elías Lopera – a member of Escobar's civic works committee, *Civismo en Marcha,* and a frontman for the apparently tyrannical Archbishop Alfonso López Trujillo, who had been made a cardinal three months earlier. The forum was held in a recently opened night-club, Kevin's, which was owned by José 'Pelusa' Ocampo, a close colleague of Escobar's. Lopera occasionally officiated as chaplain at Ocampo's vast estate around the town of Necoclí on the Gulf of Urabá (from where Ocampo exported cocaine).

Kevin's symbolized the binge-and-blow-out mentality of Medellín's drugs boom. Even its inauguration had to be postponed because its windows were shattered by a soundcheck. According to a witness, the circular walls of glass with panoramic views of the city below disintegrated under the several thousand watts pumped out by the loudspeakers. The discotheque was a gaudy labyrinth of black, white and chrome. It was the most fashionable place in town. Among the string of upright citizens who found themselves rubbing shoulders there with the mafia in 1983 was Diego Uribe, then mayor of Envigado, who, according to a mafia doorman, attended a concert by the Spanish singer Rafael when Escobar was among the guests of honour.

Escobar's economic and political power made him a force almost impossible for Colombia's leaders to ignore – not only before he was exposed as a ruthless killer, but afterwards too. By then, however, it would be too late for many: they would be compromised and trapped within his net. Betrayal, in the mind of Escobar, was a cardinal sin punishable by death or ransom-kidnap.

The drug lord's emergence into national political life alongside Alberto Santofimio, who had been jailed on fraud charges, and Jairo Ortega, occurred in the full knowledge of the Colombian business élite as to the source of his wealth. Whereas in 1978 Escobar's campaign contributions to both sides were relatively discreet, and his occupation mainly known only to Antioquia's congressmen and leading businessmen, as well as to central party leaders, by the turn of the decade his activities were common currency on the Medellín cocktail party circuit. A senior Liberal organizer, himself photographed at a party with Gustavo Gaviria, said: 'It was a secret that everybody knew. Almost every big businessman in Medellín – and in Bogotá and Cali – had had some relationship with Escobar at some time. The traffickers were buying up the best land in the country and very few people refused to sell. We realized during the campaigns in 1981 that Escobar and his people were on their way to taking over Colombia. No politician, with very few exceptions, could prosper without their money. There was a permissiveness around and it was kind of normal to accept it, so both presidential campaigns and almost all congressional candidates did so.'

According to the same source and to evidence given by Lehder in the Noriega trial, the meeting at the Hotel Intercontinental with López Michelsen only took place because the Liberals 'were sure that Escobar's cousin Gustavo Gaviria had just given 200 million pesos' (more than $3 million) to Belisario Betancur, the Conservative candidate leading a coalition, at a breakfast in a private house in Bogotá. Not that the Liberals were necessarily hard done by: Carlos Lehder claimed that during his campaign López Michelsen had received two payments from the Medellín cartel amounting to $920,000. 'Two airplanes and a helicopter were loaned to him to travel throughout the country,' Lehder told a US court. 'He was also given ten new vehicles for his committee, with the drivers and costs totally paid for.'

Initially, Escobar's political group placed itself under Luis Carlos Galán, a young Liberal reformer seen by many people, in rather an erroneous and romantic fashion, as the true inheritor of the mantle of the assassinated Gaitán. Although little attention was paid at the time, Galán had expelled him in February 1982, in what amounted to the first public challenge to Escobar's reputation.

From 1981, aided by his priests and with the backing of two

radio stations he owned, Escobar started to build up a powerful support base beyond Envigado in the poorer districts of Medellín and nearby municipalities. The 'Robin Hood' showered money around in such a way as to become an instant local legend. Apart from building floodlit soccer pitches (he played in the opening matches), Escobar gave away tractors and bulldozers, and planted trees. He gave out cash directly to widows, cripples and the most needy, sometimes to all who asked. Tales of Escobar's generosity spread like wildfire. Of how, after receiving a letter from a woman who lived under a bridge with her two children, he had bought her a house. Of how, on passing a *peón* (farmhand) labouring in a field, he had sent for the farmer, bought the land and given it to the *peón*.

'You tell me how many rich people are that generous,' challenged Francisco Flores, one of the original inhabitants of the Pablo Escobar district, where Escobar built 160 houses and gave them to families who had previously lived in hovels beside Medellín's municipal rubbish dump. 'Only a man like Pablo Escobar would do these things, noble and simple like the poorest of the poor.'

One day, the story went, Escobar had turned up with some friends at the rubbish tip on the side of the river. Along with the rats and the dogs scouring for scraps were the multitudes of vultures, strangely ubiquitous in Colombia, their black and bloated bodies scuffling for meat bones. Escobar, after looking upwards for a while at the huts built out of the debris, and at the human figures, young and old, crouched over it and searching for food, was moved to say, 'Blessed God, I have to do something for these people.' 'What are you thinking of doing?' said his friends. 'I am going to organize these poor beggars,' he answered, 'I am going to buy land and I am going to build on it, so that these beggars can go and live there.' And so it was. The land was bought and builders and materials were provided and the houses were built and the poor beggars moved in.

'What government has ever, ever done anything like that?' said Francisco Flores, watering his garden. A gold-coloured card with a newspaper photograph of Escobar stuck on it was perched just inside his door. 'Don Pablo was the father of the poor in Medellín, in Antioquia and in many areas. We are orphans without him. Christ was persecuted because he did miracles, and Don Pablo because he did favours for the poor.' Every two weeks, the drugs lord had sent a lorry load of food and supplies to share out amongst the families in the neighbourhood.

Escobar was already going ahead with the housing project when he discovered that Flores' wife, Irene Gaviria, was a second cousin. Irene, the daughter of a half-brother of the father of Escobar's mother, Hermilda, said: 'Don Pablo was inaugurating a football pitch in La Moravia [near the rubbish dump] when we worked out the link. He hugged me and said we would be the first to get a house and we would never be in need.' She recalled how, during *La Violencia* in the 1950s, Hermilda had made a vow before the Niño Jesús de Atocha in their mutual birthplace, the village of Frontino, in north-west Antioquia. Alongside young Pablo, Hermilda had sworn that if God saved her family from the Liberals she would one day build a chapel in the Niño Jesús de Atocha's name. That vow was fulfilled in the Pablo Escobar district: a few metres away from the Flores' home, there stands a neat, brick chapel. It is dedicated to the Niño Jesús de Atocha.

By the time he was building the houses, Escobar was already a member of Congress. Medellín's main newspaper, *El Colombiano*, the second biggest, serious daily in Colombia, remained not only mute about Antioquia's latest public celebrity – from whom it received ample, weekly advertising – but, apparently, at his beck and call. Its article describing the housing project was a masterful exercise in factual chicanery conspiring to hide the truth and to speed up local government co-operation. 'The money has been collected via public shows,' it ran, 'such as . . . a bull fight . . . however, individuals have made important contributions. The only thing that could delay completion would be the delay by the official authorities.'

The article appeared almost word for word in Escobar's own

publication, *Medellín Cívica*, which proclaimed itself 'Colombia's first ecological newspaper' and was edited by a relative. The same issue, which featured a photograph of Father Elías Lopera greeting the Pope, carried a column by Escobar denouncing deforestation. The article's headline could not have been more ironic. While people were getting rich turning a blind eye to his cocaine trafficking, and getting killed if they did not, the headline ran: 'Crime without Witness'.

On the outskirts of Medellín, at the end of the so-called golden mile of gleaming, ultra-modern office blocks whose grandeur and self-confidence put Bogotá to shame, and just before Envigado, lies the seat of the Antioquia élite. The lush grounds of the Club Campestre sprawl for several hectares up into the hills, the main club house a proud, white colonial-style building whose rustic luxury epitomizes traditional *paisa* values and ideals. It bespeaks status. It is status.

The sun shone gloriously behind me as Fernando Arboleda, the manager, received me in his office. Sports trophies lined the shelves. The committee's long, shiny wooden table stood along one wall. Impeccably elegant and charming, Arboleda invited me to review the club records for the years 1982 and 1983. I declined. To have accepted his offer would have been discourteous, to have doubted his word; and, judging from the livid response my inquiry had already provoked elsewhere, the information I was seeking would in any case have been magically deleted long before his time.

Pablo Escobar had applied to join the club. The club now denied it. Two people with whom I had spoken clearly recalled the application posted on the notice-board. One of them, a member whose father had for several years been a highly respected and senior member of the committee, said: 'It was there for all to see, just like anyone else's.' However, he was unable to remember the names of the proposers.

What my friend did remember well were his father's reports

as to the fate of Escobar's application. Under the club rules, one negative vote by a committee member was sufficient for the applicant to be turned down. Escobar received two or three such votes, one of which was deposited by my friend's father. The remaining committee members of Antioquia's most exclusive club, which prides itself on admitting only the finest and most honourable families of the region, had endorsed the application of a known cocaine trafficker.

An office secretary employed at the time confirmed to me that Escobar had applied to the club between 1982 and 1983; that he was refused by the administrative committee; and that his dossier had been filed in the folder of 'rejected applications'. With refreshing honesty, she added: 'Pablo Escobar was a person who did a lot of bad things but a lot of good things, depending who you were. In those days he was a politician who had his problems with drugs trafficking but was not very badly viewed here in Colombia.'

One woman club member, from Medellín, said: 'When I was seventeen years old, it was an honour to be a friend of the *mafiosos*. Several of my school-friends were given gold chains and jewels by Pablo and the others. One of them ended up cut up into little pieces in the United States, I don't know what for. People bought into the mafia's loads – someone would hear of a portion of a shipment, they would split the finance, say, five ways, and hand the cash to an intermediary. In a certain time they would get back two or three times their money. The mafia was totally accepted.'

In revenge for being turned down by the club, Escobar was reputed to have subsidized a four-month strike of its staff in 1984. One of his Envigado cronies, Gilberto Saldarriaga, a former Club Campestre golf caddy who had smuggled emeralds before moving into cocaine, responded to his rejection in a more baroque manner. He tried to buy the club. Rebuffed, he built his own.

In spite of corroborating the whitewash regarding Escobar's application, the club's manager Arboleda admitted that a number of 'daddy's boys' at the 1,300-member club had invested in cocaine shipments. He added that, in the early 1980s, there existed a permissive attitude towards the mafia: that, in the eyes of some, the traffickers, too, had turned into 'figures of status'.

Alfonso López Trujillo was made a cardinal in February 1983. A student friend of Camilo Torres, the Communist priest who was killed fighting with the guerrillas of the National Liberation Army (ELN), of which he was a leader, López Trujillo was at the opposite extreme. Yet, by the end of the 1970s, his fervent, militaristic anti-Communism, with his scaremongering about the Communist menace in the Church's midst, was widely seen as a means to ingratiate himself with the new Pope as much as to intimidate the Colombian Church into bending to his will. He quickly endeared himself to the president, Julio César Turbay Ayala, by annulling the president's thirty-two-year-old marriage to his cousin – they were by now grandparents – on an ecclesias- tical technicality.

So hated was López Trujillo that 280 priests threatened to resign from their parishes if he were made archbishop of Bogotá. Around the same time, in 1977, the archbishop whom López Trujillo was trying to ease out, Cardinal Aníbal Muñoz Duque, reportedly told a group of priests in Rome: 'Don't speak to me about that son of a prostitute; [consecrating López Trujillo as bishop] is the biggest sin I have committed in my life.' López Trujillo was finally persuaded to accept the lesser archbishopric of Medellín. To enhance his prestige, the Pope nominated him cardinal; never before had an archbishop of Medellín carried the title.

Leading a clergy that was proud of its historical and geo- graphical role in the development of liberation theology in Latin America – Medellín being the site of the 1968 bishops' conference that had drawn up what became known as the 'preferential option for the poor' – some kind of a clash was inevitable. But nobody could have been prepared for the viciousness that wrecked the pastoral work in his diocese at a moment when it was most needed and for which López Trujillo, directly and hierarchically, was ultimately responsible.

According to his enemies, the cardinal converted the Church into a business machine whereby priests were forced to squeeze as much money as possible out of their parishioners. Charges for baptisms, marriages, funerals, Catholic colleges and marriage annulments were sharply increased. One priest said: 'The cardinal took everything he could, demanding cash from everyone. He was always calling for parish quotas and even demanded we take out loans if we didn't have enough.' Magdalena Toro, a member of a lay Catholic group, *Signos de Vida,* claimed that parish priests were forced to hand over to the cardinal their cash as well as candelabra, oil paintings and other works of art.

While much of his clergy was determined to live humbly, López Trujillo – in great contrast with his immediate predecessors – was famed for his sumptuous tastes and habits. Serving French liqueurs at the seminary, and ordering fresh bars of soap to be laid out for him when he visited vicarages, hardly ingratiated him with priests who not only identified with the frugal *paisa* culture but also believed that to identify with the poor, and to live alongside them, was crucial to preaching the gospel. Neither did the cardinal's tendency to drive around in a large, black limousine with darkened windows accompanied by bodyguards.

Although the cardinal always denied he had any contact with Pablo Escobar, or with other drugs traffickers, there was abundant testimony indicating the contrary. Father Sierra, a keen bullfighting enthusiast, said: 'In December 1981 or 1982, in the bullring at [the town of] Girardota, a journalist showed me a letter he had received in which López Trujillo asked the journalist to put him in touch with Pablo Escobar.' Sierra said he was also told by a famous Medellín personality, a flamboyant homosexual nicknamed 'La Macuá' (macaw parrot) how the latter had brought back a pectoral cross as a gift from Pablo Escobar to the cardinal.

According to priests in Medellín, the pectoral cross was made of ebony. It was said to be studded with emeralds, pearls and diamonds. Although the cardinal claimed that it was a present from the Pope, Escobar's mother, Hermilda, confirmed to me that it was a gift from her son. Was it true, I asked her outside the jail where she had just visited her surviving son, Roberto, who had recently been blinded by a letter bomb, that López Trujillo had received the cross from Pablo? 'Yes, it is true,' she answered. A little later, near the drug lord's grave, she added: 'The cardinal asked for donations from my son and then turned into one of his worst enemies.' She would not elaborate. A nun came up and hugged her.

Escobar, who was also reputed to donate a communion chalice to the cardinal, was allegedly witnessed visiting him at the seminary around 1980. A priest from the town of Caldas claimed: 'I saw Escobar arrive with three or four jeeps, just before dark. He stepped out and was let into López Trujillo's residence. The priests living in the seminary said he visited him several times.'

Escobar was by no means the only drugs trafficker with whom the cardinal was implicated. According to Father Sierra and another priest related to the family, the Ochoas acceded to several of his requests for money. Finally, so the priests were told by the Ochoas, the family decided enough was enough. In response to an early morning call for a particularly huge 'loan', the cardinal was told: 'With great pleasure, but on the condition that you mortgage us the seminary.' The cardinal made them no further requests. Among past favours that priests said he had done for the Ochoas was to authorize a marriage on one of their private estates, the Hacienda Copacabana, after the local vicar refused because he claimed it to be illegal. Priests said that a bribe was paid.

The cardinal's bitterest foe was Father Pedro Nel Torres, who claims to have amassed more than a hundred files of documents implicating the cardinal and his allies in disreputable acts. Some of the jealously guarded files were shown to me amid great secrecy at a rendezvous in a rural vicarage. One typewritten sheet listed a few of the cases linking the Church to drugs traffickers. Thirteen priests were named as having taken gifts from Escobar.

Forty-eight priests were claimed to have received monthly cheques paid by one of Escobar's most senior lieutenants, Carlos 'Arete' Alzate, who organized contract killings from an office in the poor neighbourhood of Aranjuez; some of the priests were accused of working as mules. One priest in Caldas was accused of presenting Escobar at a political rally; a little later, it was said, the priest bought an expensive house in the town of Barbosa.

I was also shown a letter from churchgoers in the town of Fredonia, objecting to a 1 million peso or $14,000 donation received by their priest, Hernán Muñoz. The money was alleged to have been presented publicly by a notorious cocaine trafficker, Jaime Builes, in December 1982, in the presence of a delegate of the cardinal.

The cardinal was not the only high-ranking member of the Colombian clergy to be linked with drug traffickers. Bishop Darío Castrillón, of Pereira, openly accepted Church donations from Carlos Lehder, defending such gifts provided they went to the poor. The bishop, who later became Archbishop of Bucaramanga, was photographed with Lehder at the inauguration of Lehder's entertainment complex in the Quindio department in mid 1983, where he allegedly gave his blessing. Oddly enough, Lehder's first wife was reported to be related to López Trujillo.

As did Escobar once he entered Congress, so did the cardinal enjoy a certain level of judicial immunity. Under a treaty with the Vatican, Colombian bishops and their superiors were not subject to the Colombian penal justice system. The disaffected priests in Medellín, therefore, sent their complaints to the papal representative in Bogotá, Angelo Acerbi. However, instead of passing them on to the Vatican, it was believed that Acerbi returned them to the cardinal. Once they realized what had happened, up to forty priests fled the diocese. Complaints and requests for investigations were sent directly to the Vatican throughout the 1980s, but in vain. Only when the Colombian minister of foreign affairs intervened was the Vatican forced to act: in 1990, Acerbi was transferred to Hungary and López Trujillo summoned to Rome. The new papal representative, Paolo Romero, was greeted with a letter signed by scores of Antioquia priests in which they noted their 'great despondency' and pleaded for an archbishop who would 'modify the actual financial policy' and conduct himself 'without luxury, without ostentation'.

By early 1994 it was reported from Italy that Cardinal Alfonso López Trujillo, who was president of the Vatican's Commission for the Family, was among the five favourites to become the next Pope. Not only was he very close to John Paul II, but also to the head of the Congregation of Bishops, Cardinal Bernardin Gantín, a close friend of the Pope. 'He is giving banquets and presents as he always has done,' said Father Pedro Nel Torres. 'He will stop at nothing to achieve his ultimate ambition.' In spite of opposition from most Italian and Latin American bishops, López Trujillo was claimed – albeit in Colombian television reports – to be a papal front runner.

Meanwhile, in the first half of 1983, socially, politically, economically and ecclesiastically, Escobar was up with the gods. Cocaine was estimated by Colombian economists to be providing anything between 6 and 15 per cent of the country's gross domestic product and the traffickers in Medellín controlled the lion's share of the market. In spite of the city's industrial crisis its banks had remained awash with cash: indeed, their deposits had continued to increase. And unemployment, which in 1979 had been 65 per cent higher than the average for Colombian cities, was falling fast: by 1984 it was only 26 per cent higher.

The magnitude of the cocaine trade swept all before it. Or, as one Colombian columnist wrote, sucked inside all who came near it – like a black hole whose ever greater density emitted an ever more irresistible magnetic force. In a political culture where the buying of votes was very much the norm, a growing number of politicians not only felt unable to reject drug money if it were offered – which furthermore risked offending the donor – but were also obliged actively to seek it out if they were to have any chance of beating their electoral rivals. Honest politicians were brushed aside. And very shortly, politicians who adopted a public stance against 'hot money' were killed.

Ideological differences between the Liberal and Conservative parties were by now negligible, except for the latter's closer links with the Church. The parties had shared power ever since the end of *La Violencia*. Both represented the interests of Colombia's economic élite, interests which the congressmen endeavoured to square with legislation and government appointments that benefited their regions and their local political bosses – on whose electoral muscle they depended. There was no room for outsiders. Newspapers, radio and television news programmes were mainly owned or controlled by those whose families had dominated the political parties for decades.

Yet migration to the towns had broken the parties' traditional, geographic hold on local loyalties. The urban population more than doubled between the 1964 and 1985 censuses, at the expense of rural areas. Political affiliation, which had previously been an article of faith, became a matter of material favour instead. Even Francisco Flores, who had received the first house in the Pablo Escobar district, and whose life-long adoration of the drugs lord was thereby gained, said rather wistfully: 'At least in the past the violence was about *politics*.'

Material favour was what the cocaine traffickers could offer in abundance, either directly or through their Congress stooges. A political system that already operated on the basis of vote buying and influence peddling at the service of business interests was wide open to the approaches of Colombia's new breed of billionaires. That was all the more the case in a country so riddled with government corruption that the former president, Julio César Turbay Ayala, pledged during an electoral campaign to 'reduce immorality to its proper proportions'.

The attorney general recently elected by Congress, Carlos Jiménez Gómez, a surprise appointment from Antioquia and a good friend of President Belisario Betancur – whose brother, Juvenal Betancur, was later implicated in an international money-laundering case – described Colombian society as 'morally numb'.

Legal penalties, he said, 'lack repercussion, potentiality, exemplary capacity . . . in a society where nothing is bad, or where bad and good are interchangeable counters . . . Legal sanction without social sanction is an explosive without a detonator, a vehicle without wheels, a train without rails, pure junk, nothing'. At some point, Jiménez Gómez would become an interchangeable counter, too. He would switch from being attorney general to defence lawyer for the Ochoas.

The Liberal Party faction headed by Luis Carlos Galán, New Liberalism, which had expelled Escobar from its ranks and campaigned against the party's offical presidential candidate in 1982, fought to reform the party in order to eradicate its more nefarious electoral practices. It was the first to denounce drug money in politics. Enrique Parejo, a senator who advised Galán on criminal affairs, said: 'It was difficult because people were not against drugs trafficking. They had not yet realized the magnitude of the problem – the size of the trade, the danger to health, and how the traffickers wanted to use political power in their favour.'

Escobar's crucial error was not that he sought political power itself but that he sought it openly. Instead of remaining content with controlling the purse strings, he wanted to be out on the stage. Secretly, according to his friends, Pablo Escobar dreamed of being president. However, in the early 1980s there were forces noble and strong enough in Colombia to denounce a major cocaine trafficker, and a constitution and a political climate that helped the exposure to take place. Escobar's mistake was that he broke cover too soon. All that he gained in the short term were parliamentary immunity and a diplomatic visa to the United States. In only slightly longer a period, it allowed him to become the national and international symbol of cocaine trafficking. Although he relished that, it made him the number one target as well.

The United States' issue of a visa to Escobar in late 1982 was strange, to say the least. The Department of State had been informed a year earlier by the Drug Enforcement Administration that Escobar was among the 'top ten' Colombian cocaine traffickers. In getting his information, the DEA's first resident agent in Medellín, Errol Chavez, had been through a nightmare. His six informants were murdered. One of them, a cousin of Escobar, was found naked with six bullets in his back. Another, a member of the Ochoa family, had his eyes gouged out. A human tongue was thrown into Chavez's garden. He found his telephone to be heavily tapped. But in spite of his reports on Escobar, whose minions were meanwhile buying him millions of dollars of property in Florida, the US Embassy in Bogotá gave the drugs lord a visa on account of his parliamentary status. It later emerged that Escobar travelled freely to Miami, New York and Washington. Either the granting of the visa was a bureaucratic blunder, or, once again, the Department of State was not prepared to risk jeopardizing bilateral relations with Colombia by creating an open, diplomatic rumpus involving someone in government. Even if that person was suspected of being the world's biggest cocaine trafficker.

The cancerous spread of the drug traffickers' power within Colombian politics rapidly took root in the judicial system too, and throughout the public services. This was facilitated by the tradition of government jobs being divided up between the country's political groupings and distributed according to their local and congressional strengths. Mayors and departmental governors were at that time nominated according to similar criteria. Hence, although many were browbeaten by threats – and many were to be killed for standing up to those threats – a generation of public figures was soon to owe its careers to the mafia. The difference between them and Escobar was simply that, being smaller fish, the vast majority would escape national and international scrutiny. Some would rise to the top of the government.

One typical example was a young Medellín Liberal, Alvaro Uribe Vélez, a man accused of drug-related corruption as well as collaborating politically with Escobar in launching what became a successful public career – that would last long after Escobar's demise. A former head of the Aeronautica Civil, which was responsible for the country's airports and for granting pilot's licences, Uribe Vélez was, briefly, the mayor of Medellín during the government of President Belisario Betancur. The president was reported to have attended the funeral of his father, Alberto Uribe Sierra, who was known to be involved with the drugs traffickers and was murdered near his ranch.

I met Uribe Vélez in the basement dining-room of a Bogotá hotel in March 1994, to discuss politics and drugs trafficking. By that time he was a senator. One of the congressmen just elected under his political tutelage was William Vélez, who had been one of Escobar's first political allies in Envigado, receiving the drug baron's electoral backing until 1986. According to the senator's secretary, the senator had worked with William Vélez for between twelve and fifteen years.

It was when I mentioned the Vélez connection that the boyish, albeit rather superior, charm evaporated, along with the smile. Instead, his brow turned shiny with sweat and his eyes and mouth opened with amazement. He recovered in a split second, the smooth chatter about the need for 'an ethical rebirth' in Colombia dissolving into a vitriolic damnation of foreign journalists and a mockery of the millions of drug users in the United States and Europe. After he appeared to have calmed down a little, I asked him about his tenure as head of Aeronautica Civil.

That was it. A little man, he jumped up in fury and stormed past the waiters who were laying the tables for lunch, raced up the stairs and through a lobby, and did not stop until he had escaped into the arms of his bodyguards who had parked themselves outside on a terrace. Whereupon, thinking better about abandoning an on-the-record interview in such a manner, and surrounded by his bodyguards in order to back him up and to intimidate me, he insisted we continue.

'I am honest,' he repeated endlessly. I had never suggested otherwise. Somehow, the name of Federico Estrada cropped up – the senator who had patronized the electoral list that featured Escobar, and had organized his official party meeting with former President Alfonso López Michelsen and the actual presidential favourite, Ernesto Samper. In addition, Estrada had been photographed drinking whisky with Escobar's cousin, Gustavo Gaviria, before being murdered by the cartel when campaigning for the current president, César Gaviria (no relation to the former). I mooted loosely that Estrada had been a mafioso reputed to have distanced himself from his sponsors when things became tough.

A fist was suddenly shaking in my face. Behind it, Uribe Vélez was shouting that I was staining Estrada's honour and should retract my words immediately. The right fist was not just shaking, it was stabbing towards my chin (he couldn't reach as far as my nose). The bodyguard behind him took a step forward. I had no doubt that, unless I defused the senator's rage, he would hit me and that his entourage would beat me to pulp. And that I would be accused, perhaps judicially, of attacking the senator.

When, with pained politeness, I cited the photograph of Estrada with Escobar's cousin, which had surfaced alongside others that compromised senior Liberals, his sandy, brown-flecked eyes glowed with a sudden smugness. 'Ah! you didn't find me in those photos!' he said, pleased as punch. And we were off on to his reputation again. Given his aggression, his obsessive defensiveness, his ambition and his bodyguards, I deemed it prudent not to ask him about other claims.

Uribe Vélez, who at the turn of the 1990s was allowed into the United States to study at Harvard University, was a strong contender for the 1994 governorship of Antioquia, closely connected to Ernesto Samper, and hoped to be the Liberal presidential candidate in 1998 or 2002.

While Escobar was waging his civic campaigns in Medellín, Carlos Lehder launched his own political movement in the department of Quindío, the National Latin Movement, in March 1983. Unlike Escobar, whose early public declarations were restricted to his civic rallies and avoided all references to drugs, Lehder made cocaine trafficking his central political platform. Although the swaggering Lehder was considered a loudmouth by the rest of the top traffickers – and, as a transport provider, a second-tier trafficker at that – his views and attitudes, barring his fondness for Hitler, were shared. As with Escobar, it was Lehder's desire to be a public figure that would trigger his downfall. It meant that he carried the brunt of any offensive against the traffickers and enabled him to be made into a scapegoat – which would prove just as useful to his colleagues as it would to the Colombian and US governments.

In a published radio interview in June 1983, Lehder peppered his language with references to oligarchies and imperialism. It was the first nationwide broadcast of the traffickers' views, albeit wild and ridiculous in parts. Lehder claimed that the Colombian oligarchy was jealous because the profits from the cocaine and marijuana 'bonanzas' had been channelled towards 'the people'. The North Americans, he said, had been the ones who started off the Colombian marijuana trade, who consumed the drugs and who collectively raked in most of the profits. So why should they now be seeking the extradition of Colombians? Should they not rather be helping out Colombia's drug addicts instead? In the meantime, argued Lehder – apparently oblivious to the contradiction – Colombians only wanted to 'improve their position, do something for their country'. 'I am above material things,' added the man whose political party and Posada Alemana estate – comprising zoo, restaurants, discotheque and convention centre – claimed to employ 260 people. Lehder, who boasted that his party already had 10,000 members – enough to win him the Senate seat he coveted – repeatedly referred in glowing terms to the tax amnesty recently passed by President Betancur. This, he said, had allowed 'hot money' to be legalized. His only grudge with the president was that the traffickers were not being treated with quite as much latitude as the guerrillas, with whom the government was currently engaged in peace talks. Still, he had little reason to complain – yet.

Lehder, who also compared the cocaine traffickers with the Kennedy family in the United States, who made their fortune smuggling whisky during the time of prohibition, questioned the origins of the fortunes made by Colombia's political magnates too. Most vivid of all was his resentment of the USA, where he had been jailed, he said, because he was 'a leader of a Latin neighbourhood' and fought against police persecution, 'defending my race, my principles and my Colombianism'. He added: 'They say I conspired against the United States; I say that not only did I conspire but that I am conspiring and I will go on conspiring until the day the extradition treaty is cancelled.' After defending the right of people to 'take certain precautions' against being kidnapped – the cartel had set up its Death to Kidnappers Movement (MAS) – and noting that 'very big forces liquidated Gaitán', Lehder said that his party aimed to defend people who were 'extraditable' as well. Colombia was warned.

The argument that most big Colombian family fortunes were illicitly gained was put more explicitly in an anonymous, typewritten letter delivered later to General Miguel Antonio Gómez Padilla, then director general of the national police, by cocaine traffickers in Cali. It indicated five successive origins – colonial feudalism, the slave trade, tobacco and quinine smuggling, the expropriation of Church assets, and land-grabbing during *La Violencia* – before adding 'and now it's us . . . and our children will be the magnates of the future'. Unlike Lehder and Escobar, the Cali traffickers never sought a front-line political role. While Escobar would soon grow embittered that others enjoyed his money to grease their Congress careers whereas he was not only excluded but a hunted man, his Cali colleagues never suffered from such illusions. They were content with manipulating power from behind the scenes.

The battle over extradition was fuelled by the arrival of a tough, North American ambassador, Lewis Tambs, in April 1983. An ardent anti-Communist whose preferred strategy was the saturation persecution of unions and left-wing groups, together with the heavy military repression of the guerrillas, Tambs was the inventor of the term 'narcoguerrilla'. His determination to link drugs and Communism in Colombia was – at that time – a pernicious exaggeration. Although from the middle 1980s the rebels began to extort protection money from the traffickers in some areas, encouraged peasants to grow coca and built their own laboratories, it embraced a relatively small part of the trade. Focusing on the guerrillas distracted attention from the drug-related corruption eating away at the intestines of the state: its Congress, police, army, judicial system and other public entities. But the guerrillas were a softer, more North American target, even if Tambs's declarations tended to jeopardize President Betancur's peace process. However, the ambassador's energies were principally directed at persuading the president to implement the treaty on extradition.

The treaty, which had been signed and ignored by the previous government, was being ignored by President Betancur as well. The traffickers had, after all, helped bankroll the election of his Conservative government, which saw little wrong in cocaine trafficking and welcomed the profits for the economy; extradition was only going to cause trouble. However, in August 1983, under a pact with Luis Carlos Galán's dissident Liberal faction – which had denounced 'hot money' and expelled Escobar from its ranks – the president appointed one of its senators, Rodrigo Lara Bonilla, as minister of justice.

Lara Bonilla was murdered eight months later. With the United States breathing down his neck for the extradition of Lehder, who had been indicted in Florida, the minister had continued to denounce the impact of cocaine cash on politics, homing in on the movement of Alberto Santofimio, to which Escobar was affiliated. Stung by the attacks, the traffickers finally responded. It was Jairo Ortega, Escobar's Congress partner, who picked up the gauntlet. Accusing the minister of hypocrisy and double morality, he waved before Congress a cheque for 1 million pesos ($10,000) made out to Lara Bonilla by Evaristo Porras, a major Colombian importer of cocaine paste operating out of the Amazon port of Leticia, who had escaped from a Peruvian jail while held on drugs-trafficking charges.

Not only was the cheque authentic but a tape recording of a conversation between them indicated that Lara Bonilla knew the true occupation of Porras. The tape suggested that Lara Bonilla's true worry was not the ethical aspect of 'hot money' so much as the fact that it was bolstering the power of his Liberal adversary, Santofimio; and that Santofimio was reaping political dividends by becoming the main opponent of extradition. Porras presented himself as an opponent of Escobar's and an ally of Lara Bonilla's faction, the New Liberals. Nevertheless, it appeared that Lara Bonilla was tricked over the cheque itself, which was paid in through a family business. In a later judicial statement, Porras, who dismissed the Peruvian incident as a youthful caper and explained his current wealth by claiming – as Escobar had done – that he had won the lottery, said he had also given cash to President Betancur.

Lara Bonilla's response to Ortega in Congress was to accuse Escobar openly of drugs trafficking and of being a member of the Death to Kidnappers Movement (MAS). In the ensuing furore, the cheque was quickly forgotten. Lara Bonilla's rejection of two extradition requests – by way of gratitude for the president's private support – also went unnoticed. For the first time, Escobar's name and reputation were on public trial.

While Escobar initiated legal action against Lara Bonilla, the screws were turned tighter. A US television documentary accused Escobar of being Colombia's biggest drugs trafficker, worth about $2 billion. Escobar appeared on ABC television claiming that, were it not for 'hot money' or US dollars, Colombia would be suffering a grave economic crisis similar to those in other Latin American countries. Dressed in an open-necked shirt, Escobar appeared calm and relaxed as he vaunted 'all those benefits that can bring about employment for the Colombian people'. He claimed that he personally had made his fortune in the construction business.

The newspaper *El Espectador* not only gave the documentary front-page coverage but, five days later, on 6 September, pounced with a scoop from its own archives. It discovered a story from June 1976 with a photograph of Escobar after he had been arrested, along with his cousin Gaviria and others, in possession of 18 kilograms of cocaine in Itagüí. The case was still open. In a pathetically futile gesture, copies of the newspaper in Medellín were frantically bought up by Escobar's thugs in an effort to block the disclosure, which was shortly followed by the revelation that police and judges involved in the case had been threatened and murdered.

The traffickers' first golden age was over. Escobar himself would never have another one. By the end of September he had been officially abandoned by the political movement of Santofimio. In response to Santofimio's rejection, Escobar pointed out that he had built sports fields, schools and health centres long before he had entered politics, and that he had sought public office 'thinking only that from the administration one could offer a better service to the community and openly defend the people's budget'. An arrest warrant had also been issued against him and Gustavo Gaviria for the murder of the detectives in the 1976 case, although it was revoked on a legal technicality (the judge who issued the warrant, Gustavo Zuluaga Serna, was killed in October 1986). The car theft case was also uncovered, although the court-room files had been burned a few months earlier. Escobar's parliamentary immunity was lifted, too.

Meanwhile, a former minister of justice official, Jorge Edgardo González, who had appealed against Lara Bonilla's rejection of the extradition request for the two traffickers, was shot dead in his car. The murder provoked the resignation of the magistrates due to study the appeal. It was that killing which finally converted Lara Bonilla into an extraditionist – just when the Supreme Court had also approved the extradition of Lehder. 'The more I learn, the more I know of the damage that the *narcos* are causing the country,' said Lara Bonilla. 'I will never again refuse the extradition of one of those dogs. So long as Colombian judges fear drug traffickers, the drug traffickers will only fear judges in the United States.'

But, supported by the professed belief of his attorney general, Jiménez Gómez, that extradition was unconstitutional, the president ordered that the US' request for Lehder be rejected. Lara Bonilla refused to endorse the president's order. While the legal chicanery whirred ever more gently towards paralysis, Lehder revealed that Jiménez Gómez' private secretary, William Bedoya, had asked for 30 million pesos ($380,000) to get Lehder off the hook. Angry that two months had passed by without an investigation, Lehder released a tape recording of the incident. Bedoya was found dead a day or so later, poisoned.

Although the attorney general's office declared it to be suicide, both a senior policeman and a senior lawyer from the attorney general's office told me they believed that Bedoya was murdered and that the attorney general's office deliberately covered it up. The cover-up was said to have been arranged by Jaime Hernández, the attorney general's anti-drugs advisor. Alvaro López Dorado, the lawyer in the attorney general's office who eventually drew up the accusation against Escobar for the Lara Bonilla murder – and had to flee Colombia – said: 'Hernández' group got control over the attorney general by playing to his weaknesses – women and whisky – and then showing him money. DAS told me they had solid evidence Hernández was working with the mafia. I informed the attorney general but Hernández was promoted. Hernández' group killed the secretary and then organized the tale about suicide.'

Lara Bonilla was desperate to mend the damage to his reputation caused by the Porras cheque. Firmly backed by the head of the new anti-drugs unit, Colonel Jaime Ramírez, as well as the DEA, he launched Colombia's first true crusade against the cocaine trade. His fellow New Liberals, never mind the government itself, cowered away from the heat. Lara Bonilla was out there alone. Dozens of private aircraft were grounded and investigations were opened into several transport companies; most of the aircraft and companies concerned were believed to be controlled by Escobar and the Ochoas. The debate about Escobar's immunity plunged the two main parties into an acrid row about their own good names. And Escobar's court files were not the only things to vanish. He did too.

During the brief moments when the arrest warrant was valid and his parliamentary immunity was lifted, before more legal machinations closed the opportunity once again, Escobar was nowhere to be found. However, he did manage to be present at the inauguration of the floodlights he had donated to a football ground in the town of Puerto Berrío in the Magdalena Medio, which was now a haven for right-wing paramilitary forces killing left-wingers; the ground was named after the assassinated Liberal, Jorge Eliécer Gaitán. Escobar busied himself mainly with co-ordinating a campaign of intimidation against Lara Bonilla, whose telephone conversations were played back to him down the line. Death threats started. Although the minister directed the legal efforts to trap Escobar, he was blocked by one lawyer after another. One judge even criticized Lara Bonilla for 'his desire to moralize the country'.

The exposures and clampdown continued. Six football teams were named by Lara Bonilla as belonging to or being controlled by the mafia. Escobar was fined $5,000 for illegally importing his zoo animals, which were ordered to be sold off at auction. An arrest warrant was already out for Jorge Luis Ochoa on a similar offence – a few months earlier he had been condemned for smuggling in sixty fighting bulls. But by far the biggest blow to the cartel was the police raid on a gigantic complex of cocaine encampments in the jungle of the department of Caquetá. The complex was known as Tranquilandia.

Bugged ether was the key. Ether was the most important chemical in the production of cocaine. After getting wind of a Colombian order equivalent to nearly half the country's total ether imports in 1980, the DEA attached radio transmitters to two of the drums and followed the signals by satellite from Chicago to the Amazon. What they found was what the DEA's Colombia chief, Johnny Phelps, described as the 'Silicon Valley of cocaine'. Built around the confluence of two rivers and spread out over several miles were no fewer than fourteen laboratories and encampments, with fully equipped kitchens and dormitories, including washing machines and showers, for hundreds of people.

The initial police raid was a complete surprise. Forty workers were arrested at the main encampment, although the managers, one of whom later emerged to be Carlos Lehder, managed to flee. The workers elsewhere escaped also. Although automatic rifles, pistols and shotguns were seized, there was little sustained resistance apart from the occasional outburst of sniper fire. During the next fortnight in March 1984, Colombian police destroyed 7 airstrips, 7 aircraft, nearly 12,000 drums of chemicals and almost 14 metric tons of cocaine or cocaine paste. The cocaine was estimated to be worth about $1.2 billion. By quantity, it was nearly half as much again as had been seized by the US Customs in the whole of the previous year.

The Medellín cartel, and particularly José Gonzalo Rodríguez Gacha, who had invested heavily in the laboratories, were upset.

By 1984 Colombia, and especially Medellín, was a much more violent place. The national homicide rate of 9,721 the previous year was more than double its 1970 level in a country whose population of 30 million had increased by only half over the same period. Furthermore, the nature of the violence was changing. Knives were being replaced by guns. The heavier use of firearms was linked to and accompanied by a big increase in political killings, which, from being a mere 1 per cent of killings in 1980, had jumped to 8 per cent three years later.

In Medellín itself nearly twice as many people died a violent death in 1984 as in 1980; 75 per cent of the killings were caused by firearms, up from 65 per cent. By 1988, that figure would be 80 per cent. The combination of the ideological justification for violence promoted by the guerrilla groups expanding in both rural and urban areas, with the competition and vendettas deriving from the get-rich-quick cocaine business, along with a morally permissive Church prepared to sell its blessings at any price, was bad enough. But the climate of killing was inflamed further both by the smuggling in of sophisticated weapons by the drug barons and by the government-backed creation of civil defence groups which rapidly degenerated into police and military-linked death squads.

The smuggling of weapons started with the launch of the Death to Kidnappers Movement (MAS). A convicted North American drug trafficker, who worked for the Medellín cartel before turning state witness under the name of Max Mermelstein, claimed he sent 100 Uzi, Ingram and MAC-10 sub-machine guns and machine-pistols to Colombia in late 1981. The weapons, along with 60 Browning revolvers and 50,000 rounds of ammunition, were bought legally in Miami with the proceeds from a cocaine shipment. They were flown to the Ochoas' La Veracruz ranch before being distributed by Escobar and Rodríguez Gacha among the bands of killers they were training near Medellín and in the valley of the river Magdalena. The import of arms in this manner slowly became a torrent.

'You buy a weapon where drugs are sold, on the corners, in bars, in taverns,' one young killer told the newspaper *El Colombiano* in the early 1980s. 'Weapons are rented out according to the type of job. It is not the same thing to do a tavern as it is to damage a guy, or when you are doing a big contract . . . [although] the guy who rents the weapons is not interested in what it's for. That's somebody else's problem and the less said the better – it could even be to kill him. There's no contract . . . your life is the guarantee. That's why you need an intermediary, he's the guarantee. Weapons are coming in like rice, usually from Panama's free-trade zone.'

Guns were smuggled back in along the same routes that cocaine was smuggled out on, not only for the traffickers' personal purposes but also, like any other contraband, to sell on the burgeoning black market provided both by the guerrillas and the private security trade. The fact that the weapons might end up in the hands of an enemy hardly worried anybody. It was the business that counted. In a gruesome spiral, the influx of weapons in turn stimulated the building of home-made guns for those not rich enough to buy anything better, but in need of them either to defend or to assert themselves in a world where the gun ruled.

When MAS metamorphosed into the more politically mature, anti-Communist paramilitary organization, ACDEGAM, in July 1984, in the valley of the river Magdalena, it merely represented the legalization of private justice. General Fernando Landazábal, a former minister of defence, was among the defenders of people taking justice into their own hands: 'If the government is not in a condition to guarantee the honour, lives and assets of its citizens, the population has to defend itself,' he said at the time. In an interview the following decade, the general elaborated: 'In 1982 and 1983, the army worked to create self-defence groups in the Magdalena Medio to fight the guerrillas and by 1984 the guerrillas were crushed. But the Communists caused such an outcry that the army was forced to suspend operations, and the civil defence groups that were then set up by landowners who hired people to defend their interests, to protect them, fell into the hands of the drug traffickers.'

However, the traffickers' MAS organization had been solidly identified with the initial army repression as well. The army's helicopter bombings of villages occurred alongside exemplary murders reminiscent of *La Violencia*: peasants from the hamlet of El Delirio told how one MAS member grabbed a pregnant woman 'and alive – excuse me – cut open her stomach, took out the baby and said, "Look! this is what you have to do because what was going to be born here is a child of a guerrilla".' Although the army was officially reined in, it would continue to run a dirty war with ACDEGAM. According to Colombia's Administrative Security Department (DAS), ACDEGAM became the power base of Rodríguez Gacha. It was also financed by Escobar, among other landowners, and funded schools, clinics, roads, bridges and shops on both sides of the river Magdalena. Local military and police commanders were on its payroll.

Municipal civil defence groups were officially launched in the valley of Aburrá around Medellín in 1980 in order to deter common crime. They were soon accused of the systematic killing of muggers, and the Envigado group was eventually put to the service of Escobar. Meanwhile, the cartel was producing its own killers. Escobar was reported to have set up a school for assassins on a ranch outside the small town of Sabaneta, next to Envigado. Its students were taught to shoot from motorbikes, firing at their victims with machine-guns as if they were making the sign of the cross. The cartel's killings of judges and policemen briefly provoked other groups into being in order to revenge them, before they, too, were overwhelmed. Dead bodies – dubbed *muñecos* or puppets – started to appear crumpled up on the roadsides. A huge signboard was erected at the start of the Bogotá highway saying: 'Don't dump corpses here.' Most of the murders were dismissed, wearily, as criminal vendettas, and therefore of minor importance.

Medellín's new newspaper, *El Mundo,* was the sole voice of protest. 'What is happening in our afflicted city is a consequence of the crumbling of our moral values,' ran an editorial in April 1983. 'It is the result of the apathy and inertia of people towards crime, it is the consequence of the reigning social and economic disorder, it is the logical and natural corollary of a community that has got used to crime and no longer values the supreme goodness of life.'

While the city's bank deposits bulged, construction soared and industry recovered itself in a large part because of the influx of cocaine profits, gangs of youths were springing up in the poorer neighbourhoods and creating a nightmarish version of throwaway, consumer culture. They were youths mostly from broken homes in young, struggling communities formed by migrants who had fled the violence and poverty in the countryside. Escobar turned them into cannon fodder. Two of the gangs originally trained at Escobar's school for assassins in Sabaneta were *Los Quesitos* and *Los Priscos.* It was the former who were given the contract to assassinate the minister of justice, Lara Bonilla. The contract, which was said to be worth 50 million pesos, was believed to have been paid not only by the leading Medellín traffickers but also, according to a senior policeman, by those in Cali. The government's rogue minister, working hand in hand with Colonel Ramírez and the US Embassy but isolated politically as well as within the government executive itself, had become too much of a menace.

Lara Bonilla died after receiving seven .45 calibre bullets from a MAC-10 machine-pistol while in his chauffeur-driven car in Bogotá on 30 April 1984. The shots were fired by Iván Darío Guisado, a hired *sicario* and ex-convict with a long and violent criminal record. Guisado, who was gunned down by the minister's bodyguards when his motorbike crashed seconds afterwards, was found to be carrying a miniature picture of the Virgin of Carmen in his underpants.

Although it was eight months before Congress finally suspended Escobar's parliamentary immunity, the murder marked the end of his political career. For years afterwards, Lara Bonilla's family believed that the traffickers were not alone in ordering the minister's death. His sister, Cecilia, a former governor of the Tolima department, claimed that 'very powerful and respected people' also had a hand in it. She added: 'The mafia itself was used by people in government. Rodrigo was killed because he knew too much and if he had escaped Colombia as planned he could have revealed it all. Within four hours of his death, his office had been cleared of all but the most trivial of papers. It is very easy to blame everything on Pablo Escobar, but it is just too easy. His power depended on people in government.'

In the crackdown that followed the murder, Escobar fled Colombia.

CHAPTER FOUR

AN EMPIRE WITHOUT FRONTIERS

Four days after the murder of the Colombian justice minister; during a national manhunt for the Medellín traffickers; following President Betancur's grave-side pledge to enforce extradition; and after receiving the unusually short notice of 48 hours to attend Panama's presidential elections as an observer, a tall, bald, elderly and bespectacled former Colombian president held a rendezvous with Escobar and Jorge Luis Ochoa in a Panama city hotel.

Alfonso López Michelsen, the Liberal Party patriarch, was described by Lehder as the 'cartel's protector'. (His son Felipe was the main owner of Colombia's leading news magazine, *Semana*, which had dubbed Escobar a Robin Hood.) López Michelsen was said privately by an Antioquian senator to have been accompanied by Alberto Santofimio, the former justice minister jailed for six months following corruption allegations. A third man, Carlos Pérez Norzagaray, a long-time confidant of López Michelsen, was said by the senator to be present, too.

The gathering was organized by Santiago Londoño White, who had also set up the meeting where López Michelsen and his Liberal protégé and campaign treasurer, Ernesto Samper, had received $26 million pesos ($400,000) from Escobar, Jorge Luis Ochoa and their colleagues in 1982. According to López Michelsen, who was forced to acknowlege the encounter three months

100

later, the traffickers denied any responsibility for the Lara Bonilla murder and indicated that they were prepared to dismantle their 'global infrastructure' and hand over laboratories, airstrips and coca plantations as a show of goodwill. 'They said they constituted the head of the cocaine organization; an organization which, according to them, had taken ten years to form and which worked in co-ordination with people from Brazil, Peru, Ecuador and with accomplices in the United States . . . in a business that produced several thousand million dollars a year.' López Michelesen added that the traffickers claimed to pay regular bribes to government officials as well as to the army, alongside which they battled against the guerrillas. The former president said he had dissuaded the traffickers from making the cheques public on the grounds that nobody would believe them.

López Michelsen, who for all his cynicism was one of Colombia's elder statesmen and an engaging and worldly intellectual, declared the offer a positive 'promise of absolute surrender'. In fact, the offer was an absolute fraud. López Michelsen passed the traffickers' message to the president. In late May, Carlos Jiménez Gómez, the attorney general, flew to Panama in a private jet owned by the Londoño White family. With him was Jaime Hernández, his anti-drugs agent. It was Hernández who was believed to have been behind the murder of Jiménez Gómez's secretary in the Lehder affair.

The second meeting in Panama produced a six-page memorandum in which the traffickers formalized their offer to abandon the cocaine trade, in what was no more than a bid to acquire immunity before Colombian law while continuing with their business. They claimed to control between 70 and 80 per cent of its total volume, which produced an annual income for them of about $2 billion. Their withdrawal from the market, they said, 'would mean, in the short term, an increase in the prices of the final product abroad, a drop in quality, difficulty in buying, and, as a consequence, a reduction in the number of consumers'. They said their involvement in politics had been exclusively for the purpose of lobbying against the extradition treaty.

The traffickers volunteered to take part in campaigns to eliminate drug consumption in Colombia and to encourage 'the rehabilitation of addicts'. In the mid-term, they promised to repatriate their profits as well as themselves 'within the absolute framework of the law'. Among their suggestions were that extradition not be applied for offences committed prior to a proposed revision of the extradition treaty, that extradition appeals be permitted before the Council of State – and that Colombia's drug laws be tightened up in order to be more dissuasive.

Like its guerrillas and like its tax evaders, Colombia's cocaine traffickers wanted an amnesty. In return, they were offering to bring back their cash. If the country's governments had historically been prepared to pardon the rebel groups, then why not them as well? *La Violencia* had ended with a general amnesty in which the political leaders during the period, in which at least 200,000 people were killed, were let off with a handshake. Land and money were parcelled out to the Liberal guerrillas, and their party leaders such as López Michelsen went on to become presidents; meanwhile, the fact that President Laureano Gómez had inspired the Conservatives' atrocities did nothing to prevent his son Alvaro from also becoming a major political figure.

General Fernando Landazábal, President Betancur's first minister of defence, said: 'We've always been at war in Colombia and amnesties have become a way of life. But they destroy the state of law. The country is profoundly permissive – today's political class is mostly sustained by drug money. People don't want social discipline. If you apply it they accuse you of being a dictator. Rebels against the state always receive benefits from it in order to make peace.'

By the time the offer had surfaced publicly – after being scorned by the United States embassy – it had already been rejected. And López Michelsen's cousin and trustee, Jaime Michelsen Uribe, who was hiding from Colombian justice in Panama, had been exposed as a money launderer of the Medellín cartel. During a raid in the department of Armenia following Lara Bonilla's murder, a letter had been found from Carlos Lehder to

Michelsen Uribe written in December 1981, when Michelsen Uribe was president of the Grupo Grancolombiano banking conglomerate prior to its collapse. After noting recent talks between them, Lehder wrote: 'We also want to confirm our interest in the Grupo Grancolombiano being the means for channelling our foreign money resources, produced by our businesses abroad, amounting to about $20 million a year, which we would be ready to transfer to the country [Colombia] via your bank branches.' The letter thanked Michelsen Uribe for his interest and 'the magnificent attention' provided.

The traffickers' plea for an amnesty also coincided with two discoveries which proved that their promise to abandon the cocaine business was a carefully premeditated lie.

In May the Panamanian army raided a big cocaine laboratory on the river Quindio in the Darién jungle, about 80 kilometres from the Colombian border, and arrested twenty-three Colombians. In return for a payment of $5 million to senior military officers in Panama, the Medellín cartel had been switching its operations there from Colombia since late 1983. A large part of the fee was said to have been paid to General Manuel Noriega, the Panamanian strongman and a pivotal force in Central American and Caribbean politics. Having installed his presidential candidate through fraudulent elections, the pockmarked-faced general double-crossed the traffickers to gratify his principal patron, the United States. The Darién laboratory raid occurred whilst Noriega, who had also received $1 million for providing sanctuary to Escobar, was abroad. It was only through the mediation of Fidel Castro, the Cuban Communist dictator with whom Noriega shared a mutually respectful relationship and through whom the cartel had negotiated a truce with Colombia's M-19 guerrillas, that the dispute was resolved. If Lehder's later court evidence was to be believed, López Michelsen mediated in the dispute on behalf of the Medellín cartel, in Cuba 'López Michelsen had re-established diplomatic links between Colombia and Cuba in 1975.' The Darién laboratory workers were released and about $3 million was returned to the cartel.

Infinitely more damaging to the traffickers was the revelation of their links with the revolutionary Sandinista regime in Nicaragua (Escobar claimed that it was M-19 who had originally put the Medellín cartel in touch with them). A US pilot who had flown about 300 tonnes of cocaine for the cartel – earning himself $75 million – had turned into a DEA informant after finally being caught. The pilot, Barry Seal, said that the cartel had told him of a deal with some Nicaraguan ministers whereby an airstrip near the Managua capital was going to be used as a refuelling stop. There were also cocaine laboratories being built nearby. Equipped with hidden cameras in the nose and rear of a bulky C-123 transport plane, Seal flew into Nicaragua on 25 June. Because it was early days for the Nicaragua arrangement, which had politically explosive implications if it leaked out, and because the traffickers were flitting between there and Panama anyway, Escobar and Rodríguez Gacha were both repeatedly present at the loading of the drug. They, as well as Seal and an alleged Sandinista government official identified as Federico Vaughan, were all apparently photographed filling up the airplane – nicknamed the 'Fat Lady' – with 25-kilogram bags of cocaine. Escobar, however, later claimed it was a frame-up and that Nicaragua was a refuelling rather than a drug-loading point.

Nevertheless, Seal's shipment, of 750 kilograms, was busted by the DEA in Florida in such a way as to make it seem an accident. The cartel decided to go ahead with its plans. Thousands of kilograms of Bolivian cocaine paste stockpiled in Colombia were to be flown to its new Nicaraguan laboratories, prior to being taken by Seal aboard the 'Fat Lady' to northern Mexico, from where the cocaine would be transported on small aircraft into the United States – just in time for the Olympic Games in Los Angeles. In what promised to be a potentially crippling blow to the Medellín cartel, the DEA hoped its leaders could be lured to Mexico for what would be a sensational arrest.

Other parts of the US government had other plans, however. Lieutenant Colonel Oliver North, President Ronald Reagan's National Security Council adviser who was organizing clandestine aid to the Contra rebels in Nicaragua, was anxious to win a forthcoming Congress vote on official aid to the Contras. Evidence of a Sandinista link with cocaine trafficking was likely to prove conclusive. He was advised of the DEA operation. Either North or the US Central Intelligence Agency, which had installed the Seal cameras, were believed to have leaked the Sandinista information in early July through the head of the US Southern Command in Panama, Lieutenant General Paul Gorman.

The DEA was forced to catch who it could, quickly. On 18 July Seal's Miami contacts were arrested; the cartel leaders, however, were outside its net. Instead, Pablo Escobar and Jorge Luis Ochoa were indicted the same day by a federal court in Miami for conspiring to import and distribute cocaine in the United States. Although the charges meant that the threat of extradition now hung like an axe above their heads, and although the evidence of their continued trafficking revealed what López Michelsen called their 'promise of absolute surrender' to be a cynical trick and torpedoed any chances of its acceptance, at least they were free. The United States government executive had placed its geopolitical interests in Central America firmly above the battle against drugs.

While the Sandinista incident enabled the US government to wax lyrical about links between Communism and the cocaine trade – granting President Reagan's wife, Nancy, extra moral high ground in her 'Just Say No' anti-drugs campaign – the White House, CIA and State Department continued to turn a blind eye to their allies' involvement in the cocaine trade. The latter had included the right-wing Nicaraguan dictator, Anastasio Somoza, who according to Escobar was a close ally of the Medellín cartel and who was toppled by the Sandinistas. In the Iran–Contra scandal, it was alleged that, as well as illicitly funnelling money to the Contras from arms sales to Iran, Lieutenant Colonel North had also enabled the Contras to arm themselves with funds from cocaine. Lewis Tambs, the US ambassador in Colombia who was switched to Costa Rica in 1985, and who had coined the phrase 'narcoguerrilla', was forced to resign his post when accused of assisting North in his Contra supply network.

In late 1984, the US Embassy in Bogotá initiated a bizarre cover-up of Colombia's incipient opium trade. Reports of opium seizures had started in the late 1970s, after the seeds were brought in by Mexicans. The plantations were said to be in the departments of Cauca, Tolima, Meta and Cundinamarca. In late 1984, a British journalist and drugs expert, Timothy Ross, bought 2 grams of heroin in Bogotá and filmed it for ABC Television. To test the purity, he gave half to a toxicology clinic and half to the DEA. Not less than 65 per cent pure, said the clinic. It has no opiate content whatsoever, said the DEA. 'It was the first indication that something was weird,' said Ross, who then secured another sample, this time a 10-gram blob of opium which he bought off a Cauca poppy grower. With no reason to distrust the DEA, with whom he was on good terms, Ross asked them to test it for morphine content. 'The effect was extraordinary. A few weeks later, they denied getting the sample. The secretary who had received it from me was transferred abruptly, inexplicably, and nobody said where to, so there was no way I could prove I had ever given it.'

Meanwhile, a propaganda visit by five members of the Afghanistan anti-Soviet resistance movement was organized. 'A friend in the attorney general's office told me that two of them stayed on, and that it was reported they were helping Colombians to make proper quality heroin,' said Ross. 'My friend had already claimed that an Israeli agronomist had been brought in to improve poppy cultivation. I was naïvely chatting with the embassy about what I was hearing when they suddenly got very weird with me.' One week of what Ross described as 'serious terror tactics' culminated in his being summoned by the embassy security officer, who pointed his finger at him and declared: 'You are going to lay off this story or you are going to die.'

'He was playing it as a warning but I was sure that it was a threat,' said Ross. A few months later, the White House anti-drugs adviser, Carlton Turner, initially refused him an interview in the Ecuadorian capital of Quito because Turner had been told that ABC's report on Colombian opium had been faked using Mexican footage. When persuaded otherwise, said Ross, 'he was

delighted, saying "it all fits" and that he would "kick some butt"'
back in Washington. Turner would explain no further. However,
according to Ross, Turner was extraordinarily open about shipments of cocaine to Afghanistan, saying they were being sent in
order to hook the Russians ('like they did to us in Vietnam').

When the Iran–Contra scandal broke, Ross discovered that he
featured in North's diaries. A note written in 1985 ran: 'Should
Timothy Ross (ABC News) be invited to Florida to talk with
district attorney about Sandinista trafficking?'

Bearing in mind these allegations, and considering Turner's
assertion that cocaine was being shipped to Afghanistan, was it
not feasible that the cocaine was being traded for heroin, a much
more profitable drug, which was then sold by or on behalf of the
Contras in exchange for arms? And that the Colombian production of heroin had been encouraged simultaneously? The insatiable US heroin market was running dry because the Mexican
suppliers had been heavily repressed, so demand was high. And
was it possible that North even planned that the heroin be aimed
at the Sandinistas to hook them 'like they did to us in Vietnam'?
Many of North's ideas proved to be equally daft and impractical.
Even if only the cocaine part were true, in North's secret battle
with Communism he deliberately stoked up drug addiction.

The most brazen case of US duplicity was its treatment of
General Noriega in Panama. Noriega had been a long-time friend
of the US Army and CIA because of his political opposition to
Panama's previous strongman, General Omar Torrijos, who was
killed in a mysterious aircrash in 1981. The fiercely nationalist
Torrijos had signed a treaty with President Jimmy Carter in which
the US military base would be dismantled in 1984 and the canal
revert to Panama at the end of the century. The Reagan administration planned otherwise. The Fort Gulik base was known as the
School of the Americas, where Latin American military officers
had been trained for decades. And on the Pacific side of the
isthmus was a vital US listening post covering the whole of South
America. In exchange for Noriega's apparent willingness to safe-
guard the United States' strategic interests in Panama, and his

readiness to act as a go-between with Fidel Castro, the US overlooked DEA reports that Noriega was receiving protection money both for transit shipments of cocaine and for allowing the profits to be laundered through Panamanian banks.

However, as Noriega himself said, once he became commander of the Panama Defence Forces in 1983 he ceased to be the paid US puppet of yesteryear. The man who had been a one-time friend of Casper Weinberger, Reagan's secretary of defence, proved less pliable than anticipated over the Canal treaty and refused point blank to take a hostile stance against the Sandinistas. Noriega's links with the drugs trade became first the instrument to pressure him to change back or to abandon dictatorial power, and then, when that failed – and after two federal indictments in Florida – the pretext to invade Panama in 1989.

With Noriega safely behind bars in the United States, the US sat back again as rumours swirled regarding the law firm of its new, albeit democratically elected Panamanian lapdog, President Guillermo Endara.

While bankers in Colombia, Venezuela and to the north effortlessly line their pockets with the mafia's cocaine takings, the peasants who cultivate the coca leaf itself, in Peru, Colombia and Bolivia, remain almost as poor as any small-time, primary agricultural producers in the developing world.

The sacred bush, which in Peru and Bolivia still retains its ancient social and religious value, is a symbol of Indian identity and prestige. Its little oval leaves are mixed with lime or banana ash in order to encourage the extraction of their psychoactive alkaloid. The leaves are chewed into a ball, which is then pushed into the side of the mouth; periodically, the ball is switched to the other cheek. Not only is physical pain thwarted but energy and endurance are increased. When drained of its nutrients, the green wadge is unceremoniously spat out, and replaced. Although coca is chewed on any ordinary, secular occasion such as during village meetings, communal building projects or simply while walking up a mountain or driving a bus, 'Mother Coca' is also consumed in a celebratory fashion at marriages and religious festivals. In the case of religious rites, coca is chewed in order for the Indians to feel closer to their gods, to whom the coca is simultaneously offered up in sacrifice. The leaves, which themselves are a form of currency, are openly for sale at markets. Foreign tourists are often grateful for coca teabags in overcoming the effects of altitude sickness – but woe betide them if they are caught by Customs taking a box back home for the family.

Coca bushes grow to a few metres high and thrive best in the valleys on the eastern slopes of the Andes, between 500 metres and 2,000 metres above sea level. In Peru, it was first grown intensively – mostly for medical purposes – in the valley of La Convención in the department of Cusco. As overseas demand grew, plantations sprang up in the jungle during the 1940s in the Huánaco and San Martín departments. The crop's expansion occurred alongside colonization, by coastal inhabitants as well as by Indians from the mountains. By 1975, there were about 1,000 hectares of coca growing in the valley of the river Huallaga. Five years later, as the plantations spread down the valley, that figure had sextupled; coca cultivation had also intensified in the valleys of the Amazon rivers Marañon, Ene and Apurímac. By 1990, according to United Nations agricultural experts, there were 200,000 hectares of coca plantations nationally. The Huallaga valley, with 80,000 hectares alone, was the world's single largest coca-growing zone and home to most of the 580,000 Peruvians estimated by the US State Department to be dependent on it directly for a living.

The peasants turned to coca leaf because it is easy to grow, can be harvested up to six times a year, and its average price of $1.50–$2.25 per kilogram makes it more profitable than other crops such as coffee or cacao. One hectare of coca yields about 200 kilograms of coca leaves, which produces 2 kilograms of base (this converts into a slightly lesser quantity of cocaine). Furthermore, while other crops take several days to be driven over the mountains along dangerous roads frequently rendered impassable by landslides, and encounter bureaucratic barriers erected by monopolistic business cartels at the ports, coca leaf is bought directly from their farms by middle-men who take it off to convert into cocaine paste in nearby laboratories.

In Bolivia, Indian peasants succumb to similar economic pressures. However, the illicit market is much more open and pacific than in Peru, where the presence of left-wing guerrillas in the coca zones – the Communist Party of Peru or Shining Path, and the Túpac Amaru Revolutionary Movement (MRTA) – and the corresponding army repression has triggered bloody and anarchic violence in the coca-growing areas in a tripartite battle for power. Bolivian coca farmers, on the other hand, have enjoyed top-rank military protection and channelled their protests against US eradication campaigns through hundreds of well-organized unions.

Bolivian coca was traditionally grown for local use in the Yungas valleys north of the La Paz capital. In the 1970s, when the foreign trade took off in earnest, it expanded east into the subtropical jungles of Chapare, which, like the Huallaga valley, was also a colonizing, frontier zone. By 1990, it was estimated that Bolivia's coca plantations occupied between 50,000 and 80,000 hectares. The trade is closely linked to the country's political and economic élite, particularly around the town of Santa Cruz, which is the heart of the traffickers' national, commercial and financial infrastructure.

After being harvested and dried in the sun – risky in the Huallaga where for several years US helicopters were liable to swoop down and use their blades to blow away the leaves – the crop is parcelled up, collected and taken to ramshackle laboratories hidden in the jungle.

I visited one such coca-processing plant after it had been raided by the DEA and police near the Huallaga village of Ramal del Aspusana on a sweltering afternoon in September 1989. Abandoned turkeys ran around the stilts of the wooden dormitories on the edge of a clearing barely large enough to land our gun-stacked UH-1H helicopter. A baby's high-chair, a tiny bicycle and the remains of a white cot beneath a picture of Jesus Christ attested to the lost paradise of the heir of a jungle drug boss. The inhabitants had escaped among the trees. A few hundred metres away through boggy marsh, almost hidden beneath the forest canopy and too far from the dormitories to cause any harm if it exploded, lay the remains of the laboratory itself. The dozens of concrete pits had been destroyed and the plastic dustbins and plastic sheeting jumbled together with the wrecked wooden roof frame into a gigantic, mangled heap. The cocaine base itself had been torched with the very paraffin used to release the alkaloids from the leaf in the first place.

According to the DEA, the laboratory was not merely producing cocaine paste, but the purer version, base. The paste is created by adding sulphuric acid to the initial solution of coca, together with lime or sodium carbonate, and paraffin; the acid serves to extract the alkaloids. The resulting mixture is filtered off from the paraffin. In order to make base, the paste is then dumped in another bath of sulphuric acid, along with potassium permanganate; the latter destroys the non-cocaine alkaloids. The cocaine base, which has a clay-like texture, is sold off initially in 1 kilo balls, each of which will produce 1 kilogram of nearly pure cocaine hydrochloride. According to the DEA, the Ramal del Aspusana laboratory was capable of churning out cocaine base worth about $750,000 per week on the streets in Miami.

Attempts at throttling the coca trade in Peru and Bolivia have varied from manual and – apparently – biological eradication to the blowing up of laboratories and airstrips, air interception and seductive but ultimately futile attempts by the United Nations to persuade the peasants to grow other crops instead (they simply grow them as well). Interdiction has hitherto achieved little more than to trigger leaps in the coca price and the expansion of the trade into new valleys. The corruption of civil authorities, the police and the army – and their protectors in central government – have also contributed to the impotence of drug law enforcement. In 1993, the United States closed down its 40-hectare anti-drugs base, Santa Lucía, in the Huallaga, because it was no longer considered worth the expense.

From Peru, the drug, whether in paste or base form, is transported to Colombia by road, river or airplane. Most of it is flown out in 400-kilogram loads from illicit as well as municipal airstrips, day and night. From Bolivia, the base travels to Colombia solely by air. In both the 'paste' countries, the manufacture of cocaine itself has increased slowly but constantly since the mid 1980s along with the development of their own routes and markets. However, most of that cocaine production is controlled by Colombians.

A key figure in the Medellín cartel's paste supply for more than a decade was Evaristo Porras, the man whose cheque shamed the justice minister, Rodrigo Lara Bonilla. Porras, who was born in Cali, has operated since the early 1970s out of the small Amazon port of Leticia. The small town is at the tip of a finger of Colombia wedged between Brazil and Peru, whose city of Iquitos, several hours upstream, also became a mecca for coca paste. As early as 1973, *El Espectador* wrote that drug traffickers had 'taken control at all economic, political and official levels in Leticia' and that 1,200 kilograms of cocaine paste was arriving at the airport annually from Peru. (Twenty-one years later, when the Cali cartel's biggest coca-paste supplier, Demetrio Chávez, a Peruvian, was arrested in Colombia, he was accused of importing 30,000 kilograms a month.) A few months after the newspaper report, the head of the DAS secret police in Leticia was arrested with cocaine at Bogotá airport. A few years later, *El Espectador*'s Leticia correspondent was shot dead.

Porras's first known arrest was on drug charges in 1975, in Leticia. It was followed by him being jailed in Peru in 1978 for carrying 29 kilograms of cocaine; Porras escaped. His only conviction in Colombia in the 1980s was for the illicit possession of a gun. By 1993, so complete was Porras's dominion over Leticia that, in spite of his infamous reputation nationally, he openly presided over a public political meeting in Leticia in which two Congressmen nephews of the former president, Julio César

Turbay Ayala, supported the congressional candidature of Porras's close associate, Melquisedec Marín. Meanwhile, Porras's brother, Iván, was to be the group's candidate for the governorship of the Amazonas department. If all were successful – which since they were the official arm of the Liberal Party and were supporting the presidential favourite, Ernesto Samper, was more than probable – the pyramidal nature of Colombian politics would ensure that Porras's group would sweep to power in innumerable local and regional councils, thereby controlling government entities too. In return for his official patronage of Turbay Ayala's nephews, it was reported that Ernesto Samper stood to win 300,000 votes in the departments of Amazonas, Caquetá, Huila and Putumayo.

Although national revelations of the meeting forced Samper to disown the Turbay Ayala nephews publicly, they were both elected to Congress the following year, remained in the Liberal Party and continued to support him. Samper was elected the president of Colombia in June 1994.

Coca-bush plantations sprang up in Colombia in the mid 1970s in the departments of Putumayo, Caquetá, Guaviare and Meta, south east of the Andes. Again, it was mainly peasant migrants – whose families had fled *La Violencia* – who adopted the crop. Its cultivation attracted a second wave of migrants and by the mid 1980s had fallen under the sway of the FARC guerrillas, who justified their struggle claiming they were fighting to protect the interests of the colonists from the large, predatory landowners following in the colonists' footsteps. However, the poor quality of the native coca, as well as the guerrillas' extortion of both the growers and the primary traders, ensured that its cultivation failed to prosper as fast as in Peru and Bolivia. Furthermore, the emergence of the traffickers themselves as Colombia's new landowning élite converted them into the guerrillas' natural enemies. By 1990, the US State Department estimated that only about 40,000 hectares in Colombia were planted with coca.

However, thereafter the official US figures and those of the United Nations and regional agricultural authorities differed widely. While the US claimed that the number of hectares with coca was actually decreasing, the UN was adamant that the opposite was true. According to the latter, whose impressive crop-substitution programmes served only to displace coca cultivation and were only of interest to the small-time growers, by 1993 there were between 50,000 and 60,000 hectares. That made Colombia the second biggest producer of coca leaf. Furthermore, the UN believed that the crop was expanding very fast in the Amazonian and Orinoquian regions and that, with the spread of imported Peruvian coca plants, the harvest frequency and yield were just as high as in Peru and Bolivia.

It was Rodríguez Gacha who was famed for encouraging the cultivation of coca in Colombia. His lieutenants fanned out in the lowlands, distributing the seeds to peasants who were already in frontier zones. The crop attracted migrants and hastened the development of remote areas as well as bolstering the fortunes of farmers suffering from the decline of traditional agriculture, which became more acute following Colombia's free-market reforms in the early 1990s.

Inevitably, given the minimal presence of the state in the coca-growing zones, as well as the illicit nature of the trade, coca attracted violence. The army, police and guerrillas fought for protection money. While the peasant growers tended to prefer the guerrillas, who imposed a sort of justice where there was none, the traders or middlemen themselves, who generally came from the towns, tended to side with the security forces. Furthermore, according to peasants in the department of Caquetá, whereas the guerrillas did not demand a quota from them, soldiers and police were notorious for stealing their paste or extorting their money. The security forces also extracted cash from those dealing in the main substances to convert coca into coca paste: petrol and cement. (Caquetá, a wild and underdeveloped region with only a few main roads in its western tip, consumed enough petrol and cement to fuel a large Colombian city and major construction boom.) The guerrillas, on the other hand, did attempt to extort or 'tax' the middlemen; in parts of Caquetá and elsewhere, they also ran their own, very large, coca plantations.

The port of Curillo on the river Caquetá is a typical centre for the buying and selling of coca paste. Every Saturday, the farmers bring the paste, which they themselves produce from their own coca harvest in primitive field kitchens known as *cambuyónes*, to the town. In turn, buyers at the service of regional paste collectors arrive to purchase it off them directly, and very discreetly. The buyers return to the departmental capital, Florencia, in order to hand over the paste for it to be dispatched on private or commercial flights to cocaine laboratories run by the minions of the big traffickers. At the weekends, coca harvest workers or *raspadores* also flock to the port to spend their money, like the coca farmers, on alcohol and prostitutes (who come in busloads from Florencia and boast of how many *polvos* or ejaculations they produce). The drunkenness and settling of scores ensure that a handful of people are murdered every week in a town of only a few thousand. Shortly before my visit, upon seeing her father gunned down, a ten-year-old girl had picked up his weapon and fired at everyone in sight. On the day of my arrival, there was a funeral for the father of a six-year-old boy who had shot him thinking his gun was a toy. Yet, the increasing state presence, and the guerrilla prohibition of *basuko* consumption – it was a capital offence – had reduced the violence from its previous levels.

One hour by mule off the dirt-track main road to Curillo, over gentle hills and in drizzling rain, I found Lucas and his family emptying the latest part of their forty-five-day harvest of coca leaves into the wooden pen next to the oil drums, buckets and plastic tubes that made up their *cambuyón*. Lucas had 3 hectares of coca, and with the help of the United Nations International Drug Control Programme had diversified into sugar cane, buffaloes, rubber trees and fish-ponds.

Stripped to his waist and in gumboots, a teenage boy showered the leaves with cement and kicked them around for a while. Once the leaves' alkaloid was deemed to have transferred to the cement, the mixture was doused in petrol and left for four hours in a drum. Meanwhile, the family continued with leaves from another drum, draining out the petrol – to which the alkaloid had transferred in turn. Water and sulphuric acid were then added to the petrol in order for the alkaloid to transfer to the water, which was siphoned off by mouth. Potassium permanganate and bicarbonate were mixed in order to re-alkalinize the solution; a greyish goo emerged. The mixture – which was mostly cocaine sulphate – was rewashed with petrol and water, then scooped out by Lucas's wife, wrung dry and prepared for the Curillo market. The half kilogram of washed coca paste or base was currently worth the equivalent of $750 locally. When told that their paste, by the time it was purified and converted with solvents into cocaine, would fetch up to $95,000 diluted at street level in Great Britain, Lucas's wizened face gazed silently first at me and then at the buffaloes. He was clearly unable to decide who was the more bovine.

While the added ingredients for the first stage of cocaine's production process – paraffin or petrol, and cement (for its alkalinity) – are easy to obtain in bulk, the subsequent chemicals required need to be bought from a specialist supplier. Apart from the coca itself, the only essential chemical is potassium permanganate; the small amount needed makes it impossible for governments to control. Initially, ether and acetone – which are used in equal quantities – were the solvents most in demand. They were supplied mainly from the United States. The DEA investigation that led to the bugging of the ether consignment and to the Tranquilandia raids discovered that although acetone was widely used in Colombian industry, ether's application was minimal. And yet, between January 1978 and June 1981, Colombia had imported 3.7 million kilograms of it. That was enough to produce about 250,000 kilograms of cocaine during a period when US Customs' total cocaine seizure had been little more than 4,200 kilograms. The quantity of ether exported to Colombia was gigantic: a highly volatile chemical avoided by most industries if at all possible, it represented a tenth of the United States' annual production.

The results of the ether investigation – in which its biggest importer was reported to work for Shell Colombia, the local limb of the petrochemicals multinational – were concealed from the government. Having just declared the chemicals free of import tariffs and taxes, President Turbay Ayala was not thought to be a terribly good bet. However, the incoming government – specifically the new and, at first, morally zestful attorney general, Carlos Jiménez Gómez – agreed to enforce restrictions. In December 1982, all importers of ether, acetone and some other chemicals were obliged to secure a permit from the Colombian Foreign Trade Institute as well as a certificate declaring themselves to be free from suspicions of drugs trafficking.

The following year another piece of red tape was introduced for the importers: compulsory registration at the health ministry. A year later, illicit trading of the chemicals was made a criminal act. But it made no difference. The legal inflow of the cocaine chemicals continued to increase. Between 1984 and 1986, imports of acetone, ether and methyl ethyl ketone (MEK), a substitute for acetone and ether that was regarded as just another solvent, shot up by 500 per cent. In 1986 the penalties were stiffened; in 1987 more chemicals, including MEK, were specifically brought under government control; in 1990 these controls were extended to the whole process of transportation, arrival and storage, and the supervisory powers of police and customs were expanded; and in 1991 anybody involved in any stage of the management of the chemicals was obliged to obtain a police clearance certificate.

Yet the controls simply increased the corruption. They brought more people into contact with the immense buying power of the cocaine mafia, whose ravenous appetite for the chemicals was matched only by that of cocaine's ravenous snorters abroad.

The manager of one major cargo shipping company said: 'While the clients we know to be honest have immense problems in getting all the permits together, the crooked ones produce boxes of permits as if by magic.' Once public officials grew accustomed to being paid for their co-operation, they became less than co-operative to those who saw no reason to buy it. The secret police (DIJIN), according to one executive working for a chemical distributor, used to 'come and ask for bribes, with dirty great diamond rings on their fingers; they are very unpleasant and thick as pigshit'.

The 1986 restrictions merely slowed the flood. By 1989 acetone and ether imports had doubled again while those of MEK were, according to customs figures, up by a third. One factory, Baz Rezin, which had been set up by a company that dominated a fifth of the Colombian paint market, was widely reported to be linked to Rodríguez Gacha. Baz Rezin, whose termination of MEK imports coincided with the termination of Rodríguez Gacha – killed in December 1989 – was said by a shipping agent to have 'brought in enough MEK to paint the whole of South America'. It was the assassination earlier in 1989 of the presidential favourite, Luis Carlos Galán, that sparked off a national crackdown during which the chemical imports crashed. However, by 1992, although acetone and ether supplies were still only running at something of a dribble, MEK imports had doubled once more.

MEK, which produces a less pure cocaine than acetone or ether, is safer, cheaper, and, because of its wider industrial usages – including the manufacturer of thinner, paint, glue and palm oil – easier to import. The principal ostensible buyers were paint factories. Dozens of tiny paint companies, as well as bogus ones, ordered vast amounts of the chemical with no trouble at all. By 1994 between 30 and 50 per cent of the legally imported MEK was still said by the National Council for Dangerous Drugs and the DEA to be finding its way into the cocaine laboratories. The council itself, which had always been famed for corruption, was still inclined to feign ignorance or impotence; nevertheless, it was believed to have improved. According to chemical traders, however, the DIJIN secret police officers who investigated the factories continued to be reported as totally corrupt.

Even if the chemical shipping, docks and distribution companies had wanted to turn down the permit-backed MEK orders with which they were being inundated, they claimed that they were not in a position to refuse. They risked legal action, harassment or violence. According to the DEA, in the first half of the 1990s at least fifty chemical traders who had flirted with the cocaine business were murdered. However, some international companies lusted for the business, throwing ethics to the wind.

Until the 1988 US Chemical Diversion and Trafficking Act, whose implementation the following year coincided with the start of the internal crackdown in Colombia, most of the cocaine chemicals came from the United States. The main providers and importers were Shell and Exxon. Thereafter, acetone was imported almost exclusively from the United States by Shell, mostly for a Cali cigarette filter manufacturer. Ether, meanwhile, came to be imported to Colombia mainly from Germany and Holland – as was the bulk of the MEK, which originated mainly in Germany and Austria and was shipped out from Rotterdam in Holland. The export trading companies mostly involved were Trasmarichemie and Jebsen & Jessen, of Hamburg. In Colombia MEK was mostly imported by the biggest chemicals distribution agent, Holanda Colombia, which is part of the Dutch multinational, HCI. Its MEK imports – mostly on behalf of Colombian paint factories, with all their permits meticulously in order – shot up from 358 tons in 1989 to 1,960 tons in 1992 and to as much as 4,057 tons in 1993. The chemical was said to account for only 3 per cent of Holanda Colombia's annual sales, yielding a profit of around $1.5 million in 1993. However, that year its storage and terminal sister company, which worked for other importers, too, handled 8,000 tons of the chemical.

The real profits came on the black market. This was operated through the companies who bought from Holanda Colombia, as well as by other importers/distributors and their buyers. A chain of illicit wastage came into existence whereby the MEK was diverted to about half a dozen stockpilers directly linked to the cartels' laboratories in the departments of the Valle del Cauca and Antioquia, and in the eastern plains or Llanos. It was also brought in by smugglers. Just like cocaine, the closer the MEK came to its final users, the more vastly inflated its price. According to police, the black-market price of a 55-gallon drum was normally double the legal cost. After Holanda Colombia's trading was suspended by the National Council for Dangerous Drugs in March 1994 – at which time, along with its sister companies, it was trading in up to half of Colombia's total MEK imports – the black-market price for the laboratories quintupled.

'It would be pure speculation.' The friendly Scotsman at HCI's local storage division tugged his beard on the eleventh floor of a spectacular office tower in north Bogotá. Bruce Clark was responding to the suggestion that since up to half of Colombia's annual MEK imports were believed to find their way to the cocaine laboratories, wasn't it possible that HCI was helping it to get there? 'All our clients for controlled chemicals have the correct permits,' he added, still, apparently, rather amazed at the idea.

The following day I visited another of the main MEK distri-bution companies, Química Flamingo: its MEK licence had also recently been revoked. Seeing that two similar companies had already hung up on me, I arrived unannounced. The lift opened on to the top floor of an innocuous building to reveal so luxurious and vulgar an office that it echoed a cocaine trafficker's boudoir. Sumptuous white leather sofas and chairs were scattered liberally on the grey marble floor, which was broken up irregularly by paler, spotty grey squares and black triangles. The walls surround-ing the lift were faced with thousands of pieces of frosted stone which rose to form an ugly indented archway leading upstairs. The windows, doors and partitions were pattern-frosted, too. Huge plants in carved stone and marble urns, a brass and red ceramic statue of a flamingo, and an acrylic painting of a river all screamed the same warning. And beyond, in another room, were more white leather sofas, a crystal table with marble base, huge ashtrays at its corners and, between them, a large silver box.

The manager, a former salesman at HCI, was out. I explained my journalistic interest in chemicals, left my card with the beautiful receptionist, and was not called back.

I had more luck at Arpisol, whose main owner had also worked for HCI. The tatty, two-storey premises were out near the airport, the darkened, second-floor wall of windows curiously incongruous above the heavy brown garage that took up most of downstairs. On the desk were fat, imitation Mont Blanc pens in front of a jumbo-sized calculator. The office was decorated with fluffy pink bedroom wallpaper; behind me, in a corner, was a pedestal upon which there stood the plaster figure of a lovingly sculptured Italian mafioso. It was a man in a suit, in a big hurry; all was white except for his black trilby hat band and black tie, which flew behind his head. A pair of red sunglasses had been hung on his side, and a silver chain and waistcoat watch strung around his neck. This gangster's icon belonged to an underling, not to Germán Muñoz, whose hard, brown eyes now bored into my skull.

'Mafia is a word of yours, not mine,' he said. Arpisol was the fourth biggest MEK importer having doubled its imports over the previous year. Its permits had since been cancelled for alleged book-keeping inconsistencies which underlined suspicions that it had been under-mixing MEK in its thinner and diverting the balance to the cocaine trade. 'Controlling the chemicals has simply raised the profits for their foreign producers – who put the price up – and damaged Colombian industry,' said Muñoz. Maybe, but it had not stopped MEK imports skyrocketing. 'The only thing we know about the cocaine producers is what we read in the press,' he retorted. 'Since the chemicals they use are totally controlled by the authorities, they can only come in as contraband. Like anything forbidden – like another man's wife – it just raises its value and attraction.' Would he sell MEK to a suspected cocaine producer? 'If somebody has the correct permits, it is unethical not to sell.' Meanwhile, because of the cancellation of his own permits, he had laid off thirty out of his thirty-four staff.

As the legal controls on the cocaine chemicals have tightened, so their smuggling has, indeed, increased. According to General Miguel Antonio Gómez Padilla, a former director of the national police, a large quantity is diverted from the Caribbean, where false end-user certificates are issued; the chemicals enter Colombia via Panama, whence they are mostly shipped or flown down to the Pacific coast having had their drums' identification altered. The solvents also arrive overland from Ecuador and Venezuela or are flown in from Brazil to refining laboratories in the Llanos and elsewhere. 'It's a neat, circular and highly profitable business,' said General Gómez Padilla. 'The traffickers buy the chemicals abroad with their profits, either laundering their money through legal imports or smuggling in the chemicals like any other contraband.'

The big, Tranquilandia-style cocaine laboratories of the first half of the 1980s gave way to laboratories that were physically smaller and more technologically sophisticated. Hundreds of them were scattered up and down the Andean valleys and across into the Llanos, concentrated mostly in the departments of Antioquia, Valle del Cauca and Meta. Primitive urban laboratories, in particular, were inclined to explode because of ether's high volatility in its oxidized form when spilled. Workers were regularly killed. The chemists as well as their assistants were paid according to production levels. An average worker would earn $1 per kilogram; in a big laboratory he could make $2,000 per month, more than ten times the minimum wage. The monthly income of a chemist in a similar laboratory would be as much as $10,000.

It was the need for ventilation and security that pushed the laboratories into remote areas. As the solvent controls increased in Colombia, the United States and Germany, so did the cocaine producers' ability to recycle the chemicals. Up to 80 per cent of MEK could be retrieved. At the same time, the mafia introduced mobile laboratories to stay yet another step ahead of the police and informants. Once a prefabricated skeleton structure had been erected near a road, the generators, pumps, solvents and cocaine base were brought there by lorries for one or two weeks' intensive production before being moved on to a different location. The traffickers went back and forth between about half a dozen such sites, leaving behind only the skeleton walls and solvents, until such time as they feared their security was exhausted. Although mobile laboratories were believed to have been used by the Cali traffickers since the mid 1980s – in Ecuador they were said to have been employed earlier – it was not until December 1993 that the first one was raided in Colombia. The laboratory, which was found outside the small town of Cumaral, Meta, a few hours from Bogotá, had only been in operation for four days. But it housed 3,800 kilograms of cocaine (worth about $7 million locally, up to $150 million wholesale in the United States). There were also 32,000 kilograms of cocaine base – potentially worth up to $1.2 billion if sold wholesale in the United States as cocaine.

On one side of the conference table deep inside the Division of the Anti-narcotics Police in Bogotá, there hangs the photograph of a man who fearlessly gave his life in a courageous, heartfelt battle against Colombia's cocaine trade. Colonel Jaime Ramírez, who led the unit between 1982 and 1986 when it seized thousands of lorries, cars, boats and aircraft, and arrested several thousand traffickers, was machine-gunned to death in front of his wife. (Little did the state care: on the grounds that he was not on active duty at the time, he did not receive the usual posthumous promotion until his widow's efforts finally bore fruit six and a half years later.) Opposite his photograph above the table, directly in front of Ramírez's gaze, there is a map of the world. Red, mauve and blue lines snake all over it. Each colour represents a drug. Each line indicates a route. And both the drugs and the routes have multiplied since Ramírez's time.

Repression of the cocaine trade in the face of its huge profitability and the corruption it generates, the lack of true international enforcement, willpower and co-operation, and the apparently insatiable consumer demand outside Colombia, has acted like pruning back a rose bush. Not only has the industry emerged all the stronger but it has also demonstrated a stubborn tendency to develop new and more adventurous branches – enabling it to bloom ever more prodigiously. Its ability to adapt has manifested itself in the traffickers' diversification of production techniques, routes, smuggling methods and money-laundering systems. No sooner has one option been closed than another has opened.

The three initial cocaine embarkation points in Colombia were the Gulf of Urabá, the Pacific port of Buenaventura and the Caribbean coastline east of the town of Santa Marta. In the same way that the Urabá was a traditional two-way smuggling route to Panama, Buenaventura in the department of Valle del Cauca was the main thoroughfare for contraband between Cali and California. However, it was smugglers in the Santa Marta area who had already developed the most sophisticated networks, because for a long time they had controlled the main route out for illicit emeralds coming up from the Boyacá department north of Bogotá. It was they who were also on hand to export the marijuana grown nearby in the mountains of the Sierra Nevada. Both products were moved by speedboat and on freight vessels to the Colombian free-trade islands of Providencia and San Andrés, from where they were shipped to Mexico and the United States. The islands being historic centres for contraband from Panama and elsewhere, the smugglers would return laden with contraband for distribution throughout Colombia. Smuggled goods are sold freely in all Colombian cities at special markets nicknamed *sanandresitos*.

Colombia's natural domination of South America's most direct and traditional smuggling routes to the north enabled it to gain control over the cocaine trade from the first coca producers in Peru and Bolivia, and the early refineries in Chile. As the demand for cocaine grew in the United States, so did the need to increase the size of the cargoes and to multiply routes. The introduction of light aircraft to fly the drug northwards in the late 1970s opened up scores of supply lines through the countries of the Central American isthmus into Mexico. Drug flights also took off from the north Colombian coast for Caribbean islands – Lehder's staging post in the Bahamas was only one of many, even if the most important of its time – before the cargo was shipped or flown on again to the United States. The traffickers' heyday – hazardous as it was – came when it found US pilots prepared to make the round trip to Colombia straight out of California, Mississippi, Texas or Florida.

Although extra fuel tanks and improved aircraft and navigation technology made the round trip easier, US Customs soon fought back with more sophisticated systems of radar detection and a greater capacity for air interdiction. Landing in the Florida everglades, in particular, became increasingly difficult. With demand continuing to grow, the typical light aircraft cocaine capacity of 400 kilograms was also inadequate for the leading traffickers to shift their gigantic stockpiles in Colombia. Smuggling cocaine as commercial freight by sea or by air allowed far more to be moved. However, its embarkation point had to be disguised to minimize suspicions at the final destination.

Because of this, although continuing with the northern flights and sailings, both commercial and non-commercial, the drug barons started to push cocaine straight out south from Bolivia. Having already grasped considerable control over the Bolivian trade in coca paste, the Colombians encouraged the spawning of cocaine laboratories there as well. The drug, dressed up as conventional freight, began to travel out by rail to the Chilean port of Arica, where, in wan compensation for having stolen Bolivia's stretch of the Pacific coast in the late nineteenth century, Chile allowed the free, unchecked transit of Bolivian goods. Once in Arica, the cocaine's documentation would be altered to make it appear to originate from Chile. It was then either shipped directly to Mexico and the United States, or was driven down to the Chilean port of Valparaíso, from where it was sent by sea to Mexico and the United States, or to Europe via the Panama Canal, or to Argentina and Brazil via Cape Horn. Once in the Atlantic Ocean it was dispatched to Europe, often by yet another detour via either Nigeria or South Africa (where there also happened to be a healthy internal market).

The development of the southern routes – as well as those through neighbouring Venezuela – stepped up sharply after the

Colombian government clamped down on the traffickers in 1989 following the assassination of the presidential candidate, Luis Carlos Galán. Imports of coca paste from Peru and Bolivia were semi-strangled by the implementation of greater radar and air controls; simultaneously, trafficking operations in Colombia came under intense pressure. As a result, under the Colombians' iron-clad tutelage, local Peruvian and Bolivian production of cocaine received a major boost – and new routes flowered through Chile, Uruguay, Paraguay, Argentina and Brazil.

Bolivian cocaine freight passed freely, in transit, into Brazil; so did thousands of human 'mules' who carried 5 or 10 kilograms over the border every day of the week. Paraguay was also ideal: with an economy anchored firmly in contraband anyway, and the customs officers in danger of losing their jobs if they opened anything up, the cocaine freight freely entered the country from Bolivia, was loaded on to ships and barges, sent down the river Paraná to the Argentinian city of Rosario, and transferred – enjoying full in-transit immunity – to ocean-going vessels headed, as usual, for the United States, South Africa and Europe. Bolivian cocaine entered Argentina directly with similar ease. Meanwhile, Peru's cocaine was shipped mostly out of Lima's port, Callao, to Chile. Ecuador became involved, too: the Colombians pushed cocaine out through the port city of Guayaquil, where the customs' brief was to collect import revenue, not to check exports – they did not have the resources for both.

A European customs official said: 'Like any businessmen, the traffickers are constantly looking for new opportunities to diversify. That is further stimulated by the need to stay one step ahead of police and customs. They'll send cocaine cargoes halfway around the world just to disguise the origin, thereby minimizing the risk to their investment ten-fold, even if it costs more in transport and organization.'

Initially, in the 1970s, a large amount of cocaine was smuggled out of Colombia by 'mules' on commercial flights. These couriers usually worked for small organizations, which, as their capital increased, adopted more sophisticated methods to move greater quantities. The risk of couriers being detected was minimal at the time, so little attempt was made to hide the cocaine. So confident were the traffickers that Carlos Lehder successfully sent his mother with a load, and one of the Ochoa sisters was arrested in the United States with 1.5 kilograms hidden in her bra. Soon, however, the cocaine was concealed in false-bottomed suitcases, then it was wrapped in condoms which either were inserted into vaginas or anuses, or simply swallowed – highly dangerous since, if the packages burst, the smuggler was killed by the agonizing alkaloid blast – and, in the early 1990s, the cocaine was discovered in buttock packs. These plastic packs were surgically inserted into the buttocks of the courier, who was relieved of them in a second operation upon his or her arrival. In order to deflect suspicion, the couriers often dressed up as boy scouts, nuns and priests.

Customs officers divided courier smugglers into stuffers-and-swallowers, body-packers, and clothing and suitcase-fillers. The water-soluble cocaine was impregnated in clothing; packed or inserted into everything from wigs to shoulder pads and shoe heels, aerosol cans and toothpaste tubes; solidified into ashtrays, ornaments and other handicrafts; and in a liquid solution dyed to masquerade as a soft drink, shampoo or other innocent-looking product. 'You have a million-to-one chance of spotting it,' said the European customs official.

It is in the smuggling of cocaine by bulk commercial freight that the traffickers demonstrate their true ingenuity, although the cocaine is often merely packed alongside legitimate cargo. The drug has been found masquerading in tin cans as everything from pineapple chunks to cat food. Detection almost always results from some form of intelligence or a tip-off. In July 1993, it was discovered in boa constrictors. Seventy kilograms of cocaine had been stuffed in condoms inside more than 200 snakes, whose rear ends had been sewn up to prevent their expulsion. Most of the snakes died *en route* (to a Florida zoo). Often, the drug was hidden inside huge consigments of coffee, Colombia's biggest legal export. According to foreign customs officers, who were too physically overwhelmed by the volume of coffee shipments to be able to check them properly, up to 5 per cent of Colombia's coffee sacks were estimated to contain cocaine.

A fundamental strategy was to conceal the drug in exports whose examination was either difficult, time-consuming and unpleasant, or simply ruined the legal product. It was found inside huge Peruvian cotton bales, whose expansion on cutting their wire rendered repackaging a nightmare; inside Venezuelan bitumen barrels, which could only be checked by tipping out the contents; within big, refrigerated food loads whose melting destroyed the meat or fish; within flowers and fresh fruits – especially Jamaican coconuts – which depended on reaching their markets quickly and whose examination shortened their shelf life if the shipment were legitimate; and inside lead ingots impermeable to X-rays.

Customs officers have discovered cocaine compressed and coloured to appear like coffee beans; mixed with cellulose in the manufacture of cardboard boxes; and combined with glass fibre and other substances to create hard material that can be moulded into any shape desired. In 1992 US federal narcotics agents seized dog kennels each of which could be ground down and treated with chemicals to extract cocaine with a street value of about $450,000. 'The drug cartels have reached an all-time high in terms of technology,' said a spokesman for the US Federal Bureau of Investigation, John Hoos.

In the same way that cocaine trafficking could only prosper in Colombia because of police, judicial, government and financial corruption, so, too, could it only thrive along its routes and in its foreign markets because of similar complicity there. Apart from Panama, where General Noriega was accused by Lehder of receiving a commission for every kilogram that passed through and for every dollar that was laundered, the staging-post countries most noted for cases of high-level cocaine corruption included Peru, Bolivia, the Bahamas, Mexico, Cuba and Venezuela.

In Peru the 1980 electoral campaign of the American Popular Revolutionary Alliance party (APRA) was largely financed by Carlos Langberg, a businessman with close links to the outgoing military government, the army and police, who was jailed for cocaine trafficking two years later. Shortly after APRA's Alan García became president in 1985, the explosion of a cocaine laboratory in Lima lead to the imprisonment of Reynaldo Rodríguez, 'The Godfather', a major, Langberg-linked drugs trafficker who was an adviser to a senior police chief. Meanwhile, the APRA minister of interior, Agustín Mantilla, and a defence minister under García, General Julio Velásquez, were widely said by Peruvian and foreign intelligence, military and drug-enforcement sources to extract cocaine protection money. A senior western diplomat said that drug-related corruption under García's government went 'right to the top'. Congressmen and supreme court judges were also implicated.

When, a decade later, García was openly accused of links with drugs traffickers, an official APRA communiqué was issued noting that Reynaldo Rodríguez' lawyer was Vladimiro Montesinos, the strongman of the following president, Alberto Fujimori. It was Montesinos, a former army captain cashiered after being accused of working as a double agent for the United States, who masterminded Fujimori's seizure of absolute power in April 1992, and became head of government intelligence. Montesinos, according to APRA, had also defended the Medellín cartel's baron of cocaine paste, Evaristo Porras, who escaped from Peruvian custody while being 'taken to a judicial proceeding requested by Montesinos'. According to a foreign drugs enforcement officer, as well as Peruvian intelligence and military sources, Montesinos siphoned off protection money from the army officers whose appointments he engineered in the coca zones.

An intelligence asset of old, Montesinos' drug-linked activities went unchallenged by the US State Department. At a moment of national crisis in Peru, brought about mainly by the advance of the Shining Path guerrillas but also by years of economic misman-agement, the United States was prepared once again to turn a blind eye to a friend through whom it could exercise leverage, especially during a battle against Communism. Regarding Montesinos, Fujimori remarked with absolute aplomb: 'If these drug trafficking charges were true I'm sure that the intelligence service of the United States would not maintain such a close relationship with the National Intelligence Service [of Peru].'

Bolivian democracy, which was a far frailer creature than in Peru, had been thwarted by a military coup backed by cocaine traffickers a decade earlier, in July 1980. Its leader was General Luis García Meza, a friend of the last dictator, General Hugo Bánzer, whose own government's cocaine links had been ignored by the United States because of his strong anti-Communist, pro-US stance. Indeed, the coup organizers tried to justify their expulsion of the interim government on the grounds of eliminating Communism too. Their visceral hatred of it was real enough – as the subsequent torture and murder of hundreds of alleged left-wingers demonstrated – but the real motive was to seize the reins of the cocaine trade. Colonel Luis Arce Gómez, the head of military intelligence and a relative of Roberto Suárez, then Bolivia's biggest coca-paste trafficker and a supplier of Pablo Escobar, was appointed minister of interior. Not only did he and General García Meza organize the army's systematic extortion of protection money from the major drug traffickers – recalcitrants were murdered – but they also used paramilitary squads to stamp out the smaller dealers in Santa Cruz, the commercial heart of the cocaine trade. The squads were set up with the assistance of the Nazi, Klaus Barbie.

Although the cocaine regime lasted little more than one year, during which time the United States cut diplomatic relations with Bolivia, it enabled the big traffickers to dig deep into the country's institutions. When García Meza was captured in Brazil in 1994 for extradition to Bolivia, where he had been condemned for economic crimes and human rights abuses, he claimed that his coup had been supported by the banking and business sectors, the main political parties and some unions. Arce Gómez was jailed in the United States after being spirited out of Bolivia with the co-operation of the government of President Jaime Paz Zamora in 1989. Barbie was extradited and died in France in 1991 after being convicted there for war crimes. However, top-level corruption persisted.

Paz Zamora, whose presidential term ended in 1993, was himself linked with the traffickers. His appointments of Faustino Rico Toro, García Meza's former intelligence chief, as head of the special anti-drugs force, and Guillermo Capobianco, who the US embassy openly accused of being on the drug barons' payrolls, as minister of interior, were overturned only after extraordinary US pressure. It later emerged that President Paz Zamora was a close friend of the man then regarded as Bolivia's biggest cocaine trafficker, Isaac Chavarría. Confronted in 1994 by evidence that Chavarría had bankrolled his political campaigns and dictated his senior military appointments, Paz Zamora – a charismatic man who had earned wide respect as president – admitted that he had made some 'errors'. Meanwhile, seemingly oblivious to the fact that its anti-Communist military aid had built the Bolivian army into the beast that it became, and that attempts to involve the Colombian and Peruvian armies in fighting drugs had only produced deep-seated corruption within their ranks, the United States opted to bolster the Bolivian military to enable it to launch anti-drug operations.

Elsewhere on the continent cocaine corruption was not so conspicuous at so senior a level. In Venezuela, however, which apart from becoming a major cocaine export route to Europe was also an equally major money-laundering centre, suspicions focused on a couple of presidents. Jaime Lusinchi, who was president from 1984 to 1988 and later stripped of his parliamentary immunity to face corruption charges, married his former private secretary twelve days before she was acquitted of corruption charges relating to the $200-million fortune she was reported to have made while working for him. Lusinchi's deputy foreign minster, Adolfo Ramírez, a former governor of Caracas, was jailed after being accused by police of being linked with a major Colombian drug-trafficking organization. Lusinchi's successor,

Carlos Andrés Pérez, suffered a more humiliating fall from grace. In 1993, he was forcibly ejected from office, and later imprisoned, for allegedly embezzling $17 million of public funds. Pérez's links with the Ochoa family were such that Fabio Ochoa senior declared they had given him a $20-million mare called Porcelana. Meanwhile, the DEA claimed that Pérez was a witness at the wedding of the son of Pasquale Cuntrera, one of three notorious brothers extradited to Italy on drug-smuggling charges in September 1992.

According to the DEA, the Cuntreras had arrived in Venezuela in 1974 in order to launder the profits of the Italian mafia's heroin trading there and in the Bahamas. They soon became the bridge between the Corleonese mafia and Escobar. By the time of the Cuntreras' extradition, they were accused of handling most of the cocaine shipments passing through the country. Their arrest laid the foundations two months later for Operation Green Ice, a massive, transcontinental police swoop that severely hit the New York and Italian mafia groups, as well as the Colombian cartels from the cities of Medellín, Cali and Pereira. Requests for the Cuntreras' extradition had been ignored by the Venezuelan government for years. After his expulsion from the presidency, Carlos Andrés Pérez was also accused of being implicated in the scandal of the Bank of Credit and Commerce International, from which he was believed by US judicial authorities to have received bribes; the bank, which had branches in Venezuela, laundered drug money on a massive scale before its operations were suspended in 1991.

Venezuela continued to be seen as a money-laundering paradise. So blatant was the cocaine corruption that the president who succeeded Andrés Pérez, Ramón Velásquez, was tricked into signing a presidential pardon for a key Venezuelan trafficker who had worked with Rodríguez Gacha. By the time the pardon had been annulled and a string of employees arrested – including the president's private secretary, the cabinet secretary and the director general of the ministry of justice – the trafficker had long since vanished.

In the Bahamas, where the prime minister Lynden Pindling was knighted one year before a 1984 British Royal Commission of Inquiry minority report hinted very strongly that he had been the recipient of cocaine bribes, the political system was riddled with kickbacks from both drug traffickers and money launderers. Sir Lynden, who remained in office until 1992, was always believed to be the man who collected the lion's share at the top of the protection pyramid. In 1987, the CIA was reported to possess photographs of Sir Lynden at a party hosted by Lehder. As a tax haven, and with excellent financial links with Europe, the United States and Canada, the Bahamas' banking secrecy laws made it a mecca for organized crime. Present at Sir Lynden's investiture was his close friend and Cabinet minister, Kendal Nottage, who three years earlier had been accused of laundering money for an indicted US mafia boss, Salvatore Caruana, who, in turn, had worked with the Cuntrera brothers of Venezuela. By the mid 1980s, the US State Department estimated that cocaine, marijuana, and heroin-related activity in the Bahamas made up 10 per cent of GDP – in spite of it not being a drug-producing country.

Although US–Bahamian diplomatic relations reached a critical low point in the mid 1980s because of the corruption, the US state department had initially placed them first and foremost above fighting the cocaine trade. It was reported by the US television channel, NBC, that a plan by the Federal Bureau of Intelligence to carry out a sting-arrest on Nottage was aborted because the US embassy in Nassau feared it would jeopardize talks regarding a US submarine-testing base. By the 1990s, the United States had ceased its criticism of Sir Lynden and his cronies in return for the prime minister's muted co-operation; at times – as is frequently the case in other countries involved in the cocaine trade – this was little more than a public relations exercise designed, in addition, to salvage the political pride of US governments. Although a US Customs radar station was installed and US aircraft were permitted to overfly Bahamian airspace, among other agreements, the islands continued to provide financial succour to the cocaine traders as well as to remain a transit point for the drug itself.

In so far as the US did succeed in applying pressure on the Bahamas, it simply pushed more of the traffic westwards through Mexico. Police reported that the main drug traffickers worked out of the towns of Juárez, Sinaloa, Tijuana, Matamoros and Jalisco. The extent to which the drug traffickers had penetrated Mexican public life was starkly demonstrated by three assassinations. In May 1993, Cardinal Juan Posadas was killed in an alleged case of mistaken identity during a gun battle. In March 1994, Luis Donaldo Colosio, the presidential candidate of the ruling Institutional Revolutionary Party (PRI), was shot dead, as was the PRI's secretary general, Francisco Ruiz Massieu, in September the same year. In all three cases, the hand of the drugs traffickers – in the latter allied with politicians – was either strongly suspected or blatantly evident. 'There exists an ominous, disguised narco-power, symbiotic with the structures of government and the PRI,' declared the Mexican writer, Carlos Fuentes, after the killing of Ruiz.

Since 1986, apart from commercial retaliation, the main direct threat hanging over cocaine-trafficking countries has been that of losing US aid if not declared to be co-operative in fighting drugs. It was not until 1993 that Peru, Bolivia and Panama were 'decertified' for the first time; they were promptly let off with a warning. And, with the exceptions of the Bolivian and Panamanian generals, Luis García Meza and Manuel Noriega, the only other leader of a western block country tackled head-on over drugs corruption was Norman Saunders, the chief minister of the innocuous Turks and Caicos islands, a British colony south of the Bahamas. Saunders was arrested on drugs charges in a sting operation in Miami in February 1985.

The role in the cocaine trade of the Cuban dictator, Fidel Castro, remained unclear. Lehder's claims that Castro's permission had been required for drugs-trafficking aircraft to make fuel stops in Cuba were supported by a former Cuban intelligence officer in declarations to the British television programme *Dispatches* in June 1991. While Castro's long and close links with Noriega and Colombian guerrilla movements lent credence to the allegations, the political consequences of being caught by the United States militated against him taking such a risk. However, in July 1989, four senior military officers were executed after admitting that they had collaborated in cocaine shipments for the Medellín cartel; they described meetings with both Pablo Escobar and an M-19 leader, Ramiro Lucio. Among the officers were General Arnaldo Ochao, a Cuban hero in the Angolan war, and Colonel Antonio de la Guardia, who held a senior post in the Ministry of Interior. Seven other generals in the ministry were fired and the minister himself, José Abrantes, was jailed for twenty years. Castro's critics argued that Castro had used what were essentially show trials to conduct a political purge and to demonstrate to the world a commitment to fighting the drugs trade while secretly permitting it. In 1993, Castro's brother, Raúl, was accused before a Miami court of direct involvement with the Medellín cartel.

By 1994, cocaine was being shipped through no fewer than seventy countries, mostly in the Americas, the Caribbean and Europe. Colombians, Cuban exiles and other Latin American immigrants handled the lion's share of the distribution in the United States, while the Italian mafia groups were the Colombian cartels' main bulkhead in Europe. Cocaine's principal ports of entry were in Spain and Holland, where there were the least controls, followed closely by Italy and Belgium. However, the collapse of the Soviet empire was enabling the traffickers to open up many more routes to disguise the origin of cocaine cargoes, as well as to develop new markets there. Feeble policing in many of the former eastern bloc countries, and especially the social, political and economic chaos in Russia, lent itself to the growth of all organized crime – of which the drugs mafia were at the cutting edge.

The amount of cocaine hitting the market remained impossible to determine with any exactitude. The US state department claimed that in 1993 there were about 195,000 hectares planted with coca, yielding approximately 790,000 kilograms of cocaine. Using the state department's estimates for the price in the United

States, which is much lower than in Europe, if two thirds of that cocaine were to have actually arrived on the street its sale would have been worth anything between $50 billion and $100 billion. However, the United Nations' estimates for coca cultivation were much higher: the UN believed that in Colombia alone the figure was double that given by the US. With total earnings that far exceeded the gross domestic product of most of the countries in the region, it was hardly surprising that cocaine corrupted whole governments.

During the 1980s, there emerged two kinds of cocaine user, two kinds of stereotype that represented a racial and racist divide: the slick white yuppie and the slack black junkie. The former snorted cocaine through rolled-up banknotes while pulling off multi-million dollar deals and featuring in Harold Robbins novels. The latter smoked crack-cocaine, which had been reverted to its much more addictive and destructive form as cocaine base – lived off the state in big-city ghettoes and figured in the annual crime and unemployment statistics. Neither group was taking pure cocaine. The drug was mixed with everything from talcum powder, cornflour and bicarbonate of soda to heroin and LSD. The purity of the cocaine at street level averaged between 30 per cent and 40 per cent. 'Most accidental overdoses happen because people do not know what they are getting,' said a European drugs enforcement officer. 'They buy something that is either much stronger than what they are used to, or that has been mixed with another drug, and their body cannot take it.'

The man who more than anybody else was responsible for driving the drugs trade overseas and for protecting it at home, Pablo Escobar, spent the early part of the decade travelling widely abroad. Immediately before the enforced exile in Central America following the killing of Colombia's justice minister, Rodrigo Lara Bonilla, he had visited Spain, Brazil and the United States to develop routes, distribution and money laundering.

In October 1982, a few months after he had been voted into

Congress, Escobar attended the official celebration of the electoral triumph of Felipe González, whose party had just been swept to power. Escobar accompanied Alberto Santofimio, his friend and immediate political patron, to the festivities offered by the Spanish Socialist Workers Party at Madrid's Hotel Palace. Santofimio was invited by a prominent Spanish businessman, Enrique Salasola, who was reported to have close links with Carlos Andrés Pérez and to be married to the sister of a former Colombian minister of development. While in Spain, Escobar was believed to have cemented links with drug traffickers in the region of Galicia.

The same year, Escobar took advantage of his official, parliamentary passport, which granted him diplomatic immunity, to visit Florida, New York and Washington. Apart from overseeing business, he and his son Juan Pablo posed for a photograph in front of the White House. Escobar, who was penetrating governments across the western hemisphere, was also posing a serious challenge to US foreign policy. Rattling at the White House gates must have felt appropriate.

CHAPTER FIVE

WAGING WAR ON EXTRADITION (1985–87)

Memories were blurred as to the cause for celebration. Or exactly in which year it took place, although it was probably early 1984. The last image recorded by one guest was of Ernesto Samper attempting to insert a brass trumpet between the doors of the elevator. Samper, who was noted for his high spirits and infectious sense of humour, was anxious for his guests to stay. He wanted the party to go on. Cocaine, pot and cocaine base or *basuko* were freely available alongside wine, whisky and rum. Waiters in black bow-ties stooped to empty ashtrays, taking care to rescue any smoking reefers; white-gloved hands would, with due respect, then return these to their perch. One of those present said: 'At the time there was no social stigma about taking drugs. There was no awareness of the murderous nature of the mafia behind it, there was no terrorism.' Drug taking was only a minor offence. Samper had himself written a tract in favour of marijuana legalization a few years earlier, while head of the National Association of Financial Institutions.

Following the killing of Lara Bonilla in April 1984, the permissiveness towards illicit drug consumption – which was fashionable in Colombia just as it was in the United States and elsewhere – faded but in no way disappeared. At parties, cocaine went off the coffee table and into the bathroom. The uncomfortable paradox of consuming a drug whose illicit production generated endemic violence was all the more acute in the main country that produced it. Yet a certain tolerance of both consumers and traffickers remained. From it, there slowly emerged a silent, even conspiratorial, consensus of opinion against the hypocritical countries which were bullying Colombia to clamp down on a drug which, by the end of the decade, was described by *The Economist* magazine as the world's most profitable commodity. As Colombia began to suffer the consequences of enforcing prohibition on such a lucrative product, the fires of nationalism were stirred: it did not seem fair to Colombians that they should bear the weight of international opprobrium for supplying a product for which there was only a market because of the massive demand abroad. At the same time, in a country whose per capita earnings in 1970 had ranked it the fifth poorest in Latin America according to the Organization of American States, cocaine was serious money. A weak and corrupt democracy had little chance of surviving its onslaught, for good or for bad, even if it had wanted to.

President Belisario Betancur signed the extradition order for Carlos Lehder one week after Lara Bonilla's funeral. In spite of being compromised by the large sums of money he allegedly received from the mafia during his electoral campaign, according to Lehder's evidence in the Noriega trial, Betancur was finally engaging in the war of extradition to be waged by the traffickers for the next seven years. It was a war led by Pablo Escobar and the Medellín cartel. However, it was directly supported by the other traffickers – including those in Cali, who only threw off Escobar's yoke in 1987 when the two groups were battling for dominion over foreign markets.

Extradition of its citizens to the United States struck a raw nerve in a country where there was still a lingering resentment for the US' part in robbing it of Panama, and where left-wing guerrillas had blackened the US image with decades of anti-imperialist rhetoric. Colombian national pride was at stake. To enforce extradition was also to admit the inadequacies of its own criminal justice system. The act was politically humiliating, at home and overseas. Each extradition tempered the US' image as a bearer of justice and Colombia's as a country of criminals. To rub salt into the wound, it was the United States that was the biggest consumer of cocaine.

In March 1984, Escobar had directly confronted the outspoken US ambassador in Colombia, Lewis Tambs, after Tambs accused him of owning the raided Tranquilandia laboratories. Dismissing the accusations as 'tendentious, irresponsible and badly intentioned', Escobar said in an open letter to the ambassador that he had a 'calm conscience' and that he had not been judicially linked to the case. Hiding behind the law by giving it sacrosanct status and proudly brandishing its idiocy was common practice by Colombian delinquents. The 'infamous calumny', claimed Escobar, was part of a chain of persecution designed to secure the extradition of 'some of the sons of Colombia', something that the United States 'would never permit' of its own. 'And to conclude, *señor* ambassador, as a Colombian citizen and a member of the Congress of the Republic,' wrote Escobar, 'I want to express my most energetic and patriotic protest over the improper interference of North American boats and authorities in Colombian territory, in a way that entails the most flagrant violation of the sovereignty of our motherland.'

Although President Betancur had endorsed the Lehder extradition order and launched a big police crackdown, his government was prepared to negotiate with the ringleaders in Panama all the same. Similarly, the traffickers – who later claimed, although it was probably a lie, that they had also volunteered to pay off the $11 billion foreign debt – were not only developing new routes but also threatening the Supreme Court judges being called upon to rule on whether extradition was unconstitutional. The dialogue was a farce.

The new Minister of Justice, Enrique Parejo, according to whom the Cali traffickers were also present at the Panama talks, insisted that extradition was the only way to defend Colombia from being bought up by the mafia. 'The police maintained that corruption made it impossible to get the leaders,' he said. 'Extradition was the only available weapon.' Parejo heard there were plans to kill him. 'My secretary received telephone threats directed at me, a radio station called to say they'd got a message advising that I was to be "executed", and a tap on my telephone line was discovered in the garage next to the ministry.' An assassin finally caught up with Parejo after he was dispatched as ambassador to Budapest in an attempt to escape the heat. But the man the drug traffickers dubbed the 'cadaverous minister' struggled, tossed and turned in the snow in such a way that the four bullets he took failed to snuff out either his life or his spirit. A Liberal Party dissident, he ran for president in 1994.

Meanwhile, in July 1984, the United States indicted Escobar, Jorge Luis Ochoa and Rodríguez Gacha for their cocaine trafficking through Nicaragua. The indictment enabled the US embassy to request their extradition from the beleaguered judges of the Supreme Court. More than a dozen drug traffickers were now in a similar position. Escobar, who was already being chased on smuggling charges regarding the elephants, rhinoceroses and the other zoo animals that he had slipped into the country without anybody noticing at the time, was also tied to the murder of Lara Bonilla. Nevertheless, because of a succession of supposed legal technicalities and a mysterious lack of a quorum, among endless other postponements, Escobar retained his parliamentary immunity until December. By that time, Tambs had survived an attempted car-bomb attack on his residence, been advised that one of his bodyguards had been paid to kill him, and ordered US staff with children out of the country; a car bomb near the embassy had killed a passer-by. The DEA's Medellín office was closed and Tambs was recalled to Washington.

In spite of the pressure, Escobar was prospering. While in Panama his Nápoles stronghold had been raided by the police, along with the Ochoas' Veracruz estate, in a gigantic hunt for the Medellín cartel leaders in which his aircraft, amphibious vehicles, a helicopter, weapons and radio equipment were seized, and scores of people were briefly detained, including the cocaine-paste baron Evaristo Porras and the Ochoas's horse-dealer father. Once this initial police crackdown had faded, in mid 1984, Escobar returned to Medellin. He threw a big party for the christening of his daughter Manuela, attended bullfights with his wife and bodyguards, and rescued his father from kidnappers after mobilizing 5,000 gunmen and killing his father's bodyguards and every hood involved. And while the wholesale price of cocaine in Miami – which had doubled after the Tranquilandia raids cut the supply – fell back to its usual level, Escobar and Rodríguez Gacha were expanding coca cultivation in the Llanos departments and opening up more routes through northern Mexico, whence the cocaine was easily moved over the 3,239-kilometre border with the United States. As with Florida, the border trade was again mixed up with Latin American immigrants and again following in the footsteps of marijuana. The connection with the Mexican traffickers, who had previously dealt in marijuana, was made by Rodríguez Gacha through a Honduran vagrant, Juan Ramón Matta Ballesteros, who had met Rodríguez Gacha while looking for emeralds after being deported by the United States to Colombia because he held a false Colombian passport. The Mexican route not only made Escobar billions of dollars but also cemented his close friendship with Rodríguez Gacha. Their bond – a bond between peasant sons – was at the heart of the terrorist machine taking on the Colombian state.

Escobar's other main partner, Jorge Luis Ochoa, was proving less fortunate. Spanish police arrested him and Gilberto Rodríguez Orejuela, the leader of the Cali mafia, in November the same year. The two were old friends whose drug-trafficking interests, and better social standing than Escobar and Rodríguez Gacha, had bonded them together since the early 1970s. By 1975, they were listed as joint owners of the First Interamericas Bank in Panama, which the government later closed down. Tailed for more than two months before their arrest, it was clear they were working in unison. According to the Spanish police, holding companies were set up through which the men opened bank accounts and bought luxurious properties and a string of Mercedes Benz. The men, who had false passports, met regularly for business as well as socially with their wives. The relationship demonstrated how close the Medellín and Cali traffickers really were, and that it was the Ochoas who were the link between them.

Following their arrest, a marathon legal battle ensued. The United States filed for extradition. So, however, did Colombia. In the case of Ochoa, Colombia was suddenly keen to press the charges for his smuggling 128 Spanish fighting bulls into Cartagena. In the case of Rodríguez Orejuela, it was more difficult – but the same ruse was employed by Colombia for each of them. Their US indictments (the Cali leader faced drug-trafficking charges in Los Angeles and New York) were simply copied and re-filed in Colombia, thereby reinforcing its request. More than a year and a half later, after a labyrinthine legal struggle conducted by a battery of highly paid lawyers working for the drug traffickers on both sides of the Atlantic, Colombia won the final appeal. Rodriguez Orejuela was dispatched to a jail in Cali and acquitted several months afterwards, rendering the US indictments unusable because he could not be re-tried for the same offences. Ochoa was bailed in Cartagena and promptly disappeared. In spite of the existing US extradition requests to Colombia, the attorney general's office had done everything to assist the repatriation of two of its most notorious cocaine traffickers, knowing that they would make the usual mockery of national justice on their return. The Minister of Justice, Enrique Parejo, said: 'The attorney general, Carlos Jiménez Gómez, helped initiate the Cali case against Rodríguez Orejuela through his delegate in the Valle del Cauca department, in order for it to serve as a basis for the extradition here rather than to the USA.'

By 1985, the attorney general's office was, with some few and noble exceptions, allegedly rotten to the core. According to Parejo, Jiménez Gómez 'was doing everything he could to frustrate and block the extradition processes'. A senior police officer added: 'I knew that if I gave the attorney general's office any opportunity, it was going to impede my work.' However, four Colombians were extradited, including a well-known Medellín banker, Hernán Botero, who was convicted in Miami for money laundering and jailed for thirty years. The rapidity of the conviction, the length of the sentence and the sight of Botero in chains inflamed Colombian public opinion – and terrified the traffickers. Simultaneously, the twenty-four Supreme Court judges being called upon to issue judgement on a suit against the treaty, brought by an obscure lawyer, suffered ever graver and more systematic threats.

A letter received by one of the judges, Ricardo Medina, was typical of the brutish intimidation. 'We, the Extraditables, are writing to you because . . . we know that you have said publicly and cynically that the extradition treaty is constitutional . . . we are not going to ask or beg or seek compassion, because we do not need it. VILE WRETCH. We are going to DEMAND a favourable decision . . . we will not accept stupid excuses of any kind: we will not accept that you go sick, we will not accept that you go on holiday, and we will not accept that you resign. The decision will be made by you within fifteen days of the arrival of the recommendation of the attorney general's office.' (The authors of the letter, a group calling themselves 'The Extraditables', clearly knew what that recommendation would be.) Medina was told that his police bodyguards were members of their 'organization' and that rather than give him a 'wooden smoking jacket' they would prefer to send him the quartered bodies of his family. The note concluded by paving the way for a bribe, followed by the warning: 'We swear before God and the life of our children, that if you fail us or betray us, you will be a dead man!!!'

At least thirty judges had already been murdered in the previous five years when the judge leading the investigation of the Lara Bonilla killing, Tulio Manuel Castro Gil, was gunned down in Bogotá in July 1985. He had dismissed his official bodyguards nine months earlier because he could no longer afford them. As with Lara Bonilla, his was a death foretold, a death waiting to happen. 'Only God grants a man's life. Nothing is done without his will,' he wrote in the run-up to his killing. 'I have fulfilled a mission entrusted to my sacred function ... I am sure they want to kill me.' Three weeks later, motorbike *sicarios* murdered a Bogotá prison warden who had thwarted an escape attempt by the Honduran, Juan Ramón Matta Ballesteros; Ballesteros, Escobar's Mexican link, had been arrested in May 1984, and was facing extradition for the murder of a DEA agent in Mexico.

There seemed no limit to the cartel's reach: it was slowly ripping away at the soft underbelly of the Colombian state. Politicians, judges, prosecutors and police were succumbing one by one to the traffickers' threats and bribes in so dogged and sinister a fashion that people could no longer trust their colleagues or swear to the integrity of their friends. The money and fear were too much. Backed up by the knowledge that failure to tow the line would probably mean death, $50,000 for a signature was an offer you could not refuse. 'Nobody passes the test,' said one police infiltrator of the mafia. 'They cannot afford to.' There was only one public institution that still stood outside the strict margins of party political influence, boasted a tradition of judicial, if élitist, independence and appeared to be beyond the drug-traffickers' reach: the Supreme Court.

In late 1985, that changed. At 11.40 a.m. on Thursday, 6 November about fifty M-19 guerrillas – some dressed in suits and ties – armed with assault rifles, machine-guns, rockets and grenades stormed the Palace of Justice in the centre of Bogotá. They made straight for the upper floors in order to take hostage the judges of the Supreme Court. The intention was that their demands be published in the newspapers and broadcast on radio, and a show trial of President Betancur be staged. The guerrillas' declaration accused the government of double-cross in peace talks and of blanket oppression by the 'leading class' and 'high military officials'. However, its most telling demand was that the Supreme Court judges decide 'here and now' whether Colombia should continue to surrender not only its natural resources but also 'through an unpopular and scandalous extradition treaty ... our jurisdiction, the most recent and novel of all the surrenders, which is a mortal blow against national sovereignty . . . Hundreds of our countrymen are seriously threatened . . . by the legislation of alien countries'.

The hand of the drug traffickers was only too evident. In the aftermath of the 1981 kidnap of Martha Nieves Ochoa, a sister of the Ochoa brothers, the Medellín cartel and M-19 appeared to have engaged in more than merely a truce. It was reported that Castro – who had granted succour to M-19 guerrillas after a previous spectacular, the seizure of the Dominican Republic embassy in Bogotá – had permitted cocaine shipments through Cuba provided that the traffickers flew back weapons to M-19. Much later, an M-19 leader and future senator, Ramiro Lucio, was named by the Cuban colonel shot for cocaine trafficking, Antonio de la Guardia, as being the colonel's intermediary with the Medellín cartel; Lucio was also rumoured to be closely involved with the notorious Baz Rezin company, which had 'brought in enough MEK to paint the whole of South America'.

According to official documents made available to the newspaper *El Espectador*, the rebels agreed to raid the Palace of Justice in exchange for weapons and money from the cocaine mafia. Several expert witnesses reported that some guerrillas made a beeline for where the extradition files were stored. These were duly burned in the nightmarish inferno that followed. Two years later, there also surfaced a copy of a draft rejection of a law suit denouncing the extradition treaty; the constitutional arm of the Supreme Court was to have started considering the suit the very day of the palace's seizure. A close henchman of Escobar's confirmed in a written interview: 'The storming of the Palace of Justice was organized by Pablo Escobar, with [Jaime] Bateman, an M-19 leader, and [Andrés] Almarales; the objective was to negotiate non-extradition, but as there was not a dialogue, it was decided to burn the archives.' Burning the archives was exactly what Escobar had done with those incriminating him for car theft and murder in Medellín two years earlier.

WAGING WAR ON EXTRADITION (1985–87)

Minutes after the rebels took over the building – a big, ugly, imposing structure built after the previous one was burned down during the *Bogotazo* following the assassination of Gaitán – it was surrounded by police and soldiers. The guerrillas were heavily dug in and spraying gunfire at all who approached, inside and outside. Armoured vehicles were the only option to break the strategic gridlock – the only option, that was, once dialogue and the fate of the 300 hostages had been almost instantly discarded by the government. Four tanks and two armoured cars entered the square. Bomb explosions shook the palace basement. At 2 p.m., the first tank smashed its way into the building through the main door, whose porch bore the inscription: 'Colombians, weapons have given us independence, laws will give us freedom.' The words rang somewhat caustic in the circumstances. Flocks of pigeons fleeing the tank were the third component of an image of the prelude to tragedy that embedded itself in the national consciousness. Two more tanks penetrated the Palace of Justice shortly afterwards, forcing the guerrillas to retreat to the upper (fourth and fifth) floors; helicopters landed police storm-trooper units on the roof. Explosion after explosion shook the building, which was already holed by tank shells, and a column of smoke began to emerge.

While scores of people were evacuated, the guerillas remained huddled with their principal captives, the most senior judges in the land. Among them was the president of the Supreme Court, Alfonso Reyes, whose desperate entreaties for the security forces to stop shooting were simply ignored. 'Please help us, stop the firing,' Reyes implored of President Betancur in a telephone appeal to a radio station (he had failed to get through to the president himself). 'We are surrounded by people from M-19, please stop the firing immediately . . . this is urgent, it's a matter of life and death, do you hear me?' But no such order was issued and the military continued its assault. Asked about Reyes' appeal, the colonel in charge of the tanks replied: 'If someone shoots at me, I shoot back.' Reyes' line went dead at 5 p.m. while he was talking to his son. A series of rocket and dynamite explosions followed, before fire broke out on the upper floors of the east wing. By midnight, more people had been evacuated, the government had offered the guerrillas a fair trial if they surrendered, and the army had taken the third floor. But the flames continued, and at 2 a.m. there were more explosions and the battle burst into life again – resulting in the killing of Reyes by the M-19 leader, Andrés Almarales.

At dawn, an army urban anti-guerrilla unit entered the building, leading to another full-scale fight. The Palace of Justice was little more than a smoking shell. At midday, the soldiers took the fourth floor; the guerrillas hurled dead bodies down the marble stairs. With one last, tremendous explosion at 1 p.m., the siege was over. The charred corpses of more than forty rebels, about a dozen police and soldiers, and around fifty employees of the Palace of Justice were slowly exhumed from the rubble and the ash. Eleven of the twenty-four Supreme Court judges were among the victims, including all four judges of its constitutional arm – who had been shot at close range. Six thousand case files had been incinerated in the blaze.

The court had been effectively destroyed. Its survivors were staggered by the government's nonchalance. Humberto Murcía Ballén, a judge whose artificial leg had been shattered by a bullet and who had spent most of the siege heaped among other hostages, both living and dead, before being pushed into a grenade blast that he miraculously survived prior to being thrown down a stairwell, told a radio station: 'What I don't understand is that in a country where people are talking of peace, where dialogues are under way and where the government and the peace commission send delegates to the Uribe, the Hobo and I don't know where, that it stands by impassively and lets the lives of the country's leading judges be sacrificed.' What further enraged the judicial system was that the plan had been detected a month earlier, prompting a meeting of the Security Council. The justice minister, Parejo, said: 'Police vigilance was stepped up as a result, but, curiously, although I did not know at the time, two days before the seizure the police were replaced by a handful of private security guards.' Once again, it was, as Murcía Ballén noted, the story of a tragedy foretold.

Survivors boycotted President Betancur at a memorial mass. The judicial system launched an indefinite national strike: it felt abandoned and betrayed by the government. Parejo admitted: 'Justice, at its highest level, was under threat, but its fate did not bother us and now we cry inconsolably for what we did not know how to defend, because defending justice is not achieved merely by force. Its best shield is the national conscience. Society failed because it did not discourage the threat with a resounding repudiation of those who, from the ranks of organized crime, plotted the assassination of the Supreme Court.' The court's new president, Fernando Uribe Restrepo, said the tragedy resulted from Colombia's 'undervaluation' of justice, which had been 'calmly decapitated'. One survivor, Gabriel Salóm, who feigned death while slowly being soaked in the blood of an expiring colleague tossed on top of him, noted: 'If Parliament had been seized, not a shot would have been fired. The political élite is untouchable, but since we neither gave votes or indulged in party propaganda, since we were independent and had no political power, nobody was interested.'

After the tragedy, the Supreme Court was crippled. Many judges and employees felt unable to return, and resigned. They, as well as those who were killed in the seizure, were replaced at the very moment when the drug traffickers were stepping up their cancerous, take-the-money-or-take-the-bullet offensive within the criminal justice system. It was a perfect opportunity to infiltrate the court; indeed, several of the new appointees were believed to have links with M-19. So low was the court's morale after what it considered to have been its abandonment by the government that its will to resist the mafia was severely hobbled – and many people refused to accept jobs there. A future vice president of Colombia, Humberto de la Calle, resigned from the court after only a few weeks. The court's new president, Fernando Uribe Restrepo, resigned five months later because of death threats; his successor quit for the same reason the following year, when two more

Supreme Court judges were assassinated and a third died after his oxygen tubes were mysteriously disconnected in a US hospital.

The storming of the Palace of Justice also marked the decisive collapse of the government's peace talks with the different guerrilla groups. The truce had been engaged in by M-19 and the Popular Liberation Army (EPL) purely to win a breathing space, to widen their political bases and to establish urban militia in the poor neighbourhoods of Medellín, Cali and Bogotá (as was later acknowledged by one M-19 leader, Carlos Pizarro). The FARC guerrillas, meanwhile, had set up the Patriotic Union party through which they planned to participate in the upcoming parliamentary elections. The peace process had already been jeopardized by increased right-wing paramilitary activity opposed to it in principle, but the Palace of Justice raid and the government's exaggerated response rang its death-knell. As a result, the drug traffickers and all the guerrilla groups were thrown firmly into each others' arms – although their relationship bore a closer resemblance to a boxers' clinch.

Having encouraged coca cultivation and its conversion into coca paste – for sale to the traffickers – the FARC guerrillas started to push for a bigger slice of the business directly and indirectly (through extortion). This brought FARC into bitter conflict with Rodríguez Gacha, who was already involved with the right-wing paramilitary squads confronting FARC in the fertile farming region in the valley of the river Magdalena, where he and Escobar owned their great estates. The Patriotic Union party was attacked head-on, and peasant murders turned into peasant massacres.

With the cocaine heavyweights fighting not one war but two, anarchic violence exploded. The state was wedged into a triangle in which its most dangerous adversary – the drug traffickers – was its principal ally against the guerrillas. This bloody tangle of interests became most evident under the Liberal government of Virgilio Barco, who succeeded President Betancur in August 1986. Like Betancur, initially Barco showed no interest in supporting extradition. By December that year, twelve people had been extradited on drugs charges from Colombia to the United States –

all the orders having been issued by Betancur. Some of the prisoners faced a lifetime in US jails. Their fate prompted a communiqué in November 1986 from the group calling themselves the Extraditables, whose letterhead maxim was: 'We prefer a tomb in Colombia to a jail cell in the United States.'

The traffickers, who remained anonymous, were under the leadership of Escobar. They set out five demands. Apart from a ban on extradition, which was claimed to be an affront to human and family rights and was declared an 'undebatable' issue, they also requested the government to repatriate Colombian prisoners on the grounds that they were 'discriminated against and abused' abroad. Other petitions were that 'educational establishments' be penalized if they excluded their children; that the Church prevent the media calling them 'drug traffickers, murderers or delinquents' when they had not been declared as such by the courts ('this would avoid disinformation and violence'); and that judges be promoted according to their professional merits and not their political interests. If extradition were outlawed, they promised immediately to suspend their 'military actions' against 'the extraditers'. The mafia signed off in defence of 'the absolute respect of people's rights'.

Such absolute respect for people's rights entailed killing anybody who was exercising their professional obligation to apply the law or to legislate, anybody who was exercising their constitutional freedom to express an opinion, and anybody who was merely keeping to the rules and regulations of their job. Where those paths were at odds with their own purposes – regarding extradition or any other aspect of trafficking – the cartel did not hesitate to blast aside the people causing the obstacle. That way, with money to grease the hinges, doors were opened afterwards – as the Honduran, Juan Ramón Mata Ballesteros, had discovered when he finally walked out of Bogotá jail in March 1986, following the payment of $2 million in bribes and the killing of the warden who had blocked his last attempt; the new warden simply resigned with his golden handshake.

The murder in July of the *El Espectador* correspondent in

Leticia, Luis Roberto Camacho, who had fought with the Medellín cartel's paste baron, Evaristo Porras, presaged that of the newspaper's brave and heroic editor, Guillermo Cano, in December. No other Colombian journalist had confronted the drugs trade so bitterly, so articulately and with such heartfelt moral outrage as Cano. He had denounced the influence of cocaine money in politics for several years, urging in vain that cocaine corruption in all sectors of public life be unmasked. In one of his last editorials, Cano raged against 'the political leaders in government, in Congress and in the parties' for failing to tackle the rising number of contract murders linked to the drugs trade. 'It seems that we have decided to live with crime and declare ourselves defeated ... the Colombian [drug] chiefs pass unpunished in public halls and in private parties ... the drugs cartel has taken over Colombia.' The newspaper's elderly family patriarch was gunned down by a motorcycle assassin armed with the archetypal MAC-10 machine-pistol as he drove out of its offices in the Bogotá industrial district of El Dorado. From that moment, *El Espectador* slowly became a shadow of its former self – a process that was hastened by a car bomb three years later.

Cano's murder followed that in November of Colonel Jaime Ramírez, the former head of the police anti-drugs squad whose dynamic grit had won him great respect nationally and internationally. Ramírez's replacement, Colonel Teodoro Campo, who was also highly regarded, was suddenly moved from his post in December following the appointment of General José Guillermo Medina Sánchez as head of the national police. Medina Sánchez was later sacked and charged with illicit enrichment amid public allegations that he had taken bribes from Pablo Escobar.

Meanwhile, the Supreme Court had reversed its original position on extradition. Escobar had won the first war. On 13 December, bribed and browbeaten, and tired of the offhand treatment of governments, the Supreme Court declared the 1979 extradition treaty to be inapplicable on the grounds that the law sanctioning it had been signed by a delegate of the then president, Julio César Turbay Ayala, and not by the president himself. 'The fact is that the magistrates and the judiciary in general became bored with being cannon fodder and decided to pass the ball to the executive and legislature,' said one court official. The president of Congress, Humberto Peláez, declared that the decision would staunch 'the absurd shedding of blood'.

An almost gleeful article in *Semana* noted that the decision had been expected because the state had been losing the war anyway, and that the ruling followed reports that Colombian prisoners were being physically as well as legally maltreated abroad (which echoed the Extraditables' claims). The mafia had waged its war, the magazine opined, not out of personal motives but because of 'offended dignity'. The mafia had been 'irritated' that judges whom they knew to be corrupt were ordering extraditions. And since the threat of extradition had scared off the minor players, the mafia could now be weakened by a dispersal of power. In Medellín, the final edition of Escobar's newspaper, *Medellín Cívico*, held no such reservations. 'Triumph of the People,' it roared.

The court's decision was based on a report by Jairo Duque Pérez, a sixty-three-year-old *paisa* who had joined the Supreme Court after the burning of the Palace of Justice. Chance played a strange hand. By drawing lots, Duque Pérez had been given the job of reconstructing the extradition report destroyed by fire. By drawing lots, Duque Pérez had then been appointed to issue the recommendation.

By the end of 1986, the Extraditables had won their battles on all fronts. Escobar had even been acquitted of animal contraband, and omitted from the list of those accused of Lara Bonilla's murder. However, the current victory was short lived. And an attempt – relayed through a Miami lawyer who met Escobar, Jorge Luis Ochoa and Carlos Lehder in Medellin – to secure an amnesty from the United States in return for offering information on Communist guerrillas and abandoning the cocaine business was scorned by the US attorney general's office. Indeed, in November the Medellín cartel leaders had been indicted *en masse* in Miami; they were charged with smuggling 58,000 kilograms of cocaine into the United States between 1978 and 1985. Although the amount smuggled was a fraction of the true figure, it was the world's biggest single cocaine case. With the murders of Ramírez and particularly of Cano, Escobar and his colleagues triggered the wrath of the new Colombian government, too. Although the judicial system was maimed, the media was muzzled, Congress was increasingly compromised and the national police was entering its era of greatest corruption, the Barco executive launched Colombia's third cocaine crackdown.

Once again, the repression scarcely touched the drug traffickers. In 1,300 raids, a mere 243 kilograms of cocaine were seized. Of the 360 people arrested, most were quickly released by judges. Just five laboratories were destroyed. And although more than 400 weapons were picked up, that was a drop in the ocean compared with the hundreds of thousands everybody knew were coming into the country. Evaristo Porras was arrested again – for illicit arms possession – but was let free a few months later. However, Barco did launch emergency decrees suspending certain individual rights, regulating motorcycle ownership – to impede *sicarios* – and heavily penalizing ownership of illegal airstrips. The president also launched a witness protection programme and offered rewards for information.

The jackpot came on 4 February 1987. Carlos Lehder was arrested in a dawn raid on a small ranch in the area of Rionegro in Antioquia. According to a DEA source, who claimed that Lehder was bisexual, he was caught after a party with young boys. Police were tipped off by a peasant allegedly complaining about noise. One of Escobar's top henchmen claimed much later that Lehder was caught because of his carelessness and lack of money to protect himself sufficiently. Yet Lehder, down on his luck, and with many of his known assets frozen by the government, had turned into a *basuko*-smoking pawn of Escobar's; and it was strongly suspected that he had been deliberately ditched by the cartel. The idea would have been to grant the government a bone to give the *gringos* by handing over somebody who, as well as no longer serving them, was also considered a security risk.

Loyalty was never one of Escobar's strong points. Lehder was convinced that Escobar, whom he referred to as the Monster, had shopped him; Escobar denied it.

Given that Lehder's extradition order had been signed by the former president, there was no legal obstacle to his immediate removal to the United States. Eleven hours later, Lehder was flown out of Bogotá to Tampa, Florida, on a DEA aircraft. More than a year later, after unprecedented security and the calling of 115 prosecution witnesses – the most damning ones being Lehder's former comrades who were in jail themselves – Lehder was found guilty of conspiring to smuggle 3,300 kilograms of cocaine into the United States. His jail sentence was deliberately exemplary: life without parole, plus 135 years. At one point, Bob Merkle, the US prosecuting attorney, predicted that the Medellín cartel would be destroyed by its predilection for violence. Time would very shortly reveal how right he was; what he failed to forecast was that, in the meantime, other, subtler traffickers led by the Cali cartel would not only ride on its back, but also ride to a far more telling victory after Escobar and Rodríguez Gacha were dead.

On the night that the extradition treaty collapsed, gunpowder and fireworks exploded in and around Medellín as the coca trade celebrated in traditional Colombian style. Christmas had come early. Although President Barco tried to revive the treaty by re-signing it, and although the Medellín cartel responded to his efforts with ever greater violence, thereafter the traffickers held the upper hand. But those who led the battle, which was personified by Escobar, which grew bloodier and bloodier as the mafia became steadily drunker with power and with the violence itself, would pay the price. In Medellín, the war against extradition was the golden age of the *sicarios*, the hired killers drawn mainly from the poor, northern neighbourhoods who cared little for their personal longevity. The adolescent contract killers preferred to live one minute as a somebody than thirty years as a nobody; and when they died, to be wearing Nike running shoes astride a shiny Japanese motorbike, while their mothers cooed over a new refrigerator. Killing became a way of life, however short that life might be.

Homicides in Medellín, which had doubled between 1980 and 1984, had doubled again by 1986 when the figure reached 2,000 (excluding the surrounding municipalities such as Envigado, Itagüí and Bello). By that year, homicide was the main cause of death in the city. With more than 100 killings a year for every 100,000 inhabitants – three times the national level of Colombia, which already led the international ratings for countries not caught up in civil war – Medellín was the most violent city in the world. Yet poverty and social hardship themselves were not the root causes of the problem. In an environment whose moral values had caved in to the primacy of money and power, pleading economic necessity was merely an excuse to commit a crime: a convenient lie arising mainly out of the envy generated by disparities in wealth levels which the cocaine trade had made glaringly apparent. Densely packed though they were, Medellín's so-called communes in the north no longer consisted of endless, unlit and drainless tin and cardboard hovels. Brick houses, asphalted roads and schools were being built and the installation of basic services – telephones included – was fast catching up with the arrival of new migrants. Father Federico Carrasquilla, of the Popular district, said: 'It is usually believed that violence is because of a lack of education and jobs, and because of broken families, but that situation was far worse when the area was invaded and growing rapidly in the 1970s. In my first seven years here there were only six homicides; in 1985 there were three a week.'

What had changed was the availability of fast money from cocaine alongside the influence of the guerrillas, who in taking advantage of the Betancur peace talks had established themselves quite openly in the lower-class urban neighbourhoods. Instead of using force in the last resort to defend people's rights in an unjust and incompetent state, force became the guerrillas' *raison d'être*. Shops and small businesses grew tired of their requests for collaboration payments in order to run soup kitchens. Hence, the guerrillas extorted the cash with guns. Thus encouraged, gangs of delinquents – some of whose members had previous links to the guerrillas – did the same. Shopkeepers and distributors defended themselves, the guerrillas and gangs fought over territory, and gang and family vendettas ensued. Nobody could look to the state for help, so imposing power meant buying guns. Buying guns meant working for them in a climate where life was fast losing its value while money was fast gaining it.

Enter the contract killer, a profession already thriving under the drugs trade. The cocaine traffickers, who could hardly complain before judges, already settled their private scores with bullets. The tantalizingly vast amounts of cash they spread around – cash that could raise people from rags to riches overnight – made the traffickers the lords of the realm. At the same time, in showing it was possible to join the rich man's world, and how, the drugs mafia became the principal social model in Medellín's poorer suburbs and surrounding districts. As the gangs proliferated – there were estimated to be at least 150 in the Aburrá valley – their services came also to be used by some politicians as well as by anyone who wanted to rid himself of a debt or an awkward enemy. To manage this booming market of death, which was stimulated further by poorly paid, corrupt policemen and the existence of government-sanctioned municipal self-defence forces, offices sprang up to handle the demand and to place the contracts. By the time the contract had passed down the chain to the actual killers – thereby ensuring the anonymity of the person behind it and, so long as the hit succeeded, riskless profits for the intermediaries – it was worth a fraction of the original price. The favoured, luxury method was the motorcycle kill. According to DAS, the state security police, reported motorcycle killings tripled between 1982 to more than eighty in 1986; the true figure would have been much higher.

The *sicarios* were characterized by their adoration for their mothers, their religious superstition and their relentless consumerism. In a world in which fathers were mostly dead, drunk, unemployed or simply absent, it was around the mothers that households hinged and it was to protect and support their mothers that the sons fought. They sought both to assume the father's role and to imitate and become the strongest leader around. Priests were called upon to grant their blessing for the successful outcome of a 'job', the term given to a contract killing. Most spiritual dependence, however, was placed obsessively upon the Virgin Mary, whose image they would wear on a necklace, keep inside their pockets, or slip into their shoes to ensure a quick getaway. (When asked why he preferred the Virgin to Christ, Fabian, a fatherless, out-of-work, eighteen-year-old taxidermist in the Nuevo Horizonte district, stressed: 'She's the *mother* of God.') Money earned was spent in a binge of alcohol, women, cachet brand-name clothing, stereo systems and the latest household electrical goods; nothing was saved. Those whom the Virgin failed to protect were often serenaded at their funerals by rap, salsa and heavy metal music.

The main cemetery of San Pedro, on the border of the northern suburbs, feels more like a palace. White tomb walls soar skywards in a celestial swirl of red, yellow and electric-blue chrysanthemums. Liveried pallbearers mince around like footmen of the dead. From one marble mausoleum lit with chandeliers, the soft strains of violins and guitars issue twenty-four hours a day. Below the chandeliers, scripted in discotheque purple with pink underlining, are the words: 'Remember your Mummy, I will always be with you.' Mummy's sons were the Muñoz Mosquera boys. They were poor boys made good, making it from petty gangsters to be killer lieutenants of Pablo Escobar. The brothers ('the most beautiful thing God gave me' proclaimed another motherly banner) died in the line of duty.

Behind the musical mausoleum, a pair of youths clambered down from a ladder after paying their respects to a dead friend by knocking on his tombstone; red flies flickered on the fresh cement. The friend had been shot dead by police. 'One is born to die,' said the taller one, repeating what had become a local cliché. He had a front tooth missing and was sweating out the sickly-sweet *aguardiente* on which both were drunk. Jorge had spent two years with an evangelical church. 'I was baptised and everything, but they betrayed me. They said they would give me help but they gave me nothing. I now believe in Satan – in this bad world the good don't get anything.' Jorge still had a bullet in his thigh where it had lodged after entering his groin; he had been thirteen years old at the time. Neither he nor his scar-faced mate, Eduardo, knew exactly how many people they had killed. 'Perhaps ten but you can't always see in the dark,' said Eduardo. Both were a little embarrassed.

They had fought for the Priscos gang, in the lower-middle-class Aranjuez district, whose leaders were at the beck and call of Escobar. 'I feel some shame, but even if you can find work in a factory you are treated like slaves. We're young,' said Jorge. They hated the police. Eduardo had just been in jail for a week for stealing a carton of milk. 'The police put me in a water container and dropped an electric wire into it. My body went like this,' he said, jerking his arms up and down and making a noise like a bluebottle. 'The police are killers in disguise.'

He was interrupted by tears and wailing from the burial nearby of a twenty-three-year-old boy killed by three bullets. A woman screamed and fell, her body shuddering and her eyes shut tight. For no apparent reason, Jorge and Eduardo fled, the latter pressing into my palm a picture of the Virgin Santa María Auxiliadora, the *sicarios'* favourite religious figure. Her shrine was in a church at the nearby town of Sabaneta, where the local killers crowded in every Tuesday to pay their respects and their dues. Escobar was a regular worshipper.

I joined the funeral's pallbearers. 'Burial rites changed with the drugs traffickers,' said the senior one. 'Suddenly everybody wanted lots of flower carriers, the best [North] American coffins, and motorbike escorts – which we had to stop because we needed too many. The richest traffickers take the best spots in the cemetery, next to the chapel, where they put ugly cement angels.'

Back in their hearse, the men tuned into tangos on the radio. We passed a legless beggar propelling himself amidst the traffic on a trolley. A stuffed chestnut horse stood outside a taxidermist's. 'You will see that all is lies/You will see that nothing is love/That nothing matters to the world,' cried the tango singer. But the pallbearers were happy, humming along.

CHAPTER SIX

THE SEEDS OF A MAFIA DIVIDE (1987–9)

While Escobar engaged in his gangster terrorism around Medellín, where his *plomo o plata* (lead or silver) persuasion policy ensured the loyalty of a large segment of the city's political, judicial and economic élite as well as many throughout the poorer classes, Rodríguez Gacha was rearing paramilitary squads in the region of the Magdalena Medio. It was Rodríguez Gacha who had stimulated coca cultivation in Colombia and had thereby come into direct contact with peasant colonists in the low foothills and savannahs of the Putumayo, Caquetá, Meta and Guaviare departments in the south east. To the chagrin of Rodríguez Gacha, the colonists, with the help of the FARC guerrillas, soon discovered how to convert the leaf into cocaine base, thereby retaining a little more of the trade for themselves. Worse still for Rodríguez Gacha, although the guerrillas did not extort coca taxes from the peasants, they squeezed money out of the chains of coca-base buyers whom he had commissioned. For a while there was an uneasy truce, with the guerrillas offering security in return for their share; it was a classic protection racket. The guerrillas developed their own coca plantations and base laboratories, too.

By the mid 1980s, however, the tensions were not only too great but the land-owning interests and ambitions of the leading traffickers, and of Rodríguez Gacha in particular, were such that the two sides were at loggerheads. In a later interview with *Semana* magazine, Escobar made his position icy clear: 'That they accuse me of being a drug trafficker, so what, I am used to that and nobody proves it. But that they try to make me out as a colleague of the guerrillas, that I do not accept, since it wounds my personal dignity . . . I am a man of investments and therefore I cannot be in agreement with the guerrillas, who fight against property.'

Rodríguez Gacha had succeeded in buying up a corridor of land stretching from his original base in the small town of Pacho, not far from Bogotá, to Puerto Boyacá, more than 100 kilometres away on the river Magdalena, where he bordered Escobar's domain. By 1986, known drug traffickers were conservatively estimated to own nearly 1 million hectares in Colombia. Meanwhile, the creation of the Patriotic Union party as FARC's political arm had given it a local, legal leverage that irked the cocaine mafia and fellow landowners. By the time the Betancur peace process collapsed – leaving the members of the Patriotic Union very exposed – the traffickers and the army were champing at the bit. They were supported by other big landowners, who not only were tired of the guerrillas' extortion and kidnapping but were also as anxious as the traffickers themselves to extend their own territories – at whatever the cost to the small holdings around them.

The paramilitary organization that was an umbrella for the three forces and was patronized by Rodríguez Gacha and Escobar, ACDEGAM, had already killed hundreds of people by 1985. What started out as a self-defence group in the valley of the river Magdalena metamorphosed into a fanatical anti-Communist crusade in which any peasant even suspected of selling food to the few hundred guerrillas – who, unlike the army, bought rather than stole it – was murdered. Cattle thieves, shoplifters, beggars and homosexuals were slaughtered. The full horror – and the complicity of the army – only came to light when a central government investigation was launched after more than fifty peasants were massacred near the Gulf of Urabá in early 1988.

The investigation led straight to ACDEGAM and implicated a string of local government officials, politicians and senior army and police officers, as well as Rodríguez Gacha, Escobar and a cartel colleague, Fidel Castaño.

However, it was the evidence of a deserter, Diego Viáfara, who was given refuge in the United States after talking to Colombia's state security police, DAS, that revealed the true scale of the paramilitary/drug-trafficking alliance. With minute details, Viáfara described ACDEGAM's military and financial activities, as well as its river, land and air transport, communications and drugs-trafficking infrastructure in four central, northern departments – Boyacá, Cundinamarca, Santander and Antioquia – and its satellite support networks and operations elsewhere. The paramilitary squads were dispersed between bases set up on their bosses' land all over Colombia. And on 31 December 1988, claimed Viáfara, he had witnessed Rodríguez Gacha, Fabio Ochoa and other ACDEGAM luminaries see in the New Year with the commander of the local Bárbula battallion. It emerged that active army officers were among ACDEGAM's leaders, had supplied it with weapons and had participated in operations. Most prominent among its early victims, which included two left-wing congressmen, was Jaime Pardo Leal, the leader of the Patriotic Union party. Pardo Leal, who was killed in October 1987, was preparing to run for the presidency.

Two years later, in 1989, the ACDEGAM alliance evolved into a Pan-Colombian political group, the Movement of National Restoration (MORENA). By that time, however, its bullets were giving way to bombs, and the central government crackdown of the drug lords was evolving into permanent military persecution. The focus of that military persecution would also be narrowing: the Medellín cartel would find itself increasingly alone.

By 1987, Escobar's personal enemies were mounting, not so much in the public arena as within the mafia itself. The year before, he had killed his fellow drug-trafficking 'Pablos', Pablo Arroyave and Pablo Correa Ramos, apparently over a lost cocaine load. This had been followed by the appearance in Medellín of the bodies of two Panamanians closely linked to General Manuel Noriega, one of whom was Rubén Darío Paredes, the son of Noriega's predecessor as chief of the Panamanian armed forces.

More important than these vendettas, however, was the deterioration in relations between the Medellín and Cali cartels. Cali apologists in Congress and the executive and administrative arms of government would later claim that the division occurred much earlier, before the killing of Lara Bonilla, the minister of justice. Their argument was that the Cali cartel were gentlemen traffickers who had parted company with their Medellín counterparts because they disagreed with their violent methods; in short, that they were *narcotraficantes* rather than *narcoterroristas*. This propaganda myth ignored the early criminal history of the Rodríguez Orejuela brothers and José Londoño Santacruz, who started off as kidnappers; it ignored the teamwork displayed in Spain by Gilberto Rodríguez Orejuela and Jorge Luis Ochoa after Lara Bonilla's murder; and it ignored the killings in Cali of judges and an editor of the pro-extradition *El Occidente* newspaper, Raúl Echavarría, in 1986.

According to a senior Colombian anti-drugs policeman, friction between the two cartels only began to build up in the latter half of the 1980s because of disputes between their underlings in Miami, New York and Chicago. The battle was over saturated markets. The Cali traffickers – and others mainly from Bogotá and Pereira – were challenging the market supremacy of the traffickers from Medellín. In spite of all drug-enforcement efforts, there was more cocaine getting through to the United States than ever before. This was reflected in the increased seizures by US customs officials, who impounded 75 per cent more cocaine in 1987 than the previous year. Market saturation sent the cocaine price spiralling downwards. Hence, fights were breaking out between the distributors. Once these overseas vendettas started to filter upwards to the mafia bosses in Colombia, the Cali and Medellín cartels each decided it was time to seek the upper hand;

the friction was increased by an old, personal feud between Escobar and one of the Cali cartel bosses, Pacho Herrera.

Both sides made their moves simultaneously according to the most comprehensive account of the division, which was provided by the Colombian journalist Fabio Castillo in a book (*La Coca Nostra*, or *Our Cowboys*) eventually written from exile. The cartels were to hold a summit meeting near Palmira in the Valle del Cauca, the department of which Cali was the capital, to hear a proposal by Escobar. The proposal, which had been agreed by his Medellín colleagues, was more of an imposition. With himself at the helm, Escobar sought to create a single cocaine conglomerate that would determine both its markets and its price as well as dictate political strategy. No shipment would be made without Escobar's seal of approval, all insurance had to be placed through his organization, and he would receive up to 30 per cent of the cocaine's wholesale value abroad. The Medellín traffickers wanted to swallow the Cali organization before the latter became too big a rival. But an equally, if not more important, factor for the Medellín cartel was its perception that the Cali traffickers seemed to enjoy an enviable degree of judicial immunity. Escobar and his colleagues wanted to don the same protective cloak not just for its own sake, but also because they were scared of being left in the cold.

The Medellín cartel was too late. In 1987, the Cali traffickers felt strong enough to go it alone and wanted nothing to do with the Medellín cartel's judicial problems. Requests for their own extraditions – for Gilberto Rodríguez Orejuela and José Santacruz Londoño – had been turned down by the government of President Virgilio Barco. The rejections of the orders, which had been approved by the Supreme Court, were signed by Barco's minister of justice, Edmundo López Gómez. Furthermore, one of the Cali mafia's linkmen with the Medellín cartel, Rafael Cardona, who had fallen on bad times and whose girlfriend was now having an affair with Jorge Luis Ochoa, was offering Ochoa's head on a plate. According to the journalist Castillo, who was the spinal cord of the investigative team at *El Espectador* under Guillermo Cano, it was Cardona who encouraged his Cali friends to tip off the police that on 21 November Jorge Luis Ochoa would be driving a white Porsche along the highway near Palmira, on his way to the summit meeting. Ochoa was duly stopped by police at a toll-gate, with Cardona's girlfriend in the passenger seat. Successive bribes, which started off at under $50 and finished at around $400,000, curiously failed to impress the policemen. In spite of attempts by the attorney general's office to get him off the hook, five hours later Ochoa was in a maximum security military prison in Bogotá while the United States hollered for his extradition.

Escobar, meanwhile, was taken aside at the Palmira ranch and quietly informed by an adviser of the Rodríguez Orejuelas that not only had his proposal been rejected but that the Cali cartel would no longer pay him anything at all. Ochoa's capture was a warning; Escobar himself was guaranteed a safe exit from the Valle del Cauca, but no more. For Escobar – whose paranoia about security was matched only by his lust for power – the insolence and his sudden sense of impotence were abominable. The man who more than anyone else was responsible for ruthlessly expanding Colombian cocaine exports into a multi-billion-dollar business was facing an open challenge to his authority at the very moment he had planned to enshrine it. Almost speechless with rage, Escobar was reported simply to mutter, 'But this is war, then,' before immediately abandoning the ranch.

The following day, while the cartel lawyers sank their teeth into the government in order to free Ochoa, the Extraditables tried to kidnap the owner of Medellín's *El Colombiano* newspaper, Juan Gómez Martínez. (The latter was a popular if manipulable man reputedly in the power of the local Conservative party heavyweights, the Valencia Cosio brothers, who had helped him become mayor of Medellín and then governor of Antioquia.) Gómez Martínez shot his way out of it. The dozen or so thugs took to their wheels. One hour later, a communiqué arrived from the Extraditables saying they had planned to take Gómez Martínez hostage in order for him to pass on a message to the government: that if Jorge Luis Ochoa were extradited, they would declare war on the country's political élite. The message threatened: 'We will execute the main political leaders of the traditional parties without considerations of any kind.'

Six weeks later, after some complex legal chicanery and amid sudden distractions such as a prison mutiny the other side of the city, for which only the more lowly sacrificeable heads duly rolled, Ochoa was released in time for the New Year. Rafael Cardona, who had fingered him, was already dead: gunned down in the offices of his vintage car business in Medellín.

Juan Gómez Martínez led the Medellín establishment's call for a peace agreement with the drug traffickers. 'At first, exporting cocaine seemed only to produce problems among those involved,' he said. 'It was not until they began to penetrate society and clubs, and with people having revolvers pulled on them if they complained of their driving, that there was a negative reaction, from around 1987. Meanwhile, once the bombs started, the national government did nothing to help Medellín, by sending more police or vehicles for instance. Our only defence was to seek dialogue, a pacific way out.' Strangely enough, the only time Gómez Martínez claimed ever to have bumped into Escobar was at the funeral of the murdered father of Alvaro Uribe, the fist-shaking Antioquian senator with alleged drug-trafficker links; Medellín was a small world.

Gómez Martínez's position was shared by Santiago Londoño White, the Liberal Party patriarch in Antioquia who had contacted the former president, Alfonso López Michelsen, for the Panama peace talks with the cartel in 1984. 'Perhaps the cartel would have continued business,' said Londoño White over a crab sandwich in his office, 'but there would never have been the merciless war that there was in Colombia, which destroyed a good part of our democracy and so many families.' Such voices summed up the public consensus among the bulk of the Medellín political élite: that cocaine 'exports' were less important an issue than keeping the peace. *Paisas* were, after all, conciliators. Better a bad deal than no deal at all, especially if the deal was really quite lucrative. Central government would soon agree.

*

Although Escobar had beaten off the 1979 extradition treaty, the new minister of justice, Enrique Low Murtra – whom US lawyers, flown in to Colombia to fight for Ochoa's extradition, complained of being slow and obstructive – dusted off another one signed forty-five years earlier. Warrants were promptly issued, in January 1988, for the arrest of Escobar, Rodríguez Gacha and the Ochoa brothers with a view to extradition. If captured, however, the cartel leaders were technically on safe, Colombian, ground. They had already finessed the government's move by seeing that judicial investigations regarding the crimes for which they were being charged in the United States, were brought against them in Medellín – thereby placing them out of US reach. The only fresh blots on the cartel's horizon were moves to seize hundreds of millions of dollars of their US property.

Their enemies in Cali, meanwhile, seemed to be avoiding all such problems. So far as Escobar was concerned, that was not a matter of chance. Escobar became increasingly convinced that the main Cali traffickers held a far wider, subtler and profounder hold over powerful government figures and business leaders – at a national level – than he did. Since admitting to the split with the Cali cartel indicated genuine weakness, Escobar only came to say so publicly later. It was not for nothing that Gilberto Rodríguez Orejuela was known as the Chess Player.

For Escobar, the war of extradition against the state was to develop into a simultaneous war against the Cali cartel. Escobar would win the final battle of the first war, for which the Cali traffickers – and others – were grateful, but in doing so he would lose the final battle of the second. While the battle between the cartels gathered pace, it very quickly became obvious that the security forces themselves were interested almost exclusively in attacking the mafia of Medellín. Raids in Cali were unheard of. Public speculation soon mounted that the government was deliberately giving special treatment to the Cali mafia either to damage both groups by inflaming animosities further, or to nurse the interests of the cartel that reputedly paid the higher bribes.

Sixty kilograms of dynamite heralded the new era in

Cali–Medellín mafia relations when it exploded outside Escobar's penthouse bunker on 13 January 1988. The car bomb went off in the exclusive Santa María de los Angeles district just before dawn, blowing two night watchmen to pieces, gouging a massive hole in the street and flattening houses opposite. The eight-storey El Mónaco building itself was made of sterner stuff: the bomb simply peeled off part of its concrete façade. Although Escobar's wife and son, María Victoria Eugenia and Juan Pablo, were unhurt, his daughter, Manuela, was partially deafened. 'The Doctor' himself was absent. His family immediately abandoned their top-floor duplex and, as the judicial investigation was launched, the outside world won its first glimpse of the Escobars' riches. There were paintings by Van Gogh and Salvador Dali; the marble-floored, mural-painted rooms were stuffed with porcelain and crystal; María Victoria Eugenia was revealed to possess an esti-mated 700 pairs of shoes, and in the basement were eight vintage Rolls Royces and a bullet-proof Mercedes Benz stretch limousine. Seventeen different telephone lines were connected to Escobar's room. Meanwhile, even if the building had been blown off the face of the map, it would have made little legal difference: it could not be traced on the local property register anyway.

The bomb had been placed by the Cali cartel. It was the first time that Colombia's drugs traffickers had deployed one. Although Gilberto Rodríguez Orejuela was later accused of the killings, the charges never prospered. Nobody cared much about Escobar's night watchmen – as nobody cared much about the dozens of people who were then tortured and killed on Escobar's orders because of their links with the Rodríguez Orejuelas; Medellín deserters met particularly protracted ends. Employment opportunities swelled for Medellín's *sicarios*. Escobar waged much of his offensive in the city of Pereira, which, being half-way between Medellín and Cali, provided a refuge for his local enemies and a bridgehead for his Cali ones. He also initiated a wave of fire bombings against Colombia's biggest chain of chemists, Drogas La Rebaja, which had been bought up by the Rodríguez Orejuela family.

Simultaneously, Escobar launched a curious kidnap offensive against political and government leaders. His initial targets were Mauricio Gómez, the grandson of the president who had taken office following the murder of Gaitán; Andrés Pastrana, the son of a former president and a future presidential candidate himself; and Carlos Mauro Hoyos, the attorney general. The attempt against Gómez failed. The attempt against Pastrana succeeded but was so extraordinary that Pastrana was widely suspected of some kind of complicity or at least of striking a deal. And the attempt in January 1988 against Mauro Hoyos, a *paisa* deeply trusted by the US law-enforcement authorities with whom he was collaborating closely, ended tragically after the kidnap grab was bungled near Medellín's airport in Rionegro.

Mauro Hoyos, who was pushing for a new law against illicit enrichment, was mortally wounded after his bodyguards tried to defend him. With the bodyguards gunned down, the *sicarios* drove off with Mauro Hoyos bleeding to death on the back seat from a bullet in his spine. The event was graphically recorded by Escobar, who taped his thugs' short-wave car-radio conversations. The tape, which was seized later in an army raid, bordered on black farce. The kidnappers spoke in improvised code, got their codes and lines crossed and did not know what to do with their victim or whether or not he was dead. 'No, no, it's about the car registration . . . check it well to see if you've got to chuck out the car registration or not chuck it out,' crackled Escobar's voice. 'It's that the colour has gone out of it, and everything's left white, WHITE,' was the anguished response. The corpse of Colombia's attorney general was duly abandoned on the side of the road – with eleven bullets in the face to make it look like a deliberate assassination. Deliberate or not, the celebrations in Medellín's Aranjuez district went on late into the night.

Meanwhile, a few hours before Mauro Hoyos' body was found, Andrés Pastrana had been effortlessly freed in the same area. He was under the control of just one man, who, with minimal fuss, handed over his charge to a lone policeman.

According to Pastrana, he had been kidnapped in his Bogotá office a week earlier on 18 January, driven to a ranch and flown by helicopter to another ranch near Medellín, from where he had made a 40-minute telephone call to his wife from a car telephone. Only the day before the attorney general's kidnapping, the Extraditables, in the name of two Colombians who had been extradited to the USA on money-laundering charges, issued a communiqué announcing the kidnap. The ransom demand was Pastrana's undertaking to fight for the abolition of extradition; suggested kidnap negotiators were named. What nobody understood was why Escobar, a kidnap expert, had hidden his first victim near to where the second kidnapping took place, knowing that a massive search operation would immediately ensue in that vicinity. Citing the confession of a cook at the ranch where Pastrana was held, the journalist Castillo asserted: 'That the attorney general was kidnapped in order to free Pastrana is not just a presumption, but a fact.'

Pastrana was among a group of Colombia's most illustrious political leaders invited to a reception at the Club de Ejecutivos in February 1986. The rather jaded Bogotá club was where the country's political dynasties had once been famed to plot presidential careers. The dinner was in honour of Pastrana and the editors and part owners of the highly influential *El Tiempo* newspaper, Juan Manuel Santos and Enrique Santos, for their winning of an international journalism prize. *El Tiempo* recorded the event with a photograph in which those featured were all former presidents or their sons or grandsons, with the exception of the minister of communications, Noemí Sanín, who turned down Pastrana's invitation to be his vice-presidential runner nine years later because she planned to run for the presidency the following term. The photograph showed the Santos brothers, Alfonso López Michelsen, Julio César Turbay Ayala, Misael Pastrana and his son, Andrés. The host was mentioned, but not photographed: a little-known columnist of the Conservative *La República* newspaper, owned by the cocaine-tainted Ospina family. His name was Alberto Giraldo.

That a relatively undistinguished journalist such as Giraldo could muster together, at his invitation, two of *El Tiempo*'s senior owner-editors, three former presidents and two future presidential candidates, suggested that he enjoyed some hidden pre-eminence. Although he was the host, Giraldo was not even a member of the club. The journalist, who was born in Antioquia but lived in Cali, held such close ties with Miguel Rodríguez Orejuela that he had accompanied the Cali mafia leader to the office of Mauro Hoyos one year before the attorney general's murder. Mauro Hoyos told *El Espectador* that, at the meeting in February 1987, Miguel Rodríguez Orejuela requested 'guarantees' for his brother Gilberto, whose trial for cocaine smuggling following his extradition from Spain was just opening in Cali. The drug baron let it be understood that a bribe was on offer; the attorney general refused the money. (Gilberto Rodríguez Orejuela was acquitted anyway.) Alberto Giraldo and Miguel Rodríguez Orejuela – who still faced no charges in Colombia – also tried to convince the attorney general of the legality of the Rodríguez Orejuelas' pharmaceutical chain, Drogas La Rebaja.

At the time of Giraldo's reception, Gilberto Rodríguez Orejuela was fighting for Colombia to extradite him from Spain in order to avoid spending the rest of his life in a United States jail. Alberto Giraldo never disguised the fact that he was a friend acting as a political and public relations frontman for the Rodríguez Orejuelas. The link was common knowledge in the world of the political élite. In which case, Colombia's most senior statesmen appeared to be at the beck and call of the leaders of the Cali cartel.

Giraldo and Rodríguez Orejuela's unscheduled visit to the attorney general followed the Barco government's rejection of US extradition requests for both Gilberto Rodríguez Orejuela and José Santacruz Londoño, the other Cali cartel leader who often operated directly in Queen's, New York. The rejections came immediately after the killing of the *El Espectador* editor, Guillermo Cano, amid government fears that a former president would be killed the following month unless it gave way to the traffickers.

THE SEEDS OF A MAFIA DIVIDE (1987–9)

To make up for and to cover up its caving in to the blackmail, and to respond to public outrage over the Cano murder, the Barco government launched Colombia's third military-style cocaine crackdown.

Also as a result of the Cano murder, a joint media drugs-investigation unit had been set up comprising the main newspapers and television news programmes; their reports were issued simultaneously. However, when it came to its last report in November 1987, on the Cali cartel, the unit broke up in disarray. The publishing of a chart showing the Rodríguez Orejuela business empire was vetoed. Andrés Pastrana, who was a member of the unit, left suddenly with the only copy of the chart handed out by its compiler, Fabio Castillo; the chart was shortly circulating in ministries and causing a storm in Cali. *El Tiempo* withdrew the next day and the unit collapsed. Once again, the Cali mafia seemed to exert a very special pull.

While the kidnap and release of Pastrana swept him to the mayorship of Bogotá, the kidnap and killing of Colombia's attorney general provoked another, much fiercer, military backlash against the Medellín cartel. However, events still went Escobar's way. First, there was the executive jet that had been seized with a false licence in Pereira after airport authorities reportedly responded evasively to inquiries regarding its true origins. When two people caught trying to steal the plane were released with suspicious rapidity, the Turbo Commander 1000 was flown to the military terminal next to the presidential hangar at Bogotá's main airport, Eldorado. The DEA was refused permission to examine its flight computer, whose memory would have contained the navigation and suspected drug-trafficking routes. Six weeks later, just before midnight on 1 March, the aircraft was snatched on the runway. The pilot was tracked down by the Colombian airforce to Escobar's Nápoles ranch; the plane, which had been loaded with fuel and prepared for take-off, was shot to pieces on the airstrip. Escobar complained that several people, including a pregnant woman, were killed. However, the aircraft had taken its secrets to its grave. And Escobar was granted further satisfaction when the airforce commander who directed the operation, General Mario Pineda, was asked to resign.

'The drug traffickers dominated the whole area around my base,' said General Pineda, who was later made the manager of a security firm advising top multinational oil companies. The Palanquero air combat base, the principal one in Colombia, was wedged between the estates of Escobar and Rodríguez Gacha. According to Pineda, a predecessor, General Alfredo Ortega, had been so 'very friendly with the *narcos*' that he had not only bought cattle off Escobar but allowed Rodríguez Gacha to use the officers' casino as an office during his purchase of the Gato Hermosillo estate from his ACDEGAM associate, the emerald-mining magnate and smuggler, Gilberto Molina. When Pineda assumed command, he conducted concentric helicopter reconnaissance around the base, discovered more than twenty illicit airstrips, destroyed two of them and promptly had his helicopter taken away by his superiors. 'It is for the needs of public order, don't ask me more,' was the response by the airforce commander-in-chief, General Alberto Franco, when Pineda asked why the helicopter had been removed from the base after ten years there. Pineda believed the order came from the Minister of Defence, General Rafael Samudio.

'In the Barco government, the *narcos* ruled in Colombia: they played with the military,' said Pineda. 'Samudio was a thief and involved with the *narcos* – his daughter married the son of a member of the Medellín cartel. He had no scruples. He even bought weapons for the guerrillas. The *cupula* of the police, army and airforce was corrupted. Once officers knew, they tried to get involved too. To progress, you had to be with the mafia.' In Medellín itself Augusto Bahamón, an army colonel, recalled: 'With the money obtained [from cocaine] all the state entities were infiltrated ... it happened in so many ways and was so subtle that ... I remember once that the officer who arrested

"Chirusa", the leader of the *sicario* organization of Pablo Escobar, in March 1987, told me that "Chirusa" protested angrily about his arrest and asked him if he didn't know that it was he who paid for the maintenance of the vehicles of the Intelligence Section of the Fourth Brigade ... The officer spoke with the colonel and confirmed that it was indeed "Chirusa" who paid.'

According to Pineda, $600,000 was shared out between Samudio and other officers to allow Escobar's aircraft to be retrieved from Bogotá's military airport terminal, CATAM. 'When you impound a plane, you drain it of fuel, take off its wheels and chain it up,' he added. 'However, the CATAM commander, Colonel Enrique Cueto, claimed that the airforce operations chief, General Alfonso Amaya, ordered the plane to be ready for flight. Although following orders, Colonel Cueto was thrown out of the airforce, as was an airforce officer said to have been in charge of the soldiers on the ground but who had actually been transferred three months earlier. During the operation itself, I requested ground support from the police and army but nobody, absolutely nobody, lifted a finger.'

Pineda's predecessor at the Palanquero base, General Alfredo Ortega, was made commander-in-chief of the airforce; the request for Pineda's resignation came the same day. The operations chief, General Alfonso Amaya, succeeded Ortega. General Samudio was made ambassador in Chile before being reduced to the more humble post of consul in New Orleans, USA. Meanwhile, it emerged that the man who was technically the owner of the illicit Nápoles airstrip – which was in the heart of the estate – was the brother of Alfredo Gutiérrez, Colombia's attorney general. Gutiérrez, who had succeeded the murdered Mauro Hoyos, was obliged to resign.

Escobar's second bout of good luck came with the first of his great escapes near the end of March 1988. One thousand soldiers of the Fourth Brigade launched a pre-dawn raid on his 1,000-square-metre mansion, El Bizcocho, in the lush mountain woods above the district of El Poblado. The strike was supported by tanks and helicopters; a huge cordon encircled the area for several hours. However, according to one of his leading henchmen, John Jairo Velásquez or 'Popeye', Escobar had been alerted by a perimeter guard who had spotted the troop movements below and triggered the alarm system of lights and sirens. It was also reported that Escobar had been tipped off by an army intelligence colonel and escaped in his underpants.

'There were twelve of us with him,' said Popeye. 'Our position had been given away by an informer, but there were lots of trees so the helicopters couldn't see anything although we were surrounded. We walked in a line through the woods, with Pablo in the lead, armed with R-15 rifles, MP-5 and mini-Uzi machineguns, and revolvers. Suddenly we bumped into a soldier, who put his rifle against Pablo's chest without knowing who it was. Pablo said very coldly, "Put your gun down, soldier, we're F2 [plainclothes police]." The guy swallowed the story and Pablo told us to go ahead while he identified himself. Once we had all passed, he ran for it and so did we, so the soldier started shooting and I got a bullet in my right thigh and was captured – here, look at the scar.'

Escobar walked all day to the town of Sabaneta – whose church is famous for its dazzling, celestial blue shrine of the Virgin Santa María Auxiliadora, the *sicarios*' favourite virgin whose bust featured at the entrance of El Bizcocho – before retreating to the tropical wilds of Nápoles in the valley of the river Magdalena. Inside El Bizcocho, an arsenal of weapons, munitions and radio equipment was seized, as well as documents indicating payments to lawyers, judges, judicial functionaries and politicians. By the end of the week, however, all thirty people detained in the raid were free. And Escobar's arrest warrant had been suspended by the Council of State, which acted as a court of appeal, on the grounds that the extradition treaty signed forty-five years earlier could not be applied while the status of the 1979 one was still ambiguous. 'The law of the mafia rules,' wrote *El Espectador*. 'The prevailing laws cannot be ignored for any reason, even under the pretext of public convenience,' said Samuel Buitrago, a friend of Jiménez Gómez who issued the Council of State's ruling.

'Worshipping the law saves the prestige of our democratic institutions.'

Meanwhile, Escobar received two more US indictments on top of his Florida one. Along with other members of the Medellín cartel, in February he had been indicted on drugs charges alongside Panama's General Noriega; the indictment would be the basis for the US invasion of Panama the following year. In June, a court in Colorado accused Escobar of conspiracy to import 800 kilograms of cocaine a week into the state capital, Denver. At home, the Fourth Brigade, based in Medellín, continued to hunt for Escobar while the high courts battled over the legality of his arrest warrant. In August, the Doctor received yet another arrest warrant in Colombia. This time, Escobar was accused of being one of the financial backers of ACDEGAM, the army-backed right-wing paramilitary group in the valley of the river Magdalena that was accused of massacring fifty peasants in the Urabá earlier that year. Escobar and Rodríguez Gacha responded by assassinating a string of judges who were signing their arrest warrants for the Urabá killings as well as for those of Guillermo Cano and Jaime Pardo Leal, the Patriotic Union party leader.

By August, in spite of peace-making attempts by Rodríguez Gacha, the war between the Medellín and Cali cartels was in full furore. Escobar's fire-bombing of the main Medellín branch of the Rodríguez Orejuelas' Drogas La Rebaja pharmacy chain, in which two people died, followed a wave of inter-cartel murders and gun battles in which eighty people – mostly on the Cali side – had been killed that year. The conflict was also hitting Miami, where it was reported that more than a hundred people had died in the violence. Video tapes seized by the Fourth Brigade indicated that Escobar was conducting detailed preparations to murder his top rivals in their own luxurious bunkers in the Ciudad Jardín district of Cali. The man who waged the toughest war on the Medellín cartel, playing it every bit as dirty as the drugs mafia in his apparent disregard for innocent victims, was the bullish – 'fanatic and irrational' said one senior European diplomat – General

Miguel Maza Márquez. The general, who was the head of DAS and a future presidential candidate, initially focused his investigations on the Urabá massacres; these were mainly believed to be the work of Fidel Castaño. However, it was Maza Márquez's uncovering of the paramilitary groups, and of army complicity, during 1988 that led him directly to the cartel's hard men, Escobar and Rodríguez Gacha.

In February 1989, the same month that the paramilitary-drug connection was dramatically revealed by the DAS testimony of the ACDEGAM deserter, Diego Viáfara, the Medellín cocaine cartel was exposed on yet another flank: the emerald smugglers. Rodríguez Gacha sent a hit squad dressed in military uniforms – they were later believed to be army soldiers – to gun down the veteran magnate of the emerald mines, Gilberto Molina; eighteen people were shot in cold blood.

Molina was a former friend and associate who had sold the cocaine baron some of the best land in the Magdalena valley. Rodríguez Gacha's alliance with the emerald sector in the departments of Boyacá and Cundinamarca had been crucial to his power. However, as his drugs fortune ballooned in the late 1980s, Rodríguez Gacha's landowning and emerald smuggling ambitions swelled too. Sensing that they were about to be swallowed up, and not wishing to be harmed by Rodríguez Gacha's very public reputation as a cocaine trafficker either, his former emerald-smuggling allies turned against him. Miners, guerrillas, paramilitaries, drug traffickers, assassins and their families were all sucked into the ensuing violence. But the murder of Molina cemented the emerald sector's hostility to Rodríguez Gacha. (Molina had been well connected. Not only was he a good friend of Andrés Pastrana, but when giving evidence in February 1988, regarding coca plantations in Cundinamarca, he cited as personal referees the defence minister, General Rafael Samudio, the head of the national police, General José Guillermo Medina Sánchez, and a former defence minister, General Miguel Vega Uribe.) Following Molina's killing, the miners fought a sustained battle against Rodríguez Gacha under the co-ordination of another veteran emerald smuggler, Víctor Carranza, who was nearly blown up by two car bombs.

'The fight weakened Gacha and therefore the Medellín cartel as a whole,' said General Maza Márquez, fondling a Mont Blanc fountain pen below a picture of the Christ child, or *Divino Niño*, in his Bogotá presidential campaign office. 'That helped the government in its struggle against *narcoterroristas* who wanted to take over Colombia using *sicarios*, paramilitaries and mercenaries.' In their struggle with Rodríguez Gacha, the emerald smugglers collaborated with the government by providing information about both his organization and his cocaine laboratories in the Magdalena valley and in the Llanos or eastern plains. As for foreign mercenaries, it was Diego Viáfara again who publicly disclosed their presence. They worked first for the Medellín cartel, and then for the Cali cartel. Most were British.

According to investigations by a US congressional sub-committee, which followed Viáfara's declarations, the first mercenary group to arrive in the Magdalena valley was made up of Israelis led by a retired Israeli Defence Force colonel, Yair Klein. The colonel and his men, who numbered about six, staged their first, three-week paramilitary training session in March 1988, after being hired by ACDEGAM. Klein, who claimed that Colombian military officers knew of their presence, said he was ignorant of ACDEGAM's drug-trafficking connections and understood that he was helping peasants and landowners to defend themselves from guerrilla attacks. There were said to be about fifty pupils – from the Llanos, the Magdalena valley and Medellín – who attended the infantry and weapons training. A second course was held in May, after which Klein turned his attention to organizing the shipment of 100 Uzi sub-machine guns and 400 Galil automatic rifles. The weapons, along with 200,000 rounds of ammunition, were sent to Rodríguez Gacha via the British Caribbean island of Antigua the following year. Gacha's son, Freddy, was among those trained by the Israelis.

Meanwhile, in August 1988, a team of eleven British mercenaries led by a former SAS member, Peter McAleese, who had fought as a mercenary in Africa, flew to Colombia on what was apparently more than a mere training mission. McAleese had been contacted by another mercenary, David Tomkins, whom Colombian army officers had sought out in London in order to create what Tomkins described as a 'visible asset' in the fight against the FARC guerrillas. The 'visible asset's' primary target was said to be the Casa Verde, the FARC's mountainous headquarters in the department of Meta. The mercenaries met with Colombian officers in uniform at military barracks, were supplied with full intelligence data and were introduced to former guerrillas who had come in under an amnesty programme. They were left with no doubt that their mission enjoyed complete army backing.

The mercenaries were based initially near Puerto Boyacá, on Rodríguez Gacha's Fantasy Island. While awaiting the arrival of the weapons they had requested, the occupations of those financing the operation soon became obvious from their wealth and flamboyance. Rodríguez Gacha materialized in a fleet of new landcruisers bristling with machine-guns and anti-tank rockets one moment, and among a crowd of horsemen dressed in pointed riding boots and ponchos the next. After chatting with the Mexican, the mercenaries were assigned a dozen Colombians for the Casa Verde attack. The number of Colombians eventually swelled to around fifty. However, time dragged on, the weapons never arrived, and, after being switched from one camp to another, the British ended up on a river bank in the jungle on the Ecuadorian border choking on the offerings of the cook dubbed Typhoid Mary. Around them, there was abundant evidence of cocaine laboratories. Fed up, they demanded their return to Bogotá. The plan to attack the Casa Verde, McAleese surmised, had been nothing more than 'a bait to hook us in the first place'.

True or not, the next mission led by McAleese and Tomkins was for real. Through the same original Colombian army contacts, they were asked to recruit a team whose target was Rodríguez

Gacha's biggest cocaine ally. In February 1989, the officers requested the mercenaries to kill Pablo Escobar.

The mercenaries were based in Cali, 'in a really beautiful white villa ... surrounded by landscaped gardens, mown grass lawns, ornamental trees, a swimming pool ... forests of security lights and fencing, and the largest satellite dish I have ever seen ... What a contrast to the year before,' wrote McAleese. Their supplies, which were brought by a Colombian paratroop major, arrived promptly, 'an Aladdin's cave of brand spanking new weapons, ammunition and explosives. These were not the shabby German G3s we had been given at Paradise [sic] Island, which had been cast-offs from the militia. This was the *crème de la crème*. There were American M16s, pistols, plenty of magazines, pouches, gleaming ammunition in boxes, grenades, M72 66mm light anti-tank rockets, pounds and pounds of PE4 plastic explosive, time pencils, detonators—' All to attack Escobar – and the estimated seventy men protecting him. The mercenaries trained for three months, commuting in a pair of helicopters to a camp north of the Pacific port of Buenaventura.

The assault was to take place at Escobar's Nápoles estate, which was close to where the mercenaries had previously trained the paramilitaries on his and Rodríguez Gacha's payroll. The training and the attack were minutely planned, with full live rehearsals. Once all was ready, it was simply a matter of waiting to hear when the Medellín drugs baron was at home. The word finally came from the Colombian army colonel named Ricardo who had acted as the mercenaries' main local contact on both missions. Although Escobar's gang later claimed the information had been furnished originally by DEA agents or informants, McAleese claimed the DEA was unaware of their mission. McAleese did, however, claim that the CIA had granted its tacit approval.

At 11 a.m. on 3 June, the helicopters took off from the Pacific coast, heading for a refuelling site more than two and a half hours away which was just short of the Nápoles estate in the Magdalena valley. They were joined by three other support aircraft from Cali and Bogotá. With two mountain ranges to cross, the attack helicopters never made it beyond the second. Heavy rain clouds obscured the peaks. The pilot of the leading helicopter, Lieutenant 'Tiger' González, a policeman and the son of a retired police general, Gustavo González, thought he spotted a sunny hole in the clouds. It was a mirage. The helicopter crashed straight into the mountainside at more than 5,500 metres. González was killed, Tomkins and McAleese were badly injured and the mission was aborted. Although plans were made to repeat the attempt with the mercenaries' own pilots, these were scuppered by a government crackdown on the Medellín cartel two months later when Escobar was forced into hiding, abandoning his known properties (Nápoles was seized).

CHAPTER SEVEN

MONEY TALKS

Every morning, on the fifth floor of the north Bogotá head-quarters of one of Colombia's biggest financial and industrial conglomerates, there arrives a fax from its main office in the United States. The fax gives the daily US dollar price of cocaine on the streets of New York. Immediately, the information is keyed into a computer performance chart. Two parallel lines run across the middle of the graph. When the price spikes through the upper line, it indicates a supply blockage. The scarcity of cocaine in New York means a scarcity of US dollars in Colombia. The company's domestic sales are damaged. When the price bursts through the lower line, it heralds the presence of a major new cocaine supplier and a spate of killings and informant-related seizures until the supply drops back to normal levels. In the meantime, with US dollars flooding Colombia, it is a good moment to buy them cheaply. According to a technician who worked for the conglomerate, the chart was installed in 1986.

That a leading company in Colombia should track the price of cocaine because of its impact on exchange rates and domestic business reflects the inescapable enormity of the trade. By 1993, after a decade of acidic debate regarding the amount of drug money returning to the country – be it from marijuana, cocaine or heroin – Colombia's judicial authorities claimed that the figure was around $5 billion a year. US law enforcers believed it might have been as high as $7 billion – a fraction of the amount of drugs money washed annually around the globe, which, according to a Citibank estimate in July 1994, was $400 billion. The impact in Colombia had become more evident following the relaxation of exchange controls in 1991, which in themselves considerably boosted the repatriation of drug profits through conventional channels.

At the higher end of the estimates, Colombia's annual income from cocaine and the other illicit drugs was the equivalent of its average, legal export earnings during the first four years of the 1990s. In that time, using the same $7 billion figure for cocaine earnings, they would have represented between 10 per cent and 15 per cent of the country's GDP. The days when the big traffickers merely bought up real estate, stuffed their dollars in underground holes or simply made deposits overseas were long gone. Cocaine was the country's single biggest money spinner, its profits being driven into almost every nook and cranny of the economy; it was a force that was impossible to ignore.

The influx of drug money helped to save the Colombian economy from the debt-related torment and stagnation suffered throughout the rest of South America during the 1980s. Between 1979 and 1993, its economy grew an average of 3.6 per cent a year in real terms, which was double that of other Latin American countries. In Medellín itself, this relative prosperity was reflected in lower unemployment levels, which dropped from 65 per cent above the national average in 1979 to just 10 per cent above it eight years later; this coincided with the city's cocaine-backed construction boom.

Salomón Kalmanovitz, an economist who joined the board of Colombia's central bank in 1993, said: 'Cocaine stopped the balance of payments from collapsing, which would have pushed us into the spiral of hyperdevaluation and hyperinflation that shook most of the rest of the continent, for which the 1980s were a lost decade.' As it was, Colombia continued to grow. 'Cocaine has created wealth and jobs,' said a senior foreign banker. 'It has provided the vital capital for economic expansion and in that sense has been an undeniable boon for Colombia.' So crucial to the economy did the money become during the 1980s that in moments when the cocaine supply was interrupted, or when it was simply feared that it would be because of government repression, the price of the black-market dollar leaped. After the murder of the minister of justice, Rodrigo Lara Bonilla, it soared 50 per cent.

The drugs bonanza contributed to the ferocious growth of the country's three largest, legitimate personal fortunes: those of Julio Mario Santodomingo, Luis Carlos Sarmiento and Carlos Ardila Lülle. The flood of drugs money in the late 1970s stoked booms in construction, finance, soft drinks, beer and property at a time when Colombia's new magnates were jockeying for power in each of those sectors, displacing the traditional economic groups (with the exception of Antioquia, where the older power groups finally held them off by creating the so-called Antioquian Syndicate of inter-owned companies). The meteoric rise of Santodomingo and Lülle had begun in 1968, when they sold their own brewery and drinks companies to their much larger competitors, Bavaria and Postobon, in return for shares. The buy-outs made them the single biggest shareholders. In the same year, Jaime Michelsen Uribe, who became the country's first financial tycoon but whose empire collapsed in 1984, pulled a similar deal with the Banco de Colombia. Sarmiento, who was already an important builder, assumed control of Cali's Banco de Occidente in 1972 (the following year, its assets doubled).

Alongside these men – whose fortunes blossomed with the main influx of drugs cash in the 1980s – illegitimate capital similarly conspired to engineer a transformation in the ownership of the country. Kalmanovitz said: 'Exports of marijuana and cocaine have brought about the accelerated development of a gangster bourgeoisie which has undermined the economic hegemony of the oligarchic financial groups.' By 1988, drug traffickers had bought up nearly 1 million hectares of the best land in Colombia according to Bogotá's Institute of Liberal Studies. This represented 4.3 per cent of the country's farmland

and an agrarian counter-revolution, reversing a quarter of a century of government attempts at land redistribution. By 1991, according to a survey by Alejandro Reyes of the National University in Bogotá, the traffickers owned land in a quarter of Colombia's municipalities. After consulting with the Federation of Colombian Cattle Farmers, Reyes calculated that by 1991 the drug traffickers had bought up as much as 3 million hectares, or 30 per cent of the best farming land. Their preferred areas were the huge, flat expanses of northern Colombia and the eastern plains – where they could buy up vast *latifundios* rather than going to the trouble of patching together small holdings. 'Many of the best lands were devalued because of guerrilla activity,' said Reyes, 'so the old ranchers were looking for *narcos* to buy them. Since the money was placed overseas, that contributed to the flight of traditional capital.'

Pablo Escobar was typical of the traffickers in his amassing of both land and cattle. *Paso colombiano* horses and fighting bulls – every self-respecting big-time cocaine trafficker boasted a bull ring – were added, show-off luxuries, especially for those connected with the Medellín cartel. High walls, parabolic dishes and swimming-pools in the middle of the wilds betrayed the true source of their earnings. The cocaine traffickers were the new feudal élites, displaying their wealth through their land and capable of imposing their will on guerrilla banditry – or at least, as fellow aliens of the law, thrashing out forms of co-existence. The traffickers were also Colombia's new breed of cattle ranchers, investing heavily in genetic technology and infrastructure; animal stock and meat and milk production were thereby dramatically improved in some regions.

Cattle were an attractive investment because they were like cash and could be sold within a couple of days; their owners lived chaotic, insecure lives and needed the liquidity. However, the roller-coaster nature of their careers was hardly conducive to good farming. Fleeing their ranches often meant that these fell apart. And in many cases, in spite of all the investment, the traffickers were inefficient farmers since they cared not a fig if they made a loss; if anything, losses were useful opportunities to launder money. Such an attitude was common to all their legitimate businesses. Similarly, they drove genuine competitors out of the market by effortlessly undercutting them when they so chose, and pounced on any sector in a slump. The chicken industry, in particular, fell victim in this way.

Meanwhile, the traffickers' frantic acquisition of land sent prices into a dizzy, inflationary spiral, drove peasants away and fortified paramilitary squads. 'Where the *narcos* have bought land, legitimate peasant movements have been completely destroyed,' said Reyes. 'Land ownership has become much more concentrated and there is much, much greater violence.' The culture of *sicarios*, bodyguards, security guards and paramilitary forces that surrounded the emergence of Colombia's new ruling class slowly came to permeate business practices in all sectors of the economy.

Honed in an illicit industry where the gun was the only law because life was the only limit, and the only guarantee in a deal, the mafia's mores contaminated much of both rural and urban society. The concept of private justice itself became ever more perverted in practice, until it metamorphosed into nothing but a self-righteous quest for power and survival. Such behaviour spread to the upper echelons of Colombian economic and political life, whose own twentieth-century history was already spattered with the blood of *La Violencia*. 'Colombia is very, very rough,' said the foreign banker. 'Things are quickly personalized – if you are with them, fine, if you are not, forget it. Board meetings are brutal and few people have any scruples. The state is still so absent and the judicial system so weak that feudalism rules here: people turn into despots and to defend their fiefdoms *of course* some of the biggest companies will have you killed or kidnapped. Kidnapping is the main way to pressure you.' Kidnapping became a national industry: in 1992 more than 1,700 were recorded, the highest of any country.

The traffickers' investment in land was at its height between 1982 and 1987, according to a Medellín real estate expert who acted as the intermediary in many of Escobar's purchases; parallel to this was their investment in construction. 'They were ignorant about how to handle money and wanted something they knew they could keep for ever, like property, gold bars and diamonds,' said Diego Londoño White, who was the Antioquia co-ordinator of Belisario Betancur's unsuccessful presidential campaign in 1978, the year Londoño White said he had first met Escobar. Londoño White, a member of a prestigious *paisa* family, was invited to Escobar's office because of his friendship with the Ochoa brothers, whom he had known through the riding world. (Escobar himself was not noted for his interest in equestrian sports.) 'The cartel were all looking for pretty *fincas* [ranches] and they also instigated a big construction boom for upper-class apartment buildings in Medellín; they quickly came to own about 30 per cent of the upper end of the market,' said Londoño White. Apart from the luxury apartment buildings, the mafia also invested in shopping centres, office blocks and hotels.

Medellín's industry, however, which had already been nibbled at by outside magnates who had benefited from mafia bank deposits, was rendered inaccessible by the creation of the so-called Antioquian Syndicate, which comprised an impenetrable, inter-owned block of the region's biggest companies. It was not that the Medellín traffickers themselves were interested in running industrial companies, or, apparently, in buying up what shares were available. 'If Escobar and the cartel had had good advisors they would have bought stock and ended up the owners of many of the industrial companies and of the financial system of this country,' said a leading Antioquian politician. 'They just did not have that level of education.' Instead, according to Alberto Echavarría, the Antioquia president of the National Association of Industrialists, ANDI, the traffickers preferred to take the easy, fixed income from bonds. And Jorge Lotero, an economist from the University of Antioquia, said: 'The mafia themselves were very unproductive. They simply increased general demand because of their huge capacity to spend and consume for their own ostentation and recreation.' Nevertheless, Joaquín Vallejo, Escobar's godfather and a leading Conservative politician, claimed that many stockbrokers in Medellín bought shares on the traffickers' behalf.

The Medellín cocaine-traffickers' vulgar display of wealth, which other than on *fincas* they squandered on consumer goods and services, particularly luxury cars, was in direct contrast to the conservative, tight-fisted culture of Antioquia. The extravagance – and generosity – was legion: it served to demonstrate status and power, as well as to buy friendship. (In her determination to ensure that her daughter's fifteenth birthday was well attended by her schoolmates, one 'queen of coca' promised a Renault car to everyone who attended. Receiving such presents from the mafia was ill advised: three ugly, teenage sisters were famous for sending their bodyguards to kill boyfriends who had accepted their gifts and then spurned their favours.)

The obsessive consumerism distracted public attention from those businessmen whose services the traffickers needed and used the most: bankers and financial experts. It was no more illegal knowingly to sell a bottle of *aguardiente*, a car or a ranch to a cocaine smuggler – or input chemicals – than it was to accept his cash deposits. And when the amounts of money were so large that turning down the business meant running the risk of being swallowed up by competitors who did accept it, Colombia's financial institutions – like many sectors – generally decided that they had no choice but to fight for the cash, whether they liked it or not. Worse still was the possibility that the traffickers themselves would seize control. 'It was a commonplace that either you tried to get the *narcos*' money off them or you let a group of ignorant brutes run the country,' said the engineering manager of one conglomerate.

According to a study by the economist Kalmanovitz, whose figures were higher but more complete than most other local estimates in an extremely speculative exercise, Colombian drug traffickers earned $41 billion during the 1980s. In that decade, Colombia's legal export earnings totalled exactly the same figure.

It was inevitable that capturing the mafia's money without collapsing in the process should become something approaching a national, if covert, economic goal.

Dwelling on the roots of financial crises, one of the nineteenth-century gurus of *The Economist* magazine, Walter Bagehot, wrote: 'At particular times, a great deal of stupid people have a great deal of stupid money . . . It seeks for someone to devour it . . . It finds someone, and there is "speculation"; it is devoured, and there is "panic"'. Colombia's first reaction to its great deal of stupid money was during the 1974–8 government of Alfonso López Michelsen. In response to the flood of dollars from marijuana and cocaine – as well as illicit coffee sales in a bonanza period when many exporters sought to circumvent the national coffee federation – it opened what became known as the 'side window' of the central bank, whereby foreign currency was exchanged without question at a time when its possession in Colombia was technically illegal outside its strictly controlled use for foreign trade and tourism. Meanwhile, there developed a busy black market in cheap dollars, although its existence was officially ignored.

At the same time, speculative savings funds were launched, in the local currency of pesos. Central bank regulation was minimal. The peso funds' interest rates climbed ever higher in order to attract the piles of laundered drugs cash, and sucked in innocent savings as well. As people bought up pesos, the peso revalued. In response to the glut of dollars, the 1978–82 government of Julio César Turbay Ayala relaxed import tariffs; it was the *black-market* dollar that strengthened the most. By early 1982, however, imports had developed into a flood and foreign reserves were starting to fall. A balance of payments crisis dawned. The economy had been opened up too much before it had developed sufficient productive capacity of its own. It was at this point that the Grupo Colombia of Félix Correa Maya, which had hoovered up much of the money from the speculative peso funds, collapsed in Medellín. It had outstretched itself. The 'stupid money' had been devoured. (The *coup de grâce* was purported to have been the March 1982 seizure of a $100-million cocaine shipment in

Tampa, Florida, by far the biggest cocaine seizure to date. Although the shipment's owners were never traced, it was believed to have represented investments managed through Correa.)

A major financial partner of Correa's was Jaime Michelsen Uribe, at the time the most powerful banker in Colombia, after prospering under the presidency of his cousin, Alfonso López Michelsen. Both Correa and Michelsen Uribe maintained close relationships with the Medellín cartel and received much of their cash. It was these men's forays into Antioquia, along with those by Julio Mario Santodomingo and Carlos Ardila Lülle, that caused Antioquian businesses to close their ranks to outsiders. The names of these men became dirt in Antioquia. Indeed, when the head of the National Association of Financial Institutions, the future president Ernesto Samper, vaunted Michelsen Uribe and Santodomingo as shining examples of entrepreneurial flare at a meeting of Medellín's business élite in the early 1980s, so much antipathy was generated that, according to one fellow Liberal politician, it nearly cost Samper his election a decade later.

The collapse of Correa's empire was followed two years afterwards by the collapse of Michelsen Uribe's. Under the government of Belisario Betancur, import tariffs had been raised once again to staunch the outflow of dollars. But it was too late, and manufacturing industry was undermined by the import competition. Reserves plummeted and so did the peso as the government battled with a balance of payments crisis that was saved only by the huge influx of black-market dollars. Panic struck the investors in Michelsen Uribe's Grupo Grancolombiano, whose portfolio was suddenly regarded as something of a façade. When the investors tried to withdraw their money, the Grupo Grancolombiano lost any remaining momentum and crashed. The government took over the adminstration of the group's flagship, the Banco Colombia, the country's biggest bank. The financial system itself only narrowly survived the shock. (Correa and Michelsen Uribe were sentenced to jail.)

*

The 1982–84 financial crisis was a watershed in Colombian banking history. Thereafter, not only did Medellín's cocaine traffickers – having suffered through the speculation of bankers riding on their backs – view the banks with suspicion, but the banks themselves grew much more cautious. Nevertheless, the little municipality of Envigado still boasted as many banks as Eton High Street. Among them was a branch of the Colombian subsidiary of the Bank of Credit and Commerce International. The BCCI, which was shut down by the Bank of England in July 1991, was accused by its US prosecutor, Robert Morgenthau, of having set up a corporate structure 'to evade international and national banking laws so that its corrupt practices would be unsupervised and remain undiscovered'. The BCCI, he said, had committed 'the largest bank fraud in world financial history'. It was revealed that the bank had provided legal and illegal services to international criminal and terrorist movements as well as government intelligence organizations, including the Abu Nidal gang, the CIA and M16. (Although its power rested in heroin-producing Pakistan and oil-rich Saudi Arabia, it was registered in Luxembourg, its operational headquarters were in London and its ownership recorded in the Cayman Islands.) Accounts at the BCCI were used for the illicit sale of US weapons to Iran and to channel US funds to the *mujahadeen* in Afghanistan. The BCCI's complex financial engineering defrauded individual, corporate and government investors of up to $10 billion, according to US investigators.

The bank had rocketed from nowhere after the Bank of America bought a 25 per cent stake in the United Bank of Pakistan in 1972. The new bank, the BCCI, was run by a Shiite Muslim Pakistani called Agha Hasan Abedi. At the time of its demise two decades later – after achieving close links with world leaders such as, among many others, the former British prime minister, Lord Callaghan, the former US president, Jimmy Carter, the Panamanian dictator, Manuel Noriega, and the Peruvian president, Alan García – it possessed $21 billion in assets spread over 400 branches in seventy-three countries. In order to become the world's seventh largest privately owned bank, manipulating the world's leading financial institutions, it had indulged in fraud, conspiracy, bribery, falsification of records and theft.

Drug-money laundering was its speciality. The BCCI had won access to the US financial system through its illegal purchase of the First American Bank using US nominees at the turn of the 1980s. It acquired a hot line to the cocaine industry in an apparently similar way: using Colombian nationals to secure full control over the Banco Mercantil. 'This was done by granting "loans", without obligation to repay, to the nominees to purchase the shares,' alleged US investigators. 'The nominees then pledged the shares to BCCI, signed blank transfer powers to BCCI, and gave it the right to vote shares.'

This occurred during Colombia's financial crisis, when many of the Mercantil's manufacturing clients were suffering badly from cheap imports – resulting from policy originally inspired by the big influx of cocaine dollars – and the bank was suffering accordingly. At least one leading member of the Banco Mercantil's board had very close links to the Rodríguez Orejuelas of the Cali cartel. Also on the board at the start of its take-over by the BCCI – which already had an office in Bogotá, run by a Pakistani later jailed for money laundering after a mass sting operation in Florida – was the future Conservative presidential candidate, Andrés Pastrana. Pastrana was fined – although this fine was later quashed under a statute of limitations rule – in connection with a loan of about $2 million paid by the Mercantil to a financial group of which he was also a board member. The BCCI took over the Mercantil shortly afterwards and the loan went unpaid after Pastrana's financial group, Promoviendo, went into liquidation. The so-called loan had all the appearance of a BCCI political sweetener to the Conservative government. (Juvenal Betancur, brother of the then president, Belisario Betancur, was implicated in money-laundering operations uncovered by the United States in 1982.)

The Mercantil was renamed the Bank of Credit and Commerce (BCC) and, under the Pakistanis' initiative, launched a massive effort to capture deposits nationally and internationally. It focused particularly on the earnings from cocaine, much as its parent bank had initially chased after the wealth of the oil sheiks. Between 1985, when the BCCI's control over the Mercantil was finalized, and 1989, the BCC doubled its Colombian branches. Among those eighteen branches were those opened in tiny Envigado and its neighbouring municipality, the town of Itagüí; by 1989 these had amassed the bank's highest peso deposits in the country. 'From the beginning, the work of the new shareholders focused on the massive procurement of new resources,' wrote *Semana* magazine, 'within a few years, the [bank's total] deposits rose from 8 billion pesos to 38 billion pesos.' The BCC offered a no-questions-asked security for drug money.

A former manager at the bank's central branch said: 'The central objective of the Pakistanis was to obtain dollar deposits of rich Colombians overseas – deposits which were illegal for Colombians – as well as international credit lines. In spite of the deposits being illegal, they even imposed quotas on branch managers to collect them. In exchange for overseas deposits, companies received low-interest loans in Colombia. Also, fictitious exports were arranged for dollars to arrive here and be changed into pesos. Cocaine dollars poured in. By 1989, the bank had about $600 million owned by Colombians in the Cayman Islands, Europe and Miami – it was all to cover the BCCI's thefts elsewhere.' (Fictitious exports were a major money-laundering mechanism: between 1979 and 1980 alone, the Colombian Institute of External Commerce detected an extraordinary, 50 per cent increase in exports to Panama, where the drugs cash was received from the United States. The working capital of at least sixty exporters was reported to bear no relation to their alleged shipments.)

Meanwhile, strange operations conducted on an upper floor of the BCC's Bogotá headquarters were uncovered by Colombia's banking superintendency in March 1987. It emerged that another bank, the Banco Mercantil of Nassau, had its operational centre on the third floor rather than in the Bahamas, and that it was working secretly and illegally in conjunction with the BCC in order to evade Colombian exchange controls and regulations; its foreign exchange dealings were six times greater than its host bank. Among the clients whose names were discovered was Camilo Zapata, who was closely linked to Rodríguez Gacha and the Medellín cartel. Many accounts, however, were coded. The office was found to receive certificates of deposit and to finance international commerce: a United States indictment later accused BCCI subsidiaries of assisting the Medellín cartel in buying certificates of deposit and issuing 'sham loans' in return. Although Colombia's banking superintendent penalized the BCC over its upper-floor operation, this was later quashed by the superintendent of foreign exchange controls because of an alleged lack of proof.

The US indictment of the BCCI came eighteen months after the BCC's upper-floor operation was exposed in Bogotá, incriminating one of Escobar's closest associates, Gerardo Moncada. The BCCI, which pleaded guilty, was accused in Florida of laundering $14 million in drug proceeds. One undercover customs agent described how he was assisted in placing nearly half a million dollars – which BCCI officers were told came from cocaine sales – in a Panama branch, from where it was transferred through the First American Bank in Washington and then to the BCCI in Geneva. In what was known as a 'counter-balancing loan scheme', the agent received an apparently unrelated – and unreturnable – loan for the same amount, minus a small fee, from the BCCI's Panama branch. The agent discussed cocaine profits with BCCI officers in London, Geneva, Paris and Los Angeles. Documents seized by British customs supported US Senate allegations that General Noriega had himself similarly laundered millions of dollars of drug money through the BCCI.

It emerged that a more primitive method – 'smurfing' – was for the cash to be deposited in small amounts in the United States, transferred to BCCI accounts of front companies in Panama, and for the Colombian traffickers then to receive signed, open cheques from the BCCI to make over to whom they wished. The Colombian linkman who pleaded guilty to thirty-three drug-trafficking and money-laundering charges in the BCCI indictment was Gonzalo Moro, who was alleged to be a financier for the Medellín cartel. Further evidence connecting the BCC with the Medellín traffickers was provided by the discovery in the BCCI's Luxembourg subsidiary in 1989 of transactions the BCC had authorized through front companies in the Virgin Islands, the Isle of Man and Panama; the companies were owned by relatives of Rodríguez Gacha. Meanwhile, it was discovered that Escobar himself had kept accounts in the BCCI's Cannon Street branch in the City of London.

More sordidly, the cheque paid out for the car in which the mortally wounded attorney general Carlos Mauro Hoyos was kidnapped, with Pablo Escobar personally directing operations, also belonged to the BCC. The cheque was a symbol of the symbiotic, if inevitable, relationship during the 1970s and 1980s between drug traffickers and their bankers. In not concerning themselves with the origins of the money they fought to attract, in many cases doing everything possible to solicit deposits they knew came from the drugs trade, and in order to help the traffickers hide it from government authorities, bankers in Colombia and abroad enabled the cocaine mafia to conduct their business as bloodily and discreetly as they pleased.

'Most Colombian banks were dedicated to money laundering in the 1980s,' said one local bank official, 'either through holding the cocaine mafia's overseas deposits or through knowingly participating in fictitious export transactions whereby the mafia received pesos in Colombia. The banks had to compete for the deposits to survive, to stay competitive.' Complicity in the over-billing of exports and under-billing of imports was common. Just like many of the country's politicians, judges, police, army and airforce officers, never mind its private sector, taking the mafia's cash was often the only way to survive and prosper professionally or commercially when there was always a competitor waiting to receive it in the wings. From the mid 1970s, Colombian banks expanded their foreign agencies accordingly, in the Caribbean, the

USA and South America. One former BCCI manager estimated that during the 1980s at least 10 per cent of Colombia's external commerce was financed through illegal banking operations dependent on cocaine money, and that the same proportion again was conducted through illegal foreign exchange houses (all attempts to regulate the latter once they were legalized having failed).

When the BCCI closed down in London in 1991, its Colombian subsidiary was the only one worldwide not to be liquidated. The government, fearful of triggering another financial crisis, forced it to sell out. The successful buyers – the bank was a snip at $3.5 million – were Isaac Gilinsky and his son, Jaime. They were said to have raised the money by purchasing for a premium the Colombian loans in the liquidated BCCI Panama subsidiary. Two years after the purchase of the BCC, which was renamed the Banco Andino, the Gilinskis went on to buy one of the biggest banks in Colombia, the Banco de Colombia. Prestigious foreign banks supported the deal. The international financial magnate, George Soros, bought a substantial stake in the bank soon after. Coincidentally, it was Soros who provided the funds for a pro-drugs legalization foundation in New York, the Lindesmith Center.

Methods of laundering drug money grew ever more sophisticated in the bid to remain two steps ahead of international investigators, and of the gradually more effective legal tools at their disposal. At the same time, the visible presence of the Colombian mafia slowly faded from the banking world. In the 1970s, Jorge Luis Ochoa and Gilberto Rodríguez Orejuela had been bold enough to run their own Panama bank, the First Interamericas, to cut costs and to save inconvenience. Rodríguez Orejuela even secured 70 per cent of the shares in Colombia's Banco de Trabajadores; and was appointed president of the board. Escobar was among the traffickers who laundered millions of dollars through the bank before its reputation forced Rodríguez Orejuela to sell out in the early

1980s. The new owner, Rafael Forero Fetecua, was nevertheless alleged to be a Rodríguez Orejuela *testaferro* or frontman.

The use of frontmen and front companies to disguise the true origins and ownership of drug money became crucial to the money-laundering process. The safest frontmen were people linked to the drug traffickers' families; however, they also used those who in some way were in hock to them, whether it be their chauffeurs, lawyers or bankers. The thinner the link, the safer the cash from public investigation; but the more vulnerable to betrayal. The penalty for betrayal was, as always, death. However, crooked notaries were easily found to sign undated transfer documents returning the assets to the traffickers; these remained in the traffickers' possession and could be activated at any moment.

The networks of frontmen and front companies grew ever more complex. Occasionally, they would be penetrated in spectacular, international undercover police and customs operations, such as Operation Polar Cap in 1989, in which US investigators traced $1.2 billion of drugs cash through a Los Angeles gold and jewellery business that was the headquarters of a labyrinthine, inter-continental money-washing machine run by one of Escobar's main financial wizards, Eduardo Martínez (who was later extradited to the United States from Colombia). Martínez' favoured bank was the Banco de Occidente, whose Panama branch pleaded guilty in August 1989 to laundering $411 million for the Medellín cartel. It was the biggest money-laundering conviction obtained against any bank. Branches of the Banco de Occidente in other countries were deeply implicated, including the parent, Banco de Occidente of Colombia, which only escaped a US indictment after the personal intervention of President Virgilio Barco following the freezing of half the bank's $163 million assets. The president of both the Colombian bank, whose base was in Cali, *and of the Panamanian* – which was launched in 1982 – was Luis Carlos Sarmiento. The case went under-reported in the Colombian media after the banking magnate launched a blitzkrieg of advertising. A few years later, Sarmiento – whose bank was virtually alone in prospering during the 1982–4 crisis, when its assets doubled –

had also bought the Banco de Bogotá and presided over Colombia's biggest financial conglomerate. In 1994, the US magazine *Forbes* declared Sarmiento the richest man in Colombia, followed by Julio Mario Santodomingo and Carlos Ardila Lülle.

Each successful, international anti-drugs money operation revealed another maze of investigative channels. Chasing cocaine cash became a new law-enforcement speciality, ideally demanding highly sophisticated computer programmes, the mathematical talents of an accountant, great legal expertise and the imagination of the president of a multinational corporation. Hunting for the money demanded the skills of those who were moving it. In Colombia itself, the judicial and police system had nothing like the required legal or technical capacity, never mind the political will. Banking practices worldwide, particularly the secrecy afforded by such fiscal paradises as in the Caribbean, the Isle of Man, Gibraltar and Switzerland, along with the globalization of the financial markets, rendered the tracing of cocaine money a nearly impossible task during the 1980s. Although certain banking regulations were tightened – and banking secrecy relaxed in the case of drug investigations, for instance in Switzerland – new ways were constantly being dreamed up to salt away the cash, much as new routes and smuggling methods were constantly being found for cocaine. 'While consumers want cocaine, it will always reach them, and the profits will always find a home,' said a senior European police officer. 'Our struggle on both fronts is only 5 per cent effective.' After long experience in battling the drugs trade, he was moving in favour of its legalization.

Until Colombia's foreign exchange controls were abolished in 1991, millions of dollars were smuggled back into the country in hard cash, which was the form in which most drug deals were made. The supply fuelled a lively black market in foreign exchange whereby money changers regularly masqueraded as financial consultants. At a time when the peso was not trusted, dollars were the preferred currency in which to save, even though local dollar accounts were illegal; since central bank sales of dollars were strictly limited, drugs provided them. 'Being caught with dollars was worse than being caught with cocaine,' recalled one Medellín shop owner, 'but everybody wanted them.' The imported dollars also found their way illicitly into offshore accounts, as with the BCCI's Banco Mercantil of Nassau. Importing dollar bills, however, was often the product of financial ignorance, and of the lack of any conventional business infrastructure. Rodríguez Gacha and the Moncada/Galeano families of Itagüí held so much more cash than they knew what to do with that they buried millions of dollars in holes in the ground. Often, the money rotted – as did $24 million belonging to Escobar in a Los Angeles warehouse. He had been unable to find anywhere else to put it.

The Medellín mafia tended to concentrate on land and construction (as well as gold), partly because the transactions could more easily be conducted in cash, whether dollars or pesos. Often, the money would never enter Colombia; it would simply be transferred between one foreign account and another. The more intelligent traffickers, and particularly the leaders of the Cali cartel, preferred to develop investments in banking and industry; as the law-enforcement pressure grew, they used *testaferros*, whose status was nevertheless perfectly obvious to their peers in any given sector. 'Escobar was stupid. He bought land and houses,' said one public prosecutor. 'He didn't know you had to buy the banks.' The art was in hiding the money in productive investments. Like the rest of his cartel, Escobar, whose public profile worked against him anyway, appeared to invest his cash in a manner that was both indiscreet and inefficient. Real estate was not only too vulnerable to bombs and seizure; it also gave him too little economic – and political – national leverage.

By 1987, Escobar was said by *Forbes* magazine to be the fourteenth richest person in the world, with an estimated wealth of $3 billion. *Fortune* magazine simultaneously assessed him to be worth more than $1 billion. The *Forbes* figure was based on the assumption that Escobar controlled 40 per cent of Colombia's cocaine exports between 1981 and 1986, when the magazine calculated the Medellín cartel to have jointly earned $7 billion or $43,000 a kilogram. However speculative the figure was – it vastly underestimated his costs, and probably overestimated his level of participation – Escobar's wealth was always associated with real estate, in Colombia and abroad. Although many of his overseas accounts were traced, there may have been more. When, finally, Escobar was being hunted down for the kill, his key henchmen dead, jailed or working against him, his family encircled in case he approached them, his estate managers fleeing for their lives, Escobar became short of liquid cash. Desperate, he would resort to kidnapping. Access to his foreign deposits was difficult and his hundreds of thousands of hectares – which were expensive and awkward to manage – could not provide him with ready money.

A favoured system of converting cocaine dollars into local currency was through contraband. Textiles and electrical goods such as televisions, video recorders, sound systems and refrigerators flooded illegally into Colombia from the late 1970s onwards. It was common knowledge that the drug traffickers used their cocaine export routes to import contraband bought with their dollars in Panama and the United States. The smugglers took advantage of Colombia's free-trade zones in order to sell the goods wholesale for their subsequent distribution through a national network of informal markets known as *sanandresitos*. The goods were also sneaked in by launch from mother ships offshore, particularly north of the Pacific port of Buenaventura and around the Guajira peninsula in the Caribbean. However, contraband was also smuggled in through the main airports.

The *sanandresitos*, which comprised tiny individual stalls, had initially sprung up through the efforts of migrant street vendors fleeing from *La Violencia* in the countryside in the 1960s; their name derived from Colombia's Caribbean islands of San Andrés and Providencia, free-trade zones where, in ant-like fashion, families first flocked to buy electrical goods for resale on the mainland. The illicit market-places spread to cities and towns throughout the country, fuelled by import restrictions that were circumvented through the bribery of customs and port officers by either the wholesalers or the small buyers themselves. In 1985, the contrabandists formed an official organization, ASAUNDECOL, with 80,000 members. A decade later, the membership had risen to 130,000 and the markets resembled shopping centres. With at least 1.5 million people depending directly on ASAUNDECOL, which for the most part evaded tariffs, sales and profit taxes (although tariffs were cut from an average of 50 per cent to 11.5 per cent in 1991), it was a formidable electoral block. Nationally, ASAUNDECOL was capable of mustering at least 200,000 votes. Ernesto Samper, the protégé of Alfonso López Michelsen who ran for the Colombian presidency in 1994, had for a long while patronized its interests and been appointed its 'honorary president'. ASAUNDECOL's very active support – lobbying hard for its members to vote for Samper – helped to clinch his victory in an historically narrow election.

It was conventional, two-way contraband that initially launched Escobar into the cocaine trade. According to the DEA, during the 1980s Escobar remained in control of the smuggling into Colombia of the single most lucrative item, Marlboro cigarettes, which were shipped from Panama and sold to wholesalers. The National Federation of Traders (FENALCO) estimated that 70 per cent of the cigarettes smoked in Colombia were contraband, costing domestic producers $1 billion dollars a year in lost sales. Cigarette production in Antioquia dropped by nearly three quarters between 1984 and 1992. The smuggled cigarettes carried brand name cachet and were unburdened by taxes amounting to more than 100 per cent. Illicit whisky imports dominated the market even more, although bribes ensured that the bottles were always decked out in the required seals. The man believed to be Colombia's biggest wholesaler of illicit cigarettes and whisky, the gun-slinging, gold-chained Samuel 'Santa' Lopesierra, was elected to the Senate by the department of La Guajira in 1994. The National Directorate of Taxes and Customs (DIAN) believed he owned more than half of the merchandise distributed through the *sanandresito* in the Caribbean port of Barranquilla. Ernesto Samper openly endorsed Lopesierra's campaign – a link which was denounced by the family of Samper's opponent, Andrés Pastrana. As Colombia's major alcoholic drinks importers,

Pastrana's wife's family, the Puyanas, were one of Lopesierra's principal business competitors.

The drug traffickers also sold their dollars cheaply to the smugglers. 'The *narcos* launder their cash by passing on their dollars at a 15 per cent discount,' said Sabas Pretelt de la Vega, the president of FENALCO, a private association representing 15,000 companies. Tax authorities estimated the figure to be nearer 30 per cent – and claimed that, for the sake of convenience, the dollars were often traded by weight rather than value. Small-denomination bills took too long to count, even automatically.

FENALCO held the *sanandresitos* mainly responsible for the $2 billion of contraband which it estimated had entered Colombia every year since the 1980s; its attempts to confront the *sanandresitos* had resulted in the murder of FENALCO functionaries. Similarly, when the National Directorate of Taxes and Customs (DIAN) had attempted to intervene, shots had been fired. 'The *sanandresitos* believe they have gained "acquired rights",' said one tax inspector who had been forced to employ bodyguards. 'Raids create tremendous social problems and the big wholesalers, who are all linked to the drugs trade, hide behind that.' When DIAN attempted to raid a commercial centre suspected of selling contraband in the city of Pereira in May 1994, they were prevented by the president of the Senate, Juan Guillermo Angel. In the meantime, so desperate were the cocaine traffickers to find products through which to launder their money that, in 1994, according to FENALCO they smuggled thousands of tons of lavatory paper into the country from its cocaine staging post and money-laundering neighbour, Venezuela.

Cars were another prime object of contraband. During the 1970s and 1980s, importers of luxury vehicles had to pay tariffs of up to 300 per cent. The man who revolutionized the Medellín cartel's transport route in the Bahamas, Carlos Lehder, first met Escobar while dealing in Mercedes Benz and Porsches in Medellín. Most of the cars – bought overseas with cocaine money – were imported through foreign diplomats, who were allowed to pay a mere 15 per cent tariff and happy to pass the cars on to local dealers for a cut of the profits. ('It was unethical . . . but it was not illegal,' Lehder observed later.) Once tariffs were lowered in the 1990s, cars poured in and drug traffickers were famed for being behind many of the distributors that suddenly sprang up. If they were not being smuggled in from Venezuela, legally imported vehicles were being under-valued in declarations given to the customs – by ignoring special features that often doubled their true price. 'It is not so much that the *narcos* try to save money by eluding tariffs and taxes,' said the tax inspector. 'It is just that they do not want to declare their real wealth and risk being charged with illicit enrichment.' For the same reason, attempts to legalize the *sanandresitos* were doomed: overnight, wholesalers would have to declare a 1,000 per cent increase in their capital.

Although cocaine-stimulated contraband has gravely damaged Colombia's already antiquated textile and electro-domestic industries, drugs money can also be argued to have brought some benefits to the manufacturing sector. As in Medellín, the infusion of cash helped it to renovate itself. Industrial machinery was imported after being purchased with drugs dollars outside the country. Often, it was then smuggled in through the so-called *correo de brujas* or 'witches' mail': a mechanism operated by respectable import companies whereby the cargo is sneaked in alongside registered goods to avoid tariffs or simply the extra paper work. The service itself is cheaper, but risky.

Many deals with cocaine money, however, were on an enormous scale. The ingenuity to provide a clean, safe and productive investment for drugs cash – rather than the crass, speculative financial pyramids of the early years – was the key to extraordinary economic success. It was also a service for which the cocaine traffickers learned they had to pay up to a quarter of their deposits. Neither national nor international law was in any way equipped, nor were investigators able to understand, the mechanisms dreamed up to attract and to operate the money. Sometimes, Colombia was nothing more than a gigantic money-washing machine, lubricated by bribery, impunity and political influence, through which the cash could be laundered at will before returning overseas – where most of it stayed.

Judicial evidence to implicate leading Colombian businessmen with the systematic procurement of cocaine money is virtually impossible to obtain because of the size and penetration of their empires, in which legal and illegal activities are inextricably mixed. They enjoy the protection of the presidents and congress-men whose campaigns, vote buying and personal accounts they bankroll. Almost nobody dares to speak out against them, for fear of being pulverized in the courts, having their reputation, job prospects and career ruined, or worse.

One informant, who had been introduced casually by a mutual friend, had no doubt as to what would happen if he were identified. 'I would disappear and never be heard of again,' he said. A former employee at the management level of a Colombian multi-national company, 'Luis' had no ethical misgivings about the gigantic money-laundering schemes he described.

'Look, isn't it beautiful!' he exclaimed with the moon-faced grin of a collector of rare butterflies, having covered a sheet of paper with names, figures and flow-charts. Nothing was what it seemed. A local bank was really a group of investment funds that were really paper companies; money was transferred to the bank from Panama under an amnesty for allegedly legitimate Colom-bian capital that was, in reality, drugs cash; the money was used to buy up old industrial plants at a high price from other companies within the group; the investors in the investment funds, who were really frontmen for the drug traffickers, appeared to lose their capital because of poor management; the group's other companies built new industrial plants with the cash from the old ones and on leaseback agreements from the paper companies; two more paper companies were brought into play to take over the leaseback agreements from the first group of paper companies; these two dispatched the leaseback payments to their holding company in the United States, which in turn paid back the drugs traffickers.

'Either you get the *narcos*' money or you let a bunch of

ignorant people run the country,' said Luis, who went on to explain other schemes involving aircraft and agriculture in which the money was sucked through Colombia in a similar way, although more to the detriment of both consumers and producers. 'The art is in attracting the mafia's money but stopping them taking control. Nobody admits it to foreigners, but that has been the major challenge to the traditional Colombian élite for the last decade at least.'

Another source, a computer technician, explained how one of the country's leading conglomerates helped drugs traffickers cover their tracks after buying a ranch. The ranch would mysteriously hit financial problems and be mortgaged to the holding company; the trafficker would eventually lose it to the company, and the ranch would then be sold off to a frontman for the trafficker. Such manoeuvres were designed simply to put as much distance as possible between the traffickers and their properties, and were a response to the crackdowns on the Medellín cartel from the mid 1980s, when the government first began to seek ways of seizing their ill-gotten gains.

'There is no physical way to prevent money being laundered,' said one economist in the United States embassy, who was in favour of the legalization of drugs, arguing that it would bring the market under greater control. 'Every commercial transaction has the potential to be a money-laundering operation, and it is a fact of life in an economy in which drugs trafficking and the repatriation of profits is one of the biggest businesses going, if not the biggest. Trade liberalization makes it even easier. Traditional money laundering through bank deposits in the US and Panama is probably only the tip of the iceberg.' Money launderers discover new methods to camouflage and pass on their goods with even greater facility than the smugglers of the powder itself.

Having eaten a pizza of mozzarella, tomato, anchovy and pepperoni in northern Bogotá, I asked for the bill. Alongside my receipt came a token for a free extra pizza the next time I ordered one;

the special offer was available for one month at any restaurant in the chain. A week later, I returned with a friend. After consuming our two pizzas, I presented the token and received my bill (along with another token for the following month). The bill was a print-out ticket bearing the full price of both pizzas, with the value of my token being deducted afterwards by hand. I asked if I might keep it; instead, I was given a handwritten receipt for the sum I had actually paid. The pizza chain had just recorded twice its genuine earnings. If its accounts were going to be in order, it would have to suck in $5 from elsewhere to make up the shortfall.

Businesses such as fast-food restaurant chains, hotels, night-clubs and petrol stations were commonly bought up by the drugs traffickers, through frontmen, because they were high-liquidity concerns that offered easy ways systematically to exaggerate their income or to understate their costs – and thereby to launder money through the hole in their accounts. In creating these accounting holes, the businesses through which the money was laundered actually operated at a loss. Hence, in order to justify the true purpose of their existence, they often provided impossible competition for legitimate enterprises, driving these into bank-ruptcy or illegal practices to cut their costs. The more they undercut, the more of a loss they made and the more money could then be laundered through their businesses to make up the difference.

The determination to make a loss, which was common to money-laundering operations in all sectors, did not necessarily always mean that a business was inefficient or closed to innova-tion. But it did drive genuine competitors out of the market. Once again, the easiest and often only option available for them was to play the same game. In order to survive, formerly legitimate businesses were sometimes obliged to provide a laundry service too, washing other people's dirty money so that they could dip their prices to match their competitors'. The extent to which Colombia's economy became warped in this way was hard to determine. Although banks came under greater judicial scrutiny, the rest of the laundering market continued to operate freely beyond the reach of the law. Complaints were heard only by traders and producers undermined by the cheapness of contraband, where, in their bid to wash their money as quickly as possible, the traffickers were equally unconcerned about taking a loss in the meantime. Banks, however, never pointed the finger at anyone. Unlike the thousands of shops, farmers, factories and services who suffered because of illicit competition and who also remained silent, that may not simply have been because of fear.

'Money washing generates unfair competition that is extremely damaging to many sectors, but especially to commerce,' said a senior official at the National Directorate of Taxes and Customs (DIAN). 'The biggest chain of chemists [Drogas La Rebaja], which everybody knows is controlled by the Rodríguez Orejuelas, is making all the small, independent ones shut down because its products are so cheap; it is not trying to make a profit.' Cocaine profits abroad, he suspected, were also being used to purchase the pharmaceutical drugs imported for Drogas La Rebaja in Colombia. Ironically, money-laundering businesses generally paid their taxes on the nail to avoid any investigation into their affairs, while it was the legitimate opposition that defaulted. 'Until the introduction of the illicit enrichment law, taxes were never a problem for the drugs traffickers. Escobar always paid up,' said the tax official. 'But dodging taxes is often the only way for the honest ones to try to save themselves, and they will always tell you it is because of the *narco* competition.' In the case of Drogas La Rebaja, the easiest way out for failing pharmaceutical shops was simply to join the chain.

Another monopoly alleged to have been built on cocaine money was that of a chain of photographic laboratories, which within a decade had emerged from nowhere to control five times as many outlets as any other company. 'The machines have been imported fraudulently and the labs operate in a manner that is commercially unviable,' claimed the owner of one, albeit rather sleepy, photographic business in central Bogotá. 'With extremely expensive equipment, they locate themselves near other labs, charge very low prices and force the old, traditional labs to close. Don't give my name or I'll get my throat cut.' As its market share increased, its prices went up – although car-winning raffle tickets were given away. Aggressive, respected laboratories were stopped in their tracks. Government investigations of the company were initiated after detailed complaints were filed by the Colombian photographers' association as well as by individual traders.

Beauty queens and soccer stars also fell victim to the mafia. They were bought, they were promoted, and they were murdered. Patronizing beauty contests and soccer teams was more than just the indulgence of a whim in a ruggedly sexist country obsessed with vaunting the beauty of its women and the talents of its soccer players. The kudos of sponsoring a beauty queen or a champion soccer team was indeed immense; it reflected power and granted social status. But football teams, in particular, were also big business. They offered ways to launder money in Colombia and abroad as well as the opportunity to sanction clandestine betting networks in which the bets were enormous and the drug traffickers were the principle punters.

The mafia's involvement with beauty queens came about very simply: they invited them to their parties and made them their girlfriends and wives. Rodríguez Gacha set up a modelling studio through which to attract girls whom he then sponsored in beauty contests if they slept with him. One of the leaders of the Cali cartel, Miguel Rodríguez Orejuela, had a daughter with Miss Colombia 1974. A former *peón* [farmhand or pawn] of the Ochoa brothers, who became their head horseman, married Miss Colombia 1981; as a wedding present, his employers gave him a gold chess set so that he could 'see how a pawn can take a queen'. Miss Colombia of 1990 resigned in order to marry a notorious trafficker on the Caribbean coast; the husband, who had sponsored her, was murdered three years later. Meanwhile, the father of Miss Colombia 1993 was revealed to be a business associate of the Rodríguez Orejuelas; he was the manager and a board member of Cali Hotels, which was famed for its ties to the Cali cartel leaders. In the same way that the beauty queens transformed their features with plastic surgery, so the true identity of their sponsors was often transformed and covered up by legalistic subterfuge. The traffickers sought social prestige and acceptance; the beauty queens wanted their money.

In 1994, the Colombian national soccer team was among the favourites to win the World Cup. The squad arrived in the United States after a twenty-eight-game, unbeaten streak in which the team displayed a thrilling mixture of sparkling individual talent and collective precision. Nobody denied what lay behind its rise to glory. Cocaine money had inundated the Colombian league for more than a decade, turning its players into the best paid on the continent and massively improving the overall training and infra-structure of the main teams. However, as the World Cup finals approached, the shadows of cocaine and violence hanging over the sport were blown aside by the country's euphoric sense of impending victory. But the dream turned into a nightmare; Colombia was internationally disgraced.

It was the minister of justice, Rodrigo Lara Bonilla, who had first raised the alarm eleven years earlier. 'The mafia has taken over Colombian football,' he said, six months before he was assassinated. Lara Bonilla denounced the intrusion of 'hot money' into soccer clubs and launched investigations which resulted in large fines for two clubs accused of breaking exchange regulations. Stockbrokers had first involved themselves in the game during the 1970s in order to evade exchange controls. However, the mafia bought heavily into the game during Colombia's financial crisis in the early 1980s, when the already hard-pressed clubs could field their debts no longer and were forced to issue new shares. Eager as ever to pounce on a depressed sector, and anxious for the social prestige and the money-laundering opportunities it afforded, the leading drug traffickers invested heavily. The Rodríguez Orejuela family and their associates moved into the teams América of Cali and Millonarios of Bogotá; Gonzalo Rodríguez Gacha, however, assumed most control over the latter. In Antioquia, one of Escobar's main colleagues, Pablo Correa, became a major share-holder in the Medellín team; the other local side, Nacional, featured a major shareholder called Hernán Botero and was strongly identified with Escobar. Correa was later killed – probably by Escobar – and Botero was extradited to the United States for money laundering at the service of the Medellín cartel. Most of his operations were conducted through the Rodríguez Orejuelas' bank, the Banco de Trabajadores.

The purchase of foreign players and the transfer abroad of Colombian ones were ideal ways of soaking up cocaine cash and of evading exchange controls and supervision; the players themselves were often owned not by the club, but by its individual shareholders. Similarly, it was commonly understood that players were paid, illicitly, mostly in dollars – which naturally did not figure in the club accounts and were paid at home or abroad. While the accounts in Colombia scarcely revealed profits, the big money circulated outside the country. The 1988 transfer from Cali to Montpellier, a French team, of Colombia's most famous player, Carlos Valderrama, was officially for $1.7 million. But it was widely alleged that the real figure was half as much again and that the balance remained outside Colombia. Government investigations alone revealed that, between 1983 and 1988, at least $35 million was moved by Colombia's soccer clubs and their owners in illegal exchange operations.

The complicity between Colombian drug traffickers, soccer and the financial system was illustrated by three arrests in Luxembourg in June 1990. Edgar Garciá, a vice president of the América club – owned mostly by the Rodríguez Orejuelas – was detained, together with Franklin Jurado, a founder of the Cali stock exchange and a former economics adviser to Luis Carlos Galán, and Ricardo Mahecha, a former director of América. They were accused of money laundering and $36 million was frozen. Although Mahecha was acquitted, García and Jurado received five-year jail sentences and were later extradited to the United States.

The identification of the Colombian league with the drug traffickers was such that when Hernán Botero, one of the main Nacional shareholders, was extradited for money laundering in

November 1984, the league suspended the day's games in protest. Nacional was the team most identified with Pablo Escobar, although his name never featured in its documents. A governor of Antioquia, Antonio Roldán – for whose murder the Cali cartel leader, José Santacruz Londoño, was charged – was on Nacional's board. Almost all the main teams were in some way penetrated by the mafia. The Júnior team of Barranquilla was owned by the family of a senator and one-time minister, Fuad Char Abdala, whose alleged drug-trafficking connections were such that, in April 1994, he was denied a visa to the United States; one month earlier, Char Abdala, a Liberal, had obtained the highest vote in the Senate elections.

Another prominent figure closely related to cocaine traffickers through soccer was Manuel Francisco Becerra, a board member of América for several years under the vice presidency of Miguel Rodríguez Orejuela; Becerra was education minister during the government of President Virgilio Barco, a senator and a governor of the Valle del Cauca department. During the government of President César Gaviria, Becerra occupied the very powerful position of auditor general; one of his right-hand men, the head of internal audits, was Manuel Pinzón, the husband of Gilberto Rodríguez Orejuela's daughter, Claudia Pilar.

As with its economy, Colombia's soccer prospered during a decade when elsewhere in Latin America it was mostly in decline. Nacional's 1989 victory in the South American cup, La Copa Libertadores, signalled that Colombian football was in ascendency. No other Colombian club had ever won the cup. The following year, the national Colombian team qualified for the World Cup finals for the first time since 1962, and held Germany to a 1–1 draw. Yet violence had taken a grip on the sport. Referees, linesmen, club leaders, league officials and players themselves were being threatened, kidnapped and killed. International play in Colombia was banned for a year by the South American soccer federation in September 1990, after it emerged that six men wielding pistols and sub-machine-guns had demanded that the referees ensured that Nacional beat Vasco da

Gama, a Brazilian team, in Medellín. Heavy betting, in which the clubs themselves often attempted to fix the games, was the core of the problem.

When the Colombian team arrived in the 1994 World Cup finals in the United States, their soccer fame internationally was such that their captain, Carlos Valderrama, was featured on the front page of *Newsweek* magazine and his team was being tipped for victory by the legendary Brazilian star, Pelé. Few commented on the Cartier watch reportedly given to the team manager, Francisco Maturana, by Miguel Rodríguez Orejuela; nor on his gold-coloured Porsche, allegedly from the same patron. Reminders of the team members' domestic sponsorship by cocaine were belittled by Colombian leaders; and anyway, its World Cup sponsors were the Bavaria group of Julio Mario Santodomingo.

Yet, after all the histrionic expectations, in the first game against Romania the team was a shadow of its former self, and lost. Nerves, said the commentators. Four days later, the team lost again – this time 2–1 to the United States – and was effectively out of the cup. Amid disbelief in Colombia, it emerged that threats had been received by Maturana and some of the players. 'I am convinced that key players were paid to lose the game in order for gamblers to win huge bets at long odds,' asserted one Colombian sports journalist. The first time the ball hit the back of Colombia's net was an own goal struck by Andrés Escobar, a defender whose integrity was, however, unquestionable. Andrés Escobar was the most reputable and decent member of the team. A fortnight later he was murdered in Medellín. The assassin, whose employer was the brother of a man in jail for money laundering, fired six bullets into the footballer at pointblank range. He was heard to say before shooting: 'Thanks for the own goal.'

The impact of cocaine money on Colombian soccer was a microcosmic reflection of what had happened in the Colombian economy as a whole. The drug traffickers penetrated whatever sector possible with the primary intentions of laundering their earnings and gaining control; the profitability of the businesses themselves was invariably, initially at least, a secondary concern.

The richer the traffickers became, the more desperate they were to hide and to invest their money. In finding a home in a country where cocaine, marijuana and heroin export earnings represented more than 10 per cent of GDP, illegitimate capital tended either to drive legitimate businesses out of the market or to contaminate them too. The money slowly converted the economy into its own image, moulding it to its own needs and distorting the moral and ethical values with which it operated.

Colombia's economic and sporting development may indeed have bucked a regional trend in the 1980s with the help of the billions of dollars it earned from cocaine. However, as one 1994 presidential candidate, Carlos Lemos Simmonds, said following the murder of Andrés Escobar, the country had, in exchange, 'sold its soul to the devil and the devil [had] now demanded his share'.

CHAPTER EIGHT

A PYRRHIC VICTORY
FOR THE DOCTOR
(1989–91)

Three bullets from three bursts of an Uzi sub-machine-gun thudded into the politician, perforating his main artery. It was 8.45 p.m. on Friday, 18 August 1989. Luis Carlos Galán, a charismatic, 46-year-old left-wing Liberal whose immense popular following was expected to sweep him to the presidency in a year's time, collapsed on the podium in the town of Soacha, 20 kilometres south west of Bogotá. He died of a massive haemorrhage two hours later. For many Colombians, Galán's murder was a re-run of that of the last great Liberal hero to have promised radical reform only to be killed on the brink of electoral victory, Jorge Eliécer Gaitán. Unlike the assassin of Gaitán, Galán's killer vanished into the crowd. And unlike the murder of his predecessor, there were no riots afterwards; people were too scared as well as shocked.

The backlash to Galán's death was not so much a public as a political one. Apart from the wailing and gnashing of teeth among the chattering classes, if anything there was a stunned calm. The obvious culprits were the Medellín mafia. Galán's murder converted their persecution into a government obsession that would cost hundreds more lives; however, at the same time, Colombians began to ask why it should be they who paid the price in blood for the drug taking of millions of North Americans. The US attorney general, Richard Thornburg, sympathized: 'Without the enormous appetite of drug takers in the USA, there would not be any cartels in Colombia,' he said. The government of President Virgilio Barco moved on to the diplomatic offensive as well.

Yet who had killed Galán? Apart from having expelled Pablo Escobar from his ranks, the bushy-haired, fist-thrusting Liberal had made his mark denouncing political corruption generally and its infiltration by drugs trafficking specifically. In a similar way to Alfonso López Michelsen many years earlier, Galán had made his political ascent by establishing a dissident Liberal faction which he dissolved once he was strong enough to rejoin the party's fold as its prodigal son and presidential favourite. During the year of his death, Galán's public onslaughts on 'hot money' were quite rare; a politician to his fingertips, he was more intent on winning over the Liberal Party establishment, which viewed him with considerable suspicion. Indeed, such was the mistrust – and ambition – that it was rumoured other Liberals had conspired in his murder.

Galán's immediate family were convinced that politicians linked to the drugs traffickers, including Conservatives, had incited his killing. One of them alleged: 'About a year before his death, Luis Carlos knew of a meeting in [the department of] Tolima where Alberto Santofimio, Jairo Ortega [the congressional partner of Escobar] and Eduardo Mestre [a former banking associate of Gilberto Rodríguez Orejuela] spoke of the need to eliminate him. Luis Carlos told his colleagues and the authorities, but he was never protected properly and Maza Márquez [the head of the DAS state security police] behaved very oddly when I asked for the investigation of the new chief bodyguard who was unpopular with the others and disappeared immediately after Luis Carlos' death.'

More suspect at the time, however, were sectors of the far right. So strong was the anti-Communist alliance between the army and Rodríguez Gacha – which had led *El Mexicano* to believe he was working with the government – that it was also mooted that certain generals had backed the assassination by the drug traffickers in a bid to destabilize the state and pave the way for a military dictatorship in order to massacre the guerrillas once and for all. The army was livid at the Barco government's peace talks with M-19 and other rebel groups and may have feared Galán would continue in the same spirit. In March, José Antequera, the secretary of the Patriotic Union party, had been gunned down in the lobby of Bogotá's Eldorado airport. (Ernesto Samper, then competing with Galán for the Liberal presidential nomination, was also hit; at the time, Samper, who left hospital with four bullets still embedded in his body, was reported to believe his involvement was accidental.)

Shortly before his death, the cerebral and snappily dressed Antequera had denounced a wave of violence against his party, which was effectively the legal arm of the FARC guerrillas. Antequera claimed that more than 700 party members had been killed since 1985. 'There is no doubt that a paramilitary organization is involved, at a national level,' he said, accusing the armed forces of working hand in hand with the drug traffickers. However, the politically autonomous role of the military displayed throughout most of Colombia's republican history – a rarity in Latin America – militated against the idea of any kind of concerted conspiracy.

The involvement of Rodríguez Gacha's organization in the Galán murder was indicated by the filmed presence of one of his men, Jaime Rueda Rocha. By association, Escobar was implicated as well. 'Galán won't make it to the end of this week,' one of Escobar's colleagues had confided to a Medellín priest. Yet a lawyer friend of Escobar's who asked the drug lord if he had committed the crime was told much later: 'No, why should I have done it, Galán had already dropped extradition ... I have no reason to lie to you, just ask me.' *El Patrón* proceeded freely to admit he had ordered another murder the same day – of the Antioquian police chief, Colonel Waldemar Franklin Quintero, who a few months previously had raided one of Escobar's biggest laboratories and seized four tonnes of cocaine. 'Escobar could easily have confessed other crimes without affecting the maximum sentence he faced,' said the lawyer, 'but he refused to do so, saying he wasn't going to confess to things he hadn't done.'

The murder of Galán occurred within forty-eight hours of that of Franklin Quintero and Carlos Valencia, a judge investigating the killing of the *El Espectador* editor, Guillermo Cano. The previous month, the governor of Antioquia, Antonio Roldán, had been blown up by a car bomb (for which, strangely, the Cali cartel leader, José Santacruz Londoño, was charged). Galán himself had narrowly survived an assassination attempt while being driven from a Liberal Party lunch to the University of Medellín. Meanwhile, Colombia's judges and public prosecutors had gone on strike. The judicial employees association, ASONAL, claimed that 120 of its members had been killed since 1982, mostly by the mafia. Judges in Bogotá demanded the introduction of the death penalty. They announced in despair: 'Our sentences are considered a conspiracy against the spurious new order that drugs trafficking, economic crime and pseudo-politics . . . have imposed on us.' *El Espectador* declared that the country had plunged into anarchy.

The man who took over from Colonel Franklin Quintero was the deputy commander of the national police, General Carlos Arturo Casadiego. 'Believe me, it is on Colombia that they have declared war, not the police,' Casadiego said of the Medellín cartel – one year before he was forced to resign, following allegations that he had leaked information to Escobar; he was later shot in the face, allegedly during a drugs deal. Casadiego was a close colleague of General José Guillermo Medina Sánchez, the national police commander who had been sacked in January 1989 after also coming under suspicions of being on Escobar's payroll.

General Miguel Maza Márquez was believed, however, to express sympathies in a different direction. It had been rumoured since the mid 1980s that the head of DAS had links with the Cali cartel. In 1989, Escobar started loudly to accuse him of the same thing. Meanwhile, the lawyer to whom Escobar had confessed his guilt over the murder of Colonel Franklin Quintero claimed that Escobar had personally shown him documents, impounded by Peruvian police, which demonstrated that Maza Márquez had received payments from the Rodríguez Orejuela brothers. A few years later, the bonds between the bullet-eyed general and the Rodríguez Orejuela brothers were chillingly exposed by a telephone tap whose authenticity was never in dispute; only the most obtuse of commentators denied that the conversation indicated anything other than that the Cali cartel leaders had backed Maza Márquez's presidential campaign.

It was Maza Márquez who had been the target of the first terrorist blast by the Medellín cartel. A car bomb comprising 100 kilograms of dynamite had killed six people and wounded more than fifty when it was detonated by remote control in a congested avenue in central Bogotá in May 1989. Broken glass rained down upon the wrecked cars and human carnage as the general stepped out unharmed from his armour-plated limousine, its molten tyres stuck fast to the asphalt. Meanwhile, documents found on a retired army captain in league with the Medellín cartel indicated that military intelligence officers had conspired against him; the army was bitter about Maza Márquez's unmasking of its drug-backed paramilitary activities. The documents also showed that the Medellín cartel had full access to decisions taken at a senior level in the ministries of interior and foreign affairs, the attorney general's office and other important government institutions. President Barco, who prized the general highly, was obliged to conduct a cabinet reshuffle.

In the light of later evidence linking Maza Márquez to the Rodríguez Orejuelas, it seemed that the state was caught in a political and financial power battle between the two cartels. The war about to be waged on *El Doctor*, the Ochoa brothers and the Mexican was not against cocaine; it was *for* cocaine. The Colombian state had been reduced to no more than a complex vehicle through which the fickle interests of warring mafias were playing themselves out. So much money was at stake from the hundreds of tonnes of cocaine being snorted by US and European users that, with some very honourable exceptions, many of Colombia's key politicians, government officials, law enforcers and businessmen had consciously or unconsciously become mere pawns in a bloody chess game played out between the cocaine giants.

The Cali cartel helped the state to fight its mafia opponents in Medellín. It was later claimed that Barco's brother, Pedro, had been warned personally by Miguel Rodríguez Orejuela of the Medellín cartel's impending violence; the two were reported to have met in Europe shortly before Galán's death. The head of the Drug Enforcement Administration in Colombia between 1988 and 1994, Bolivian-born Joe Toft, said: 'The partnership between the Cali cartel and the government against Pablo Escobar started around 1988; there was not a war on cocaine so much as a war between mafias.'

The Barco govenment had been soft on the Cali cartel since the beginning; two years earlier, in 1986, extradition requests for Gilberto Rodríguez Orejuela or the Chess Player and José Santacruz Londoño had been turned down by the president following the recommendation of Barco's minister of justice, Edmundo López Gómez; it was the same López Gómez who, as minister of communications, was reported to have authorized the transfer of the Rodríguez Orejuelas' radio chain to protestant groups widely alleged to be the drug barons' frontmen, and whose name was said to have figured on a list of payments made by the Chess Player when the latter was arrested in Spain.

On the night of Galán's murder, President Barco, an honest, sixty-eight-year-old oligarch whose memory was beginning to fail and who delegated most security matters to the secretary general of the presidency, Germán Montoya, re-introduced extradition. This time, however, extradition was to be by presidential decree alone. As Galán lay dying in hospital, Barco also announced the seizure of assets belonging to suspected drug traffickers, as well as penalties for illicit enrichment (an unexplained increase in a person's wealth) and for *testaferros*, the people who fronted the drug-traffickers' money and businesses. The re-enforcement of extradition kicked off two days later with the capture and subsequent sending to a United States jail of Eduardo Martínez, one of Escobar's main money launderers. The crackdown was to be directed almost exclusively against Escobar and his colleagues.

Before the assassination, the government and the Medellín cartel had been secretly negotiating for nearly a year. It was the Cali cartel, by moving closer to the government and by encouraging General Maza Márquez's persecution of its enemies in Medellín, that had helped to jeopardize these talks. Escobar's godfather, Joaquín Vallejo, a former ambassador to the United Nations, mediated on behalf of the Medellín drug barons at the request of Escobar's most trusted lawyer, Guido Parra, who was later shot dead in Medellín by a death squad backed by the Cali cartel. Vallejo claimed he met the soft-voiced government strongman, Germán Montoya, about a dozen times between June 1988 and the day of Galán's burial. Escobar's demands were essentially the same as those he had made in Panama in 1984. He and the traffickers of Medellín, Bogotá and the Caribbean coast offered to abandon drugs trafficking in return for – no more, no less – an end to extradition, a judicial pardon and a tax amnesty.

Escobar, reported Vallejo of their clandestine rendezvous, was the undisputed leader and 'a man of bewildering intellectual calibre – he understood everything at speed and each of his questions went to the heart of the matter'. Rodríguez Gacha boasted to the former Conservative senator that the empire he was prepared to surrender was bigger than Colombia's largest corporation, Ecopetrol, the state oil company worth $650 million. The cartel believed that Vallejo's talks with Montoya, which took place in the presidential palace, formed part of President Barco's avowed peace initiative aimed at guerrilla and paramilitary groups. A draft agreement – which claimed the Cali cartel controlled only 10 per cent of the market, although according to the DEA its share was closer to 40 per cent – was even produced and discussed. The document proposed global legalization with the Colombian government retaining some kind of a commercial monopoly. However, the negotiations fell foul of the United States and were undermined by police repression which was being egged on by the Cali cartel.

'The [Medellín] cartel would not have been so stupid as to have gone on with its business,' said Vallejo in his dark book-lined study above Medellín's Parque Bolívar, where thugs were openly smoking pot and *basuko* in the morning sunshine. 'I believe the offer was genuine. The government played a double game, stepping up its persecution; it wouldn't surprise me if Galán was killed in retaliation [by the cartel]. That was an error. Escobar did not have the academic preparation to realize all the effects of what was basically a political act; it finished him.' Vallejo had also been told by Montoya, an old friend and fellow *paisa*, that US agreement was essential to any deal.

Since President Ronald Reagan had just reaffirmed his hardline commitment to the drugs war, and after two vain attempts to employ lobbyists in Washington – a company managed by the former US Secretary of State, Henry Kissinger, was allegedly approached – the cartel awaited the inauguration of George Bush. 'The Ochoas had used a lawyer in Miami who worked in the private office of one of George Bush's sons,' said Vallejo. 'The idea was for the lawyer to persuade Bush's son to talk privately to the president. The lawyer agreed but said the Ochoas still owed him $20,000, which irritated them. There was a delay, Galán was killed, and that was that.'

In the run-up to Galán's murder, a communiqué from the Extraditables demonstrated how desperate the Medellín cartel was becoming: 'We want peace. We have screamed out loud for it, but we cannot beg for it . . . We do not accept, nor will we ever accept, the numerous arbitrary raids on our families, the ransackings, the repressive detentions, the judicial frame-ups, the anti-patriotic and illegal extraditions, the violations of all our rights. We are ready to confront the traitors.'

Within a few days of Barco's crackdown, the police and army had seized more than 200 mansions and ranches, about 100 airplanes and helicopters, 30 yachts and 600 weapons. Among the dozens of properties of Escobar which were occupied and confiscated were the El Mónaco building in Medellín, the Cama Suelta discotheque in Envigado and the Nápoles estate in the valley of the river Magdalena. Hundreds of people were detained, including eight traffickers and money launderers on the US list of 'extraditables'. For the first time, the government also offered a reward for the capture of Escobar and Rodríguez Gacha: the equivalent of a paltry $260,000, a fraction of the bribes either drug lord was prepared to pay for loyalty and silence. But the hunt was on.

In response, Escobar ordered his cousin, Gustavo Gaviria, to raise the price of their cocaine, the cartel's lawyers challenged the presidential decrees in the supreme court, it lobbied Congress to order a referendum on extradition and to pave the way for a pardon, and its *sicarios* set fire to or blew up political party offices, radio stations and the homes of leading industrialists in and around Medellín. 'We will begin to go for the oligarchs and to burn the houses of the rich,' said Escobar in an intercepted telephone conversation with his cousin. In spite of his billions of dollars, Escobar appeared not to rank himself as one of 'the rich', which for him was synonymous with 'the oligarchs' who had rejected him while readily – and as invisibly as possible – taking his money.

'It's that it is very easy,' continued Escobar to Gaviria, 'because the house of a rich person only has one watchman and one goes in with three gallons of gasoline and with that we shit on them and make them cry and beg for mercy . . . You know, brother, that is the only way. This country is asking for peace and every day there are more people asking for peace. So we have to apply much harder pressure—' On the same day as the cartel's new wave of violence began, it sent another media bulletin: 'We are declaring total and absolute war on the government, on the industrial and political oligarchy, on the journalists that have attacked and insulted us, on the judges that have sold themselves to the government, on the extraditing magistrates . . . and on all those who have persecuted and attacked us. We will not respect the families of those who have not respected our families. We will burn and destroy the industries, properties and the mansions of the oligarchy.'

Escobar's terrorism strategy bore fruit almost immediately. The minister of justice, Mónica de Greiff, resigned on the grounds that she was 'a minister for times of peace' and not of war. The mayor of Medellín, Juan Gómez Martínez, called for dialogue with the drug traffickers the very day of the murders of Colonel Franklin Quintero and Galán (a former Medellín mayor was killed a few weeks later). The president of the Chamber of Representatives, Norberto Morales, who vigorously supported the cartel's extradition referendum and amnesty initiative, said: 'I have always been party to dialogue with everyone. I will talk even to the worst of enemies.' And Ernesto Samper declared, while recovering from his bullet wounds, 'If we do not turn out to be capable of winning [this war], the country will have to explore alternatives.'

Although political opinion softened – and in the same way that Medellín asked why it should have to host a war conducted by the central government, Colombia as a nation began to ask why it should have to host a war thrust upon it by the United States – Escobar and the Medellín cartel found that the police repression was being systematically stepped up. With less than a year to go, the government of President Virgilio Barco was determined to destroy them. In a powerful speech to the United Nations by Barco in September 1989, Barco called on the 'consumer countries' – those whose populations illicitly bought the cocaine – to rally behind him in confronting the violence in Colombia and to make greater efforts to stamp out illicit drugs use. 'The only law that the drug traffickers do not break is the law of supply and demand,' he said. While British mercenaries prepared, in luxurious conditions provided by the Cali cartel, to kill Escobar, the British government responded to Barco's call for help by sending over members of the Special Air Services – from whose bosom the mercenary leaders had sprung in the first place – to train élite police commando units that would join in the hunt.

A PYRRHIC VICTORY FOR THE DOCTOR (1989-91)

In Colombia itself, even the DEA praised the government's determination to hunt the Medellín traffickers. 'There was an all-out effort by Barco to get Escobar and Rodríguez Gacha and the Medellín group,' said Joe Toft, the DEA head in Colombia. 'The government had very little interest in Cali, and even for us the Cali cartel was not the number one priority. We were supporting the Colombian effort so we had twice as many people working on Medellín. Police only responded to information on Cali regarding their laboratories, nothing else.'

According to Toft, it was already obvious that the Cali cocaine leaders were playing a far more sophisticated game. 'They always tried to avoid attention,' he said, talking between sips of *aromática* herbal tea in a Bogotá doughnut shop. 'They killed people left and right – law enforcement, informants and their own people who did not play by the rules – but they always managed to cover it up or make it look as if someone else did it. In Medellín, if Escobar killed someone, he left his calling card as a warning. While Escobar seemed to be concentrating on openly intimidating the government through terrorism, the Cali crowd was penetrating and buying the government while concealing its terrorist-type activity.'

The terrorism of the Medellín cartel, encouraged by the instant dissolution of most public resistance and enraged by the police persecution, became ever wilder. In September, a truck bomb blew up the main offices, in Bogotá, of the campaigning newspaper whose editor they had already murdered, *El Espectador*. The newspaper's Medellín representatives were killed the following month, when a prominent television journalist was also shot dead and the offices of the pro-Galán *Vanguardia Liberal* newspaper, in Bucaramanga, were destroyed. Judges were killed in both Cali and Medellín, provoking another judicial strike nationally. Meanwhile, a car bomb aimed at a Bogotá bridge cost the lives of four street vendors. However, if there were a single, cold-blooded and barbarous act that left all others in the shade it was the cartel's mid-air bombing of a civilian jet between Bogotá and Cali on 27 November. One hundred and seven people were killed.

The target was one man: the Liberal presidential candidate, César Gaviria, who had stepped into the shoes of Galán. According to a leading henchman of Escobar's, the bomb was inside a case which an innocent dupe had been told to open in order to tape record conversations around him; his companion had abandoned the aircraft just before take-off. 'When the guy opened the case, it exploded,' said 'Julio', my informant. Gaviria, however, was not on board. His security chief, Colonel José Homero Rodríguez, had dissuaded the future president from taking the fatal flight with the Avianca airline. 'Julio' claimed that Fidel Castaño, the right-wing paramilitary leader and Escobar ally famed for his ruthless brutality, was chiefly behind the bombing. My informant justified the atrocity with a toothy smile. 'War is war,' he said.

General Maza Márquez, the head of DAS, survived yet another bomb a fortnight later. The general was by now openly being accused by the Extraditables of being in cahoots with the Cali cartel. This time, a bus loaded with at least 500 kilograms of dynamite exploded outside the DAS headquarters in the district of Paloquemao, Bogotá. About eighty people were killed and more than 700 injured. The blast dug a 4-metre crater, devastated the DAS building and obliterated hundreds of nearby shops. Maza Márquez escaped again unscathed, as did the five men being held there under suspicion for the murder of Galán. The five men, who claimed that DAS officials tried to kill them in their cells, were declared innocent and freed three and a half years later; they had been framed by DAS. Two of those accused of the murder were killed in 1992, one of them in jail and the other – the alleged trigger man, Jaime Rueda Rocha – while he was reported to be leading a gang in the Magdalena Medio that had just taken possession of three aircraft bombs, bought in El Salvador in order to drop on top of Pablo Escobar. As with the British mercenaries who worked first for Rodríguez Gacha and then for the Cali cartel, so close were the links between the warring mafias that Rueda Rocha appeared effortlessly to have switched from one to the other.

Similarly, although doubtless after a blitzkrieg of vain

attempts, it was eventually with the utmost of ease that in 1990 the Cali mafia infiltrated Rodríguez Gacha's organization at the innermost level, placed the informer in touch with the anti-drugs police and stood back to watch as the Mexican was killed. Ten months after Jorge Enrique Velásquez, a seaman and cocaine smuggler living in Cartagena, was contracted by an old friend from Cali on behalf of the Rodríguez Orejuela, Santacruz Londoño and Herrera families, he had wormed his way into the Mexican's confidence to such an extent that Rodríguez Gacha entrusted him with his life while fleeing from the police after they had occupied his estates north of Bogotá in the department of Cundinamarca.

Velásquez, who helped Rodríguez Gacha offload an Israeli shipment of 400 Galil rifles and 100 Uzi sub-machine-guns that came via the British island of Antigua, had nearly been killed by an increasingly paranoic Escobar. His calls to Cali had been traced and Escobar's *sicarios*, who were paid the equivalent of $13,000 for every Cali cartel suspect they murdered, were banking on their bounty. But Rodríguez Gacha had vouched for him. In early December, Velásquez alerted his Cali contacts of the Mexican's presence near Cartagena. This time, three police officers flew in to meet Velásquez on a mission known at that stage only to three generals; Rodríguez Gacha instantly got wind of it from the Ministry of Defence. However, the fugitive cocaine baron believed he had been traced through his seventeen-year-old son, Freddy, who had recently joined him after being freed from jail. (The son, an obese bully with a gold-plated motorcycle, had been arrested in May with the brother of the former deputy attorney general, Clara Inés Gregory; thirteen of Freddy's fellow prison inmates, as well as the warden, had been murdered for teasing him.) Velásquez, above any suspicion of treachery, was able carefully to draw in the net. The Mexican entrusted him to find an escape route; Velásquez gave it to the police.

Rodríguez Gacha, the son of cheese-making peasants, an emerald dealer, cattle farmer, horse breeder, soccer fanatic and one of the world's richest cocaine smugglers, had abandoned his home base of Cundinamarca in a way that Escobar never did. Having murdered one emerald tsar and tried to blow up another, the man with the snake head in his hatband, an obsession with Mexico and a hatred for God-denying Communists – he built a church dedicated to the Christ child, or *Divino Niño* – Rodríguez Gacha had won the bitter enmity of his former allies. The emerald miners were colluding both with the police and the Cali cartel (with whom Rodríguez Gacha had been trying to broker a peace). The Mexican had burned his boats. Although he could travel on friendly territory, staying at the ranches of his partners and henchmen, by the time he had reached the Caribbean coast he was very far from home.

For all his billions of dollars – millions of which were buried under the ground because he could not find anywhere else to put them or anything else to spend them on – Rodríguez Gacha was now running for his life with his only son, stripped of every luxury save his Cartier watch, a 9mm automatic pistol and an MP-5 sub-machine-gun. If captured alive, he would immediately be extradited to the United States. The man piloting him in a high-speed launch from beach to beach south of Cartagena was steering him into a trap. Around noon on 15 December, after Velásquez had found a pretext to abandon his prey in order to escape the imminent gunfire, police helicopters swooped over the wooden seaside cabin where Rodríguez Gacha had spent his last night in the bay of Coveñas. The Mexican made a dash for it in a truck, chased by the helicopters. His son and three other men jumped out. Allegedly, Freddy tried to surrender; they were all shot dead. Minutes later, Rodríguez Gacha and his two remaining bodyguards ran from the truck into a banana plantation. Surrounded by soldiers, in the sticky heat, and with the helicopter buzzing overhead, Rodríguez Gacha, according to Velásquez's version, stuck a finger at the police and blew half his head off with a grenade.

Escobar had given the police the slip twice in 1989. On the first occasion, he received a tip-off. On the second, he escaped in his underpants again (said police) after his outer security ring detected no fewer than eight helicopters making a pre-dawn approach on a ranch near his Nápoles estate, at the confluence of two rivers in the Magdalena valley. Escobar and Jorge Luis Ochoa abandoned their adolescent girlfriends (who claimed each to have received the equivalent of $250 for their sexual favours), were shot at as they took to a launch and finally fled by foot into the hills along a labyrinth of paths where supplies of money, radio equipment, food and clothing had been buried in readiness for just such an emergency. Three of their bodyguards were killed and Escobar was wounded in the arm. Somehow, the Medellín cartel leaders broke through both the police and army cordons; they knew the area like the backs of their hands.

Security became an obsession as well as a science for the Doctor, who was also known as *El Patrón*. Launches, helicopters, airplanes, vehicles and horses were dispersed throughout the rivers, mountains and forests of Antioquia, making up escape routes that formed a giant web around him wherever he moved. And when under pressure, Escobar always returned to Medellín and its surrounding hills. His immediate entourage of up to a dozen men carried short-distance VHF walkie-talkies; the outer cordons used satellite dishes and radio telephones with which they would link up to a radio operator close to Escobar. Often, what appeared to be innocent roadside food-stalls were really communication and look-out posts. In Medellín, the walkie-talkies linked up to a central office which patched them through to conventional telephone lines; beepers were also used until outlawed by the government. Escobar employed so complex, transient and impenetrable a language of codes and *noms de guerre* that some of his men were buried under their latest aliases not so much for security reasons but because their companions no longer knew their real names. The use of aliases was not only to bedevil their police pursuers; it was also to confound attempts to gather judicial proof against them. Escobar would be Number 70 one day, Victor the next. A request to make over a money draft would be an order to plant a bomb; 'send him on holiday' meant send him to his grave.

Escobar's safe houses were usually of humble appearance. Located on high ground – often at the heads of valleys – in order to enjoy commanding views of access and easy escape routes into the mountains, the refuge would be bought in the name of a bodyguard. The walls of Escobar's room were doubled, in order to improve their resistance to gunfire, and the workmen who carried out the renovation were habitually shot dead on completion. Friends, family and other visitors were received at a second, more luxurious abode, customarily built a few kilometres below the drug lord's own refuge. His inner group of bodyguards were often the leaders of Medellín gangs; it was they who tortured and killed suspected infiltrators, traitors and debtors. The guards who formed the outer ring half an hour away were usually members of their gangs.

Raid after raid by the police and army failed to catch him because Escobar kept moving between his safe houses, by night, every few weeks, and with only a few men; because his codes, telephone lines and frequencies changed; and because of errors in locating the geographical source of his calls (or because he made the calls a few kilometres from the refuge itself). Helicopters – which he nicknamed liquidizers – alerted him with their noise. But most of all, according to General Maza Márquez, Escobar was protected by his network of informants within the government security forces. Police and soldiers in key positions were bribed for tip-offs and physical protection. An army patrol once materialized suspiciously near a refuge after the police had begun to encircle it. Operations were often so big that they could hardly not be noticed beforehand. Information on the identities, careers and families of the officers chasing Escobar was regularly sold to him. He also ran telephone tapping offices in Medellín and Bogotá. Meanwhile, civilian spies near military and police barracks were paid to advise Escobar of all helicopter and troop movements – especially those of the *sombreritos*, the police from the élite anti-drugs squad who sported Australian-type bush hats.

Although he was on the run, Escobar's sophisticated communications network – which his brother Roberto helped to organize – enabled him to continue his battle with the state as well as to maintain his trafficking in cocaine. In order to pay for his political, judicial and military war on extradition, Escobar enforced a monthly quota on his fellow traffickers; dissidents were kidnapped until they paid up. The money was collected by members of his inner entourage, whose own gangs were contracted to carry out the kidnaps where necessary. Nevertheless, Escobar's victims were often unaware that Escobar was behind their kidnap, and begged for his help as an intermediary. He obliged, collected both the ransom and the commission, paid off the gang and continued to demand his quota. In one such case, in a telephone call intercepted by DAS, Escobar explained at some length how he had to preserve the 'respect' of the kidnappers and not appear to go soft; 'You understand me? I mean, all my life I have helped them, all those guys in [the districts of] Aranjuez and Manrique, everywhere I built a football pitch or gave them food or money to pay their rents, all those people, all those bandits you know, and now it has become a *city* of bandits, brother—' So efficient was the kidnap-for-debt service that other traffickers also purchased it. The accounts themselves were administered by Escobar's cousin, Gustavo Gaviria, who remained mostly in Medellín. It was Gaviria who mainly co-ordinated their continued smuggling of cocaine as well as the renting out of routes, boats and aircraft to other members of the cartel.

The kingdom of crime was underpinned only by money; loyalty was no fatter than a wad of banknotes. When, in early 1990, Escobar offered a reward for every policeman killed, the ensuing slaughter only stopped, for an instant, when he had a liquidity crisis. Escobar's lower ranking workers stuck by him mostly in the hope that somehow, if they proved themselves, sooner or later they would be given the chance to earn a fortune as a member of his inner guard – who were often allowed to share in the cocaine shipments which they helped to protect. That men and women were prepared to die for him and his colleagues in suicide car-bomb attacks was a myth: according to the infiltrator who betrayed Rodríguez Gacha, Jorge Velásquez, they were simply tricked. Such dupes were known as *suizos*, a pun on suicide.

Disinformation was another vital tool in Escobar's armoury. Not only was false information of his whereabouts fed systematically, directly and indirectly, to the police, but journalists and the owners of newspapers, radio and television programmes were bribed, fooled, threatened and murdered in Escobar's bid to manipulate public opinion. Escobar was devoted to newspaper and television news, almost as much as he was to televised soccer games. According the the DAS secret police, the communiqués Escobar issued in the name of the Extraditables were written almost solely by him, following only the occasional consultation with his brother Roberto, or Jorge Luis Ochoa. The target of many was General Maza Márquez, whom he accused of being a torturer and murderer on the Cali cartel payroll. Leaflets were issued offering the equivalent of $1.3 million for the general's head. The lawyer acquaintance who claimed to have seen evidence of Cali cartel payments to the general claimed: 'Escobar had also got hold of details of Maza Márquez's [illegal] accounts in the United States and Switzerland; he never revealed the details because everybody would have believed he was making it up.' Maza Márquez always swore his innocence.

When Escobar and Jorge Luis Ochoa were roused from their nocturnal slumber – although Escobar never went to bed before 4 a.m., rarely emerging before midday – by the raid in the Magdalena valley in November 1989, their whereabouts were apparently betrayed by an informant. The information had been crossed with telephone and radio intercepts as well as documents seized during other operations. The security forces narrowly missed Rodríguez Gacha, too. The three leaders of the Medellín cartel had planned to meet at the small ranches bordering Escobar's Nápoles estate in order to discuss the possible assassination of the United States president, George Bush, who was due to visit Colombia in two months' time.

A PYRRHIC VICTORY FOR THE DOCTOR (1989–91)

The killing of Rodríguez Gacha in December 1989 was probably the biggest factor in preventing the assassination attempt on Bush from being carried out. The Doctor lost on two fronts. Public opinion was bucked by the success of the police, provoking the fickle and weak-kneed Congress to ditch the extradition referendum. Without the Rodríguez Gacha alliance, Escobar also no longer exercised the same leverage over the right-wing paramilitary squads in the Magdalena valley, which had previously been his backyard. After the death of Rodríguez Gacha, the paramilitary squads who had fought against the emerald miners started to break ranks.

Parts of the Mexican's organization found it more profitable to form alliances with the leaders of the Cali cartel – with whom for a long time Rodríguez Gacha had even shared cocaine shipments – and hence to work with the police against Escobar, who in any case was less sympathetic to their ideological aims. The Medellín drugs baron had lost the strategic security provided him by what had almost become private armies; far from being a resource, they became a dangerous and distracting threat behind his back. Escobar was also unsure about how far they had been involved in betraying Rodríguez Gacha. Were he to launch an attack on President Bush, Escobar could not depend on their backing during the gigantic crackdown that would ensue.

At the same time, killing Bush was mainly Rodríguez Gacha's idea. His bloody plans were revealed by the seaman who had betrayed him. The Mexican allegedly confided in Jorge Velásquez about how the cartel was preparing to kill Bush at the forthcoming summit between the presidents of the United States and the Andean cocaine-producer countries. Velásquez, who was later taken under US protection, wrote: 'The Mexican spoke of his intention of killing the US president, George Bush, in Cartagena. He was planning to place a powerful charge of explosives on the route of the convoy that would transport him from the airport to the city . . . He had an obsession with terrorism and was talking with an ever greater intensity of killing President Bush.'

Instead of targeting the US president, Escobar embarked on the kidnapping of leading Colombian politicians and businessmen. Among them were the son of the secretary general of the presidency, Germán Montoya, and the sister of a son-in-law of President Virgilio Barco. The government wilted. By holding Montoya's and Barco's families hostage, Escobar had the state on its knees. Yet again, Alfonso López Michelsen, the former president, stepped in as intermediary. In a peace agreement drafted by López Michelsen, after reportedly consulting the Medellín cartel, it was proposed that in return for an end to the cartel's violence and drug trafficking they should be treated with leniency. According to General Harold Bedoya, the commander of the army's Fourth Brigade in Medellín, Escobar's response was also drafted after talks with López Michelsen – along with two former presidents, a cardinal and Germán Montoya. Escobar offered to surrender in exchange for 'legal and constitutional guarantees', which were understood to include the abolition of extradition. He promised to hand over weapons, explosives, his kidnap victims or 'hostages', and cocaine laboratories. 'We accept the triumph of the State,' declared Escobar.

President Bush, however, did not accept his word. In an effort to convince the government and the man who a few weeks earlier he had been planning to assassinate, Escobar released his hostages, handed over a huge laboratory complex near the Panama frontier together with a bus containing 1,000 kilograms of dynamite, and alerted the government to a murder contract out for a former justice minister, Enrique Low Murtra, in Switzerland. President Barco, who moved to paralyse extradition proceedings against eight captured traffickers, looked set to swallow the cartel's terms.

In a repeat performance of the 1984 Panama talks, it was pressure from the United States that finally scuppered the deal. The US president attended the Cartagena summit in January 1990, only a few weeks after 24,000 members of the US army, navy, airforce and marines had invaded Panama to capture General Manuel Noriega because of his drug-smuggling involvement. Meanwhile, Bush was boxed about the ears for the United States' inability to cut its drug consumption. As for Escobar's apparent gestures of goodwill, it emerged that several of the liberated kidnap victims were obliged to pay ransom – some of them, in Escobar's view, owed him favours anyway – and that the laboratory complex did not belong to Escobar. In addition, as car bombs would subsequently demonstrate, he still had an ample supply of dynamite. The former justice minister enjoyed nothing but a stay of execution: he was murdered by the cartel in April 1991.

In Escobar's view, his release of Montoya's son and the sister of a son-in-law of President Barco left both government leaders in hock to him. He felt he had made a deal. With the government floundering, the police and army continued to hunt Escobar down. The battle moved to the poor neighbourhoods of northern Medellín, where up to 300 heavily armed gangs of *sicarios* fought for the honour of being the cartel's cannon fodder and became a deadly daily menace throughout the city. The killing of two soldiers attempting to gather intelligence in the Aranjuez district in January 1990 provoked the invasion of the north-eastern suburbs by 5,000 of their colleagues from the Fourth Brigade. Schools were turned into military barracks and hundreds of people arrested in the maze of streets and higgledy-piggledy houses that wriggled up the side of the valley. But the operations, which spread to other areas including the towns of Bello and Envigado, were fruitless and inflammatory.

According to Colonel Augusto Bahamón, who was the brigade's second-in-command, of the 970 people arrested by October, only 86 were still in jail; the rest were dead or had been freed for lack of evidence and witnesses. While the military crackdown increasingly aggravated the *sicarios'* hatred for authority, the army itself felt furiously frustrated. And since the operations were focused on his gangs at a time when he thought he had struck a deal with the government, Escobar felt tricked. Meanwhile, the mafia leader became increasingly outraged at the police because of the torturing, disappearances and killings of people directly linked to him. The police bullying of his wife was the last straw. In March, Escobar offered nearly $4,000 for every policeman murdered in Medellín; if the victim belonged to the SAS-trained élite commando force, the bounty was doubled.

By June, at least 180 policemen had been gunned down in a human safari which marked the launch of Escobar's 'total war'. The police were shot or bombed. In his determination to terrorize the government into begging for peace, Escobar ensured that there were as many civilian casualties as possible. Hardly anybody noticed a dead policeman any longer, except for his colleagues. On Mother's Day, 1990, car bombs shook the cities of Cali, Medellín and Bogotá, killing 26 people and wounding at least 180. Car bombs also exploded in Cartagena and Pereira. In the meantime, two left-wing presidential candidates, Bernardo Jaramillo, of the FARC-linked Patriotic Union party, and Carlos Pizarro, a former M-19 guerrilla, were murdered. Jaramillo was shot by hired gunmen at Bogotá airport and Pizarro by a solitary *sicario* aboard a plane (which had also taken off from Bogotá). Pizarro's killer was promptly gunned down by his bodyguards.

Although Escobar denied responsibility for murdering the candidates, he was publicly blamed. The killings coincided with his campaign to destabilize the May presidential elections in which César Gaviria, the forty-three-year-old Liberal candidate who had replaced Luis Carlos Galán and who had vowed to continue with extradition, was the favourite to win. But Escobar protested his innocence even more loudly than usual. He had been a friend of Jaramillo and had persuaded Rodríguez Gacha to save the Patriotic Union leader from the right-wing death squads. Shortly before Jaramillo's death in March, the Communist leader had told a Colombian magazine: 'Now everything is going to be blamed on Señor Pablo Escobar. He is going to be the scapegoat for all the evils that the country has suffered during these years.' Jaramillo was against extradition and in favour of a lenient treatment for the drug traffickers. Escobar, in a public letter denying his involvement, wrote with some feeling: 'I have never belonged to the right because it repulses me. I have not had, nor do I have, nor am I going to have paramilitary groups; because I have never defended the interests of the oligarchs, nor of the landowners. I have the blood of the people.'

Similarly, after the murder in April of Pizarro, whom Escobar personally considered a *marica* or gutless homosexual, he was at pains to demonstrate his sympathies for M-19. 'I have always been a friend of almost all [its] leaders,' he wrote to the police colonel who was accusing Escobar. 'In moments of the greatest tension and difficulties I hid Alvaro Fayad and Iván Marino Ospina [M-19 leaders]; you can ask the wife and children of Iván.' The Medellín cartel had worked with M-19 ever since their pact after the kidnap of one of the Ochoa sisters. Not only had the cartel backed M-19's seizure of the Palace of Justice but they were also claimed to have jointly co-ordinated drugs and arms shipments through Cuba.

However, times were changing. M-19 had come in from the cold and signed a peace agreement with the government; it was heading for electoral success. The army and right-wingers were infuriated. But so, too, was Escobar, who resented being left out of the deal with his former allies, who he suspected might turn their backs on him.

Escobar's relationship with the paramilitaries in the Magdalena valley was by now also undergoing a dramatic transformation. Although it was true they had never been under his direct orders, he had financed them and exercised control via Rodríguez Gacha. He needed their protection, yet he had never shared their rampant anti-Communism. Indeed, police intelligence sources indicated that Escobar was entering into a protection pact with local guerrilla units of the National Liberation Army; this was later confirmed by Fidel Castaño. The two main paramilitary leaders were Henry Pérez, a humble peasant, and Ariel Otero, a devious manipulator later proved to be an army intelligence officer who eventually ran off with Pérez's wife. After the Mexican's death, they objected to being treated as nothing more than rural gangsters and they disliked Escobar's left-wing connections. 'Henry and Otero were happy to guard cocaine laboratories and to kill guerrillas, but that was it,' said a DEA agent. 'They started to give us information on Escobar.'

That information almost led to Escobar's capture in July 1990, when *El Patrón* was nearly cornered in a humble wooden cabin on stilts near the river Cocorná after 500 police from the Elite Force had launched a river, air and land search. They deployed tracker dogs and a dozen helicopter gunships, while army troops threw a supposedly impenetrable cordon around the whole area. Nine thousand kilograms of dynamite along with dozens of automatic weapons and radio sets were seized. Among the twenty-five people arrested was a brother-in-law of Escobar's, but the drugs lord himself escaped once again. Hidden amongst the hills and steep ravines of the wild, semi-tropical jungle, his bunkers and tunnels were impossible to trace. Nevertheless, the heart of Escobar's biggest communications and hideout system, spreading over thousands of square kilometres around the Nápoles estate, was destroyed. And Escobar now knew for certain that Pérez, who formed part of his security network, had betrayed him. With perfect finesse, Escobar sent his pursuers the wrong way by radioing a false destination to the paramilitary leader, thereby ensuring his escape and proving beyond doubt the treachery of Pérez.

'I am letting you know that treachery has no price,' ran Escobar's typed message to Henry Pérez. 'I shall give myself the pleasure of settling some accounts with you. Not only are you a *sapo* [toad or informant] but you allied with that gonorrhea of Major Evelio Aguilar ... but I am letting you know that I am not losing the war and even if it costs me 2,000 million pesos [about $3 million] and I have to use any method at all, I will do away with you. Doctor Echavarria.' One year later, Pérez was machine-gunned to death along with eight other people during Mass.

*

Among the objects found by the police in the remote, zinc-roofed, green wooden cabin whose stove was still warm, was a short, handwritten manuscript by Escobar. Written in the third person, the book exalted him as a hero of the downtrodden who had found a tool with which to liberate them from poverty. His ramblings, which occasionally were only semi-literate, scarcely accorded with the intelligence attributed to Escobar by lawyers and politicians who knew him. The document was self-exculpatory and disinformative, designed to whip up *paisa* and Colombian nationalism as well as hatred of the police. Yet there were some grains of truth.

In the fragments released, Escobar accused the government of submitting to foreign economic pressure in plunging Colombia into a 'fratricidal war' against the drug cartels. He raved against President Barco ('Mr Shit'), who he said was 'not spineless, nor a cripple, but a scrap of offal, a worm, as [Fidel] Castro calls people who are so servile'. Escobar was obsessed with the country's hypocrisy, lack of justice and endless fixation with laws that were never applied. He justified the killings of police on the grounds that the police were torturing and massacring the poor, and suggested that central government leaders had been bribed to pick on Antioquia.

In one bizarre passage prefaced by the quotation of a nun – 'Who is more to blame, although both do wrong, he who sins for a fee or he who pays for the sinning?' – Escobar lashed out against drug smuggling. 'The sale of cigarettes, *aguardiente*, weapons, votes, public sector jobs, patronage, import licences, grants, joints of marijuana or a dose of cocaine is something totally and completely obscene,' he wrote, adding immediately afterwards: 'Neither divorce nor prostitution are bad in themselves. They are simply rather undesirable solutions, but necessary to avoid greater problems. Personally, I could not care less, because I have not got a problem with them.'

After going off on a brief tangent to condemn the Barco government's 'false morals' and double dealing, he returned to drugs: 'Cigarettes kill 400,000 people and alcohol kills 100,000 every year in the United States. Tobacco and alcohol are two of the items that produce the highest taxes for states. Here, *aguardiente* is a [government] monopoly. However, drugs do not produce income for the treasury. Drugs do not even kill 10,000 there. But none of us is bothered because we do not smoke, we do not drink, neither do we need artificial [false-bottomed] suitcases to prop up our personality [with drugs]. One cannot say that the sales of this or that are less obscene. What can be clarified is that the sale of cocaine is NO more obscene than any of the former.'

Somewhere inside Escobar's desperately convoluted attempt to justify what had made him a multi-billionaire, he was saying that although drug smuggling was obscene, not only did drugs kill fewer North Americans than tobacco and alcohol, but also that smuggling them was no worse than other forms of corruption. Furthermore, he could not see why Colombians should give a damn since they did not use cocaine themselves (national consumption was low). Escobar's confession as to the obscenity of drug smuggling, if he genuinely believed that, was extraordinary for its chutzpah; obscene as it was, his conscience rested easy. But even if his statement was made with the same hypocritical ease with which many Colombian leaders publicly referred to 'the scourge', and Escobar said it for the sake of appearance, it troubled him not in the least to acknowledge his absolute lack of morality. In a country where, when discussing corruption, a former living president had pledged during an electoral campaign to 'reduce immorality to its proper proportions', such an attitude was not exceptional.

Escobar's defence that he was no worse than many other people – he claimed the armed forces, lawyers and politicians were all corrupt – also embraced the United States. Escobar accused what Colombians called 'the monster of the north' of exporting most of the weapons which, by 1990, were killing more than 24,000 Colombians a year. He pointed out that in a country of 30 million people such a figure was proportionately far graver than the 10,000 North Americans whose deaths were attributable to drugs. The US, he said, was simply jealous it did not control the market – and happy to divert cocaine profits to the Nicaraguan Contras in the meantime. Escobar also claimed that, with the Cold War coming to an end, fighting drugs provided a useful new enemy for an under-employed Pentagon. With the arrival of US military personnel, he gloated, 'We will shortly see how AIDS propagates itself in an exponential manner in our country.'

Oddly enough, the manuscript showed that Escobar believed his days were numbered. 'The death of Pablo Escobar is something imminent and not even with all the gold in the world will he be able to escape his destiny,' his book solemnly declared. 'The soldiers and police officers, who for so many years hid him, protected him and warned him so that he could escape in time, see a terrible dilemma looming ahead: they have to finish him off because the credulity [sic] of the United States and of the whole country in his persecution is exhausted, vanished, gone. Those who exploited him know that that mine is exhausted and that to keep their jobs they have to avail themselves of the best source of support available . . . Everyone loved Don Pablo a lot, but the law of survival demands that you do not get yourself buried with him.'

The hunt for Escobar in Medellín and Antioquia swept on under the new government of President César Gaviria, a short, squeaky-voiced economist from the city of Pereira in the centre of the coffee region. Gaviria, who took office in August 1990, had inherited the political movement of Luis Carlos Galán. It was Galán's son, Juan Manuel, who had invited Gaviria, as Galán's campaign leader, to assume his father's mantle. The invitation had been delivered over Galán's grave. Gaviria, who had escaped at least three bomb attempts as well as the Avianca aircraft massacre, swore that he would make no concession to drug traffickers. Yet the political atmosphere was changing. Gaviria's promises to fight the traffickers brought only murmurs of support at his victory speech and his two Conservative opponents had both been sympathetic to negotiation. The peace deal with M-19

– whose one-legged leader (the other leg had been blown off by a grenade), Antonio Navarro, came third in the polls – and the vote to establish an assembly to set up a new constitution, contributed to the beginnings of a climate of national reconciliation. Two other guerrilla organizations, the Maoist Popular Liberation Army (EPL) and the Indian Quintín Lame group, also appeared to be edging towards peace. So weary, and fearful of violence, was Colombia that only 43 per cent of registered voters had turned out at the ballot boxes; the discovery of four tonnes of Medellín cartel dynamite on the eve of the elections underlined their concern.

The army raids, the murders of police, the cartel's witch-hunt for Cali informants and its own systematic persecution by the security forces had converted Medellín itself into a war zone. Whereas the number of homicides nationally had nearly tripled since 1980, in Medellín the figure was more than eight times higher than at the start of the decade. According to the city morgue, in 1990 there were 5,816 homicides. Medellín's homicide rate, which would have been higher if the bordering municipalities such as Envigado were included, was 360 per 100,000 people; this was twelve times higher than New York. At least 200 people were being killed every weekend. The municipal police of Envigado's Department of Security and Control, who were directly under the control of the Liberal mayor, Jorge Mesa, a close friend of Escobar's, axed to death anybody suspected of links with the Cali cartel. The barracks of the army, which occupied Envigado with light tanks and 2,000 men, became a refuge for judges, judicial employees and witnesses.

Meanwhile, police who had been sacked for corruption from the local force collaborated with the drug traffickers by giving the names and addresses of their former colleagues, as well as the details of their movements. The targets were shot down like fairground ducks. Bombs regularly exploded outside police stations. In retaliation, from the middle of 1990 the police launched daylight massacres in Medellín's poor, northern suburbs. Plainclothes men stepped out of unmarked cars without licence plates, fired off round after round and tossed grenades into crowds on street corners and soccer pitches. The army accused the police, who in turn accused the drugs traffickers and dressed up as soldiers to escape persecution. The neighbourhoods themselves, accustomed to their gangster teenagers being arrested and tortured, had no doubt that the police lay behind much of the violence directed against them. The plainclothes DIJIN police were accused of the worst of it – particularly their commander, Colonel Oscar Peláez, a former police chief in Cali. However, one of the strangest massacres was that of seventeen young men in an expensive bar in the upper-class district of El Poblado; a group of intruders forced them to the ground and machine-gunned them in the back. Nobody seemed to know who the intruders were, or why they did it.

So macabre and so nightmarish did daily life become in Medellín that in August the Colombian Institute of Family Welfare requested an investigation into the trafficking of human organs extracted from children. It was alleged that, in the same manner that cars were robbed, stripped down within a few hours and their parts distributed through second-hand dealers in the district of La América, children were being kidnapped, killed and dissected for their hearts, livers and kidneys, which were then consigned for export. 'The crime . . . became fashionable,' said Colonel Bahamón. 'Many of Medellín's *sicarios* participated in it when the war against the police entered a stage of recess, in which the drugs traffickers suspended the killings of agents for a few days while sending their envoys to negotiate with the government.' The discovery of a surgery alongside a small cocaine laboratory in an abandoned house was enough to convince the military that the allegations were true, considering 'the extreme quantity of children who had been stolen at that time'. Even though probably an urban myth, that itself demonstrated how hellish Medellín, the City of Eternal Spring, had become.

The relentless persecution of the Medellín cartel, much of which was being co-ordinated from the Nápoles estate seized from Escobar, began to bear fruit. In June 1990 one of Escobar's most trusted *sicario* leaders, John Jairo Arias, was killed, allegedly drowned, by the Elite Force. In July, when Escobar was almost caught, another key henchman – and brother-in-law – was arrested, Hernán Henao; the same month, so was Escobar's official biographer and press and media linkman, 'The Poet'. But far more damaging was the death in August of Escobar's cousin, Gustavo Gaviria. Police reported that Gaviria was shot dead as he tried to fight his way out of a house in Medellín with the help of a US army rifle and an Israeli sub-machine-gun. Escobar, however, claimed that his oldest ally, racing colleague and gravestone-robbing accomplice had been tortured and deliberately killed. Gaviria was Escobar's hands-on manager for the production and exportation of cocaine. He also acted as accountant, co-ordinating payments to the Medellín gangs as well as to the cartel's friends in the government and security forces. Gaviria, with whom Escobar had first been caught fourteen years earlier carrying 19 kilograms of cocaine in a spare tyre, was located after police followed up information on the whereabouts of their safe houses. The main source of the tip was the Cali cartel.

Even as the hounding of Escobar moved towards what appeared to be a climax, information was being leaked to the drugs baron at a senior level within the security forces. Among the three army and police generals obliged to resign in June had been the deputy commander of the police, General Carlos Arturo Casadiego, following allegations that he was on Escobar's payroll. The Medellín police commander was transferred to the capital. So grave was the cartel's infiltration that it was mooted that all 4,000 of the city's policemen might also be replaced.

After his cousin's demise, Escobar stepped up his kidnap offensive. Since July, he had been ransom-kidnapping members of the richest Antioquia families. Among them was Julián Echavarría, a great-nephew of the industrialist with whose kidnap and murder Escobar had been credited two decades earlier, earning himself the sobriquet Doctor or Doctor Echavarría. Echavarría was killed in a shoot-out with police. Like the senator Federico Estrada, who was linked with the cartel in the early 1980s, campaigned as César Gaviria's Antioquia co-ordinator and had been murdered by Escobar in May, many of the victims were selected because the cartel leader perceived them or their families to owe him some kind of a political or personal debt. However, in August, Escobar raised the stakes with the new government by kidnapping eight journalists – including the daughter of Julio César Turbay Ayala, the former president against whom US accusations of drug-trafficking involvement were allegedly dropped in exchange for Colombia's signing of the 1980 extradition treaty.

Six days later – although the government claimed that at the time it was still unaware of the kidnappings – the president who during his inaugural speech on 7 August had repeated that he would confront drugs terrorism 'without concessions' issued the first of a series of decrees giving in to the drug-traffickers' demands. In return for handing themselves in and collaborating with the authorities, they were offered minor jail sentences and virtual immunity from extradition.

In order to wring out more favourable conditions, Escobar chose to put more pressure on the government. Not only did he hang on to his hostages but, in September, he also kidnapped two more: the sister of the former secretary general of the presidency, Germán Montoya, and the news editor of the *El Tiempo* newspaper, Francisco Santos, whose family owned it. Once again, Alfonso López Michelsen and his committee of honourable citizens, the Notables, stepped in as intermediaries. With the help of Escobar's principal lawyer, Guido Parra, a tortuous process of negotiation evolved between the Medellín cartel and the government in which everybody pretended that it was anything but and that the fate of the hostages had nothing to do with the terms of the traffickers' surrender.

In the meantime – and while fifteen of the people captured in the operation that nearly trapped Escobar were released, and the assassin who gunned down Galán walked out of a high-security prison disguised as a bricklayer – the blood-bath continued.

Bulletins from the Extraditables claimed with increasing rage that the police were responsible for hundreds of killings in Medellín's northern suburbs: 'Why have arrest warrants been exchanged for execution orders? Why are search-for posters being distributed and rewards being offered for people who are not wanted by any judicial authority?' It was a classic dirty war. The police, its intelligence services and the Elite Force – although not, apparently, the army – were responding to Escobar's bounty murders and the impotence of the judiciary. They were resorting to torture and terror tactics in which innocent lives were sacrificed in a deliberate, if desperate, bid to crush the spirit of the very families and neighbourhoods that nurtured and protected the gangs of young hoodlums who stole, extorted and killed for a living. The police involvement in massacres was so brazen it was even denounced openly by the army.

Escobar's continued attacks against his enemies in Cali reached their manic zenith with the machine-gunning of nineteen people at a soccer game in September. The hit was aimed at just one man, Pacho Herrera, the fourth leader of the Cali cartel. It failed. A squad of Medellín *sicarios* wearing police and army uniforms opened fire on the small crowd at a ranch of which Herrera was believed to be the owner. But if Herrera was present, he, like many others, escaped into the sugar plantations upon hearing the first shots. Police sources claimed that among those later picked up from the ranch was Manuel Francisco Becerra, Colombia's auditor general. According to a small-time trafficker with the Cali cartel, Escobar's special grudge against Herrera derived from an incident in the early 1980s when one of Herrera's men slept with the wife of one of Escobar's. When Herrera refused to hand him over, Escobar's colleague complained to Escobar, who demanded from Gilberto Rodríguez Orejuela that Herrera be surrendered, too. The request was refused and the question of aggrieved honour turned ever more poisonous. It was widely believed that Herrera was mainly responsible for the bombing of the El Mónaco building, which had partially deafened Escobar's daughter. Prior to the football murders,

Escobar had made at least two equally vain attempts to have Herrera killed.

The massacre, which occurred near Cali, followed warnings to the local government by the Rodríguez Orejuela brothers that *El Doctor* had sent men into the region to carry out a series of terrorist attacks. Similarly, the brothers later revealed that they had collaborated – at the direct request of *El Tiempo* – with efforts to find Francisco Santos. In a letter complaining of pejorative references to him in the newspaper, which he accused of being ungrateful, the Chess Player wrote: 'Twenty-four hours later we already knew who had him, as we told you . . . through third parties.' Gilberto Rodríguez Orejuela also claimed responsibility for alerting the authorities to a truck bomb heading for *El Tiempo* earlier in 1990.

One of the Notables was the former president, Julio César Turbay Ayala, whose daughter, Diana, was in Escobar's power. A few weeks after the kidnap of Santos and Montoya's sister, Marina, and after the renewed intervention of the Notables, President Gaviria issued a second decree offering further concessions to the drug traffickers. Under the decree, if any new charges were brought after their surrender, confessing to just one crime would continue to ensure their immunity against extradition. All charges against one criminal would be heard by the same judge, effectively chosen by the drug trafficker himself. Bribes and killings had seen to it that the mafia knew which judges they could trust to sing their tune.

Escobar was still not content. In November, he kidnapped the sister-in-law of Luis Carlos Galán, Maruja Pachón, along with a relative; their driver was killed in the act. After a flurry of letters between Escobar's lawyer, the Extraditables and the Notables, the latter issued a strange memorandum that not only presented the traffickers' position but also appeared to endorse it. The crimes of drugs trafficking and drugs terrorism were, it was argued, unique because of their collective nature. The attempt to collectivize the issue, which was reinforced by the claim that more than 200 people would hand themselves in, was in order to justify political treatment. Meanwhile, Escobar's old friend and former Liberal Party patron, senator Alberto Santofimio, who sat alongside Alfonso López Michelsen on the party's central committee, was demanding a pardon for the traffickers on the grounds that they were 'now fighting the government, which makes them a political movement, entitled to the same amnesty as guerrillas'. The Medellín mafia also declared confessions to be unconstitutional – in Colombia itself the Ochoas faced hardly any charges – and demanded still more watertight guarantees against extradition as well as the right to their own high-security jails.

Delighted by the Notables' support, which coincided with the transfer of a police colonel whom Escobar had for a long time accused of tortures and massacres, *El Patrón* released three of his captive journalists. With Christmas fast approaching, President Gaviria responded with a third decree, insisting on confession but allowing the traffickers to qualify for the full judicial benefits by confessing to one crime alone.

Doggedly hounded by police raids in Medellín – Escobar had lost more of his top henchmen and even the Ochoas were feeling the pinch – it was young Fabio Ochoa who finally took the plunge and surrendered on 17 December. Accompanied by his mother and sisters, Ochoa materialized in front of a church in the town of Caldas, about 20 kilometres south of the Antioquia capital, and handed himself over to the authorities. His surrender occurred the same day as the third decree was issued: the cartel leaders had been expecting it. One month later, his elder brother, Jorge Luis, surrendered at the same church; his bodyguards hovered outside while the world's second biggest cocaine trafficker went in and prayed. As well as by his family, Jorge Luis Ochoa was accompanied by the former attorney general, Carlos Jiménez Gómez, who was now his defence lawyer. In February, it was the turn of the third Ochoa brother, Juan David. They were ensconced in the municipal jail of Itagüí, bordering Medellín, and quietly commenced plea and sentence bargaining. Among a handful of other traffickers to have surrendered under the special decrees was the powerful Gonzalo Mejía, in the city of Manizales. Having fled to

A PYRRHIC VICTORY FOR THE DOCTOR (1989–91)

Colombia from the United States while being tried for transporting cocaine, Mejía received a six-year sentence which was halved and finally suspended. Immune from extradition, Mejía walked free.

Escobar was left to wage the closing stages of his war against extradition alone except for his brother, Roberto, and his *sicarios*. If captured, he would be extradited. If he surrendered, he could still be extradited by losing all judicial benefits if he were proved guilty of the kidnaps and murders he had ordered since the first decree had been issued in September. Escobar believed he had no choice but to fight on. And he had a fresh weapon in his armoury: the newly formed Constituent Assembly, which had been elected to draw up Colombia's eleventh constitution. Within the assembly, which was to begin its deliberations in early February, there was a powerful ground swell of opinion in favour of outlawing extradition altogether. With some financial tickling by Escobar, that ground swell could become a two-thirds legislative majority.

Although the car bombs had more or less stopped, the bloodletting was by no means over. The Elite Force gunned down the two brothers who led Escobar's veteran *sicario* gang, the Priscos, on 22 January. Since one of the brothers was paralysed, Escobar and the *sicarios* were convinced they were summarily shot. On 25 January, Escobar announced that two 'hostages' would be executed, in revenge for the decapitation of the gang from the Aranjuez district that had conducted most of his dirty work for more than a decade. The order had already gone out and one was already dead, although her corpse had not yet been identified in Bogotá. Marina Montoya, the sister of the former secretary general of the presidency, had received six bullets in the head. On 25 January itself, Diana Turbay, the daughter of the former president who had been kidnapped five months earlier, was shot in the back by her captors. The murder happened during a police raid near Medellín which was allegedly aimed at Escobar.

Three days later, amid accusations from her family that the government bore half the responsibility for Diana Turbay's murder, and after a peace protest at her funeral, President Gaviria issued a fourth decree in favour of the traffickers. This time, the special benefits – which were increased – and immunity for extradition were guaranteed in relation to all offences committed until the date of their surrender, and not simply until the date of the first decree. The concession appeared tailor-made for Escobar. He was being offered judicial privileges for the kidnaps and murders he had committed in order for the laws to be rewritten to suit his own needs. His lawyer, Parra, was so delighted that he dubbed the decree 'the Diana law'.

Thereafter, Escobar bided his time. All that he needed were the government's agreement to his jail conditions and the constitutional outlawing of extradition. The last notable murder attributed to him before his surrender was that of the former justice minister, Enrique Low Murtra, on 30 April 1991. The killing of Low Murtra, who had been delivered a little wooden coffin with a miniature Colombian flag soaked in sheep's blood when contract assassins were hunting him down in Switzerland the previous year, was taken as a warning to those members of the Constituent Assembly who had still not rallied to Escobar's cause. Three weeks later, adopting his typical stick-and-carrot policy, Escobar freed the last of his kidnap victims. Finally, Escobar's lawyers had also embarked on a campaign to bribe the Constituent Assembly.

The bribing of the assembly was revealed in a video recording made during early April at the Residencias Tequendama, a hotel in central Bogotá. The recording was made after police were tipped off through the DEA, who received the information from Ariel Otero, the second-in-command of the main paramilitary squad which was at war with Escobar in Puerto Boyacá and who was later given mafia protection in Cali. An Escobar lawyer, Humberto Feisal Buitrago, was filmed offering nearly $4,000 in Colombian pesos to Augusto Ramírez, a member of the Constituent Assembly, who was collaborating with the police. The lawyer was recorded telling Ramírez that the money came from Escobar and that another thirty-six delegates had already received the same amount. 'Everything is settled,' said Buitrago, referring to the assembly's justice commission – which was presided over by the man who became President Gaviria's second justice minister, Fernando Carrillo. The commission included Alvaro Gómez, the powerful Conservative leader who was one of the three assembly presidents and the son of Laureano Gómez, the main promoter of *La Violencia*. Since his kidnap by M-19 in May 1988, Gómez had virtually ceased to attack the drugs mafia. The justice commission also included other delegates who had previously fought against extradition.

President Gaviria, who was immediately handed the video, refused to divulge its contents, which only became public four months later at the instigation of the Puerto Boyacá paramilitaries. 'Here was clear evidence that the assembly was being bribed and if that had been revealed at the time it could have defeated the anti-extradition effort,' said the DEA head in Colombia, Joe Toft. 'Either Gaviria was bought, or he was a wet noodle.' Gaviria later claimed to have informed the assembly presidents of the video; however, all denied it. The case was deliberately smothered by an inert investigation – nobody was ever called to give evidence – which Gaviria happily pre-empted by saying that the video demonstrated nothing more than a 'failed bribery attempt'. He added that this coincided with the government's view that 'the decisions of the Constituent Assembly were taken by its members following their convictions and always thinking of the country's highest interests'. While some delegates blamed the media for creating a scandal and clamoured for a judicial verdict they knew would never be made, one of the assembly chairmen confirmed that death threats had created a 'climate of fear'.

The Constituent Assembly bribes were allegedly not the only ones paid to the central government in order to secure the drugs traffickers a soft landing. According to an Antioquia politician in whom Escobar confided, the leader of the Medellín cartel had handed over a very large, unspecified sum to a prominent minister around September 1990, when President Gaviria's government was just beginning to offer concessions. 'The minister asked for the cash from the cartel claiming it was to share out within the cabinet, including the president,' said the source in Medellín. 'He received it from Escobar in return for the launch of the surrender-to-justice policy, but I don't know if he actually distributed the money.'

'O sea, O immense sea! O solitary sea, which knows it all! I want to ask you a few things, answer me. You who keep the secrets, I would like to build a grand institute for the rehabilitation of *sicarios* in Medellín. What do you think, O sea? Speak to me, you who keep secrets, I would like to speak with Pablo Escobar, on the edge of the sea, here exactly, both of us seated on this beach—'

The speaker was an eighty-two-year-old priest, Rafael García Herreros, broadcasting his message to a prime-time television audience just before the seven o'clock news, which he knew that Escobar habitually watched. It was 18 April 1991, and the priest's television slot was called 'The Minute of God'. Father García continued: 'They have told me you want to hand yourself over. They have told me you want to speak with me . . . Tell me O sea, will I be able to do it, ought I to do it? You who know all the history of Colombia, you who saw the Indians worshipping on this beach . . . ought I to do it? Will they reject me if I do? If I do it, will there be a gun battle when I go with them, will I die with them in this adventure?'

Father García's bizarre message to Escobar was the prelude to the drug lord's surrender. The silver-haired priest, who was famous for his works of charity, had been contacted by a congressman whose wife was among Escobar's hostages. The congressman, whose offer to act as an intermediary with the government had been accepted by Escobar after they had communicated through the Ochoa family, wanted to take a back seat after seeing that the Doctor's demands were fulfilled regarding certain members of the Elite Force. At Escobar's request, several were investigated by the attorney general's office for unlawfully killing, among others, his cousin. While Escobar's lawyers, Guido

Parra and Santiago Uribe, secretly thrashed out the conditions of surrender with the Ministry of Justice, Father García was brought on stage as a guarantor that Escobar would not be double-crossed and killed. With the government anxious to deflect attention from its bargaining, and Escobar eager for the protection afforded by so popular a figure as Father García, the divine intervention was made to appear as spontaneous, miraculous and as important as possible.

Three weeks after his television prayer to the sea, Father García, dressed as always in his cassock and poncho, was drinking whisky with Escobar at a luxurious ranch south of Medellín. Escobar's primary concern was his safety, both in reaching prison and once he was inside it. The meeting ended with Escobar and his bodyguards, at their own request, getting down on their knees to receive the priest's blessing. Their gold crosses and scapularies – through which God's aid would have been invoked before sending a load of cocaine or murdering an enemy – were blessed, too. Apparently oblivious of their crimes, which included the recent shooting of the former justice minister, Father García said afterwards of Escobar: 'I looked into his eyes and could see he [was] a good man.'

During the following weeks, the priest's doting sycophancy seemed to increase alongside his ballooning ego. Colombians became mesmerized by his nightly television spot. 'The Minute of God' was The Minute of Hope, when the country tuned into Channel Two to catch a hint of when the world's biggest cocaine trafficker might turn himself in and the seven years of drug-related violence that had ripped apart the state would end. With its young president, its guerrilla peace deals, its liberalizing of the economy and the birth pangs of a judicial reform and a new constitution, for Colombia the surrender of Pablo Escobar symbolized the break with its past and heralded an era of renewal. Father García became the focus of the gathering euphoria.

Yet, while Escobar waited for the pieces to fall into place, the elderly priest nearly ruined the show. In late May, Father García began his evening message with the usual unctuousness:

'Very dear Pablo. I want to tell you that I have suffered with the thought that they are going to put you in a dungeon for years. But the president told me they would treat you very well ... Well, Pablo, here they tell me that I have produced confusion and that people do not know if when I speak of Pablo, I am referring to San Pablo [Saint Paul] or you. Here they call in to ask for the Novena [a prayer] of San Pablo Escobar. People are very silly ... Pablo, hand yourself in as soon as possible, I have a place ready for you in the University of Peace, and I will defend you.'

Suddenly, however, the priest changed tone.

'Today let's talk about you. Why did you stray from God? ... Why did you change the books you previously read for pornographic books? ... Why did you abandon your children? ... Why do you only want to make money whatever the cost? ... Why have you turned so violent?'

Escobar was so livid with the tirade that he threatened to abandon his plans to surrender – until it emerged that Father García had misread his text, which should have read: 'Today, let's not talk about Pablo. Let's talk about you—'

The farce climaxed on 19 June. Amid much public speculation as to what was delaying his surrender, it seemed not to occur to anyone that Escobar might be awaiting the Constituent Assembly's definitive outlawing of the extradition of Colombian citizens. This was partly because it had become a foregone conclusion. Colombia wanted peace. Nobody minded that the police claimed that the jailed Ochoa brothers had just successfully supervised a 1,400-kilogram cocaine shipment to Spain; the Ministry of Justice quickly denied the reports. Nobody minded that while the government was bending over backwards to grant Escobar his every desire when it came to his personal security, it had not given a thought to that of the former minister of justice, Enrique Low

Murtra, who had been murdered – almost certainly by Escobar – two months earlier. Nobody dared to question the honour of Father García, whose Minute of God charity was a national institution; he later received a horse worth 50 million pesos ($80,000) from the Ochoas and a ranch from Escobar. The lone voices of protest came from *El Espectador*, the police and one or two politicians. 'We are living in a country where the bad are given a blessing and are recognized publicly as good by the good, simply because there are no longer any good people, but bad,' wrote one journalist bitterly. One senior police officer said: 'Escobar is succeeding by appearing as the victim. None of us ever thought that this could end in such an imbecile way.'

The extradition vote took place at around midday. The Constituent Assembly outlawed extradition by 50 votes to 13. Five hours later, Escobar and two of his henchmen were scooped up by a helicopter from a ranch south of Medellín. Among those who collected him were Father García and a congressman who was a relative of one of his former kidnap victims; Escobar apologized to the congressman, Alberto Villamizar, for once having tried to kill him. Within a few minutes, Escobar, sporting a thick, dark beard and sunglasses, was set down within the prison that had been built to his own specifications a few hundred metres above Envigado. After pulling out the cartridge from his 9mm Sig-Sauer automatic pistol and handing them over to the prison warder, Escobar embraced his mother and his wife and went inside. It was time to make his judicial statement.

The jail straddled a small hill, with pine forests rising up behind it and with sweeping views of the valley below. Its simple, zinc-roofed, brick buildings had recently been constructed by the municipality of Envigado. Officially, the sanctuary had been built for the rehabilitation of drug abusers and the land had been bought from an ironmonger. Such charitable concern was strange in a municipality whose own police systematically wiped out coca base addicts and other miscreants (although Envigado was the only municipality in Colombia to subsidize the unemployed). And it eventually emerged that the ironmonger, who had obtained the land the previous year, was simply a *testaferro* for Escobar. According to a police colonel, Escobar had hidden in a refuge there while he was still on the run. The name given to the jail was that of the hill it commanded: the Cathedral.

With all his security conditions met, Escobar was in buoyant form. Environmental reasons were even cited in agreeing that the forest, which offered cover in case of an escape, would not be trimmed back from the prison perimeter. No police or soldiers were to be allowed inside the refuge – where he was to be accompanied by his top *sicarios* – and he had a soccer pitch, too. In making the confession that won him the legal privileges offered by President Gaviria's decrees, Escobar demonstrated all the contemptuous and tyrannical deceit of one who not only had made a mockery of the state but knew that he could go on and rub its nose in it. He confessed to a minor involvement in one cocaine shipment to the French island of Guadalupe, for which the French courts had sentenced him to twenty years imprisonment, and declared that the only reason he had surrendered was in order to be tried by a Colombian judge and that, anyway, the real person behind the shipment had been his dead cousin. The other people he named in the case, which he needed to do in order to obtain full judicial benefits, were insignificant. (They 'informed' on Escobar to obtain the same benefits in turn.) Escobar added that he planned to embark on a university law course, that he had paid all his taxes and that, yes, he had known Rodríguez Gacha a little, although he had never done business with him. He had met Lehder once at a soccer match and knew the Ochoas because they were involved in real estate.

'I am extraditable in the sense that I was wanted for extradition,' said Escobar, 'but I am not an extraditable in the sense of the Extraditables who made war on the government, because my fight was always a political, judicial and public relations fight against extradition. And at no time did I have anything to do with military actions.' Nobody bothered to challenge the lie. It was estimated that, unless fresh charges could be pinned on him,

A PYRRHIC VICTORY FOR THE DOCTOR (1989-91)

Escobar faced a jail term of no more than eight years. Nobody in government cared.

Terrorism and bribery had won. Although Escobar had turned himself in, it was the corrupt and weary state that had truly surrendered. *El Doctor* had achieved far greater concessions for Colombia's drug traffickers than those first outlined in the 1984 Panama proposal. They may not have achieved an actual amnesty, but the scourge of extradition was now not merely procedurally enmeshed, it was outlawed. No promises were even made to give up cocaine trafficking. Meanwhile, the government was considering a programme to repatriate Colombian prisoners – another demand of the Extraditables – and its easing of exchange controls as part of the free-market overhaul of the economy was soon conveniently to enable the traffickers to repatriate billions of dollars as well.

However, the price of victory left Escobar politically bankrupt. Not only had it cost him a lot of money, it had won him a lot of enemies. He was a witness to the shame of too many members of the country's political élite. And his foes in the Cali cartel, for whom the fruits of his triumph were also theirs, had made deep inroads into his empire, at home and overseas. As well as having begun to move their operations abroad, they had developed more elaborate trafficking routes as well as much more sophisticated, and nearly impenetrable, legal and financial networks in Colombia. Now that Escobar had actually won the war, the Rodríguez Orejuela brothers and their colleagues wanted Escobar dead more than ever before. Their collaboration with the police and government had helped mortally to wound the military structure of the Medellín cartel. When the time came, they planned to strike the final blow and then to call in the favours.

CHAPTER NINE

CHECKMATE FOR THE CHESS PLAYER (1991–93)

When Escobar, his brother and thirteen henchmen moved into the 30,000-square-metre compound above Envigado, the jail was a primitive affair. Escobar considered that its conditions made it 'extremely difficult in which to live'. Inside the original building were concrete floors, naked light bulbs and basic electric stoves. While Escobar had a room to himself, the remainder of his retinue shared a dormitory. Outside, a few hundred metres away, the encampment was surrounded by nothing more than a lowish fence topped with chicken wire. The guards appointed by the Ministry of Justice and the Envigado municipality – which was under the Doctor's thumb – were permitted within the fence, as were the prison warden and his deputy; the former shared a large room and the latter were housed simply, too. However, the 140 soldiers of the Fourth Brigade guarding the immediate environs were prohibited entry into the compound and obliged to live in tents; at night, 1,600 metres above sea level, temperatures dropped to zero degrees centigrade.

No sooner had Escobar occupied the Cathedral, around which he had bought up several ranches in order to ensure he fully dominated the hills, than he proceeded to transform it into a five-star holiday camp. Under the contract signed between the government and his frontmen in the municipality of Envigado, Escobar was able to co-ordinate his own labour force and renovations. Over the next few months, an electric fence – controlled by him – was installed around a large area including the inner building. A gymnasium, discotheque, bar and games room were constructed inside, and everybody was given their own apartment, with 64-inch television screens, video players and ultra-powerful stereo sound systems. There were jacuzzis and wall-to-wall carpets, as well as a life-size doll's house for Escobar's daughter, Manuela, to play in when she came to stay. The football pitch and a trailbike track – the inmates possessed motorbikes as well as mini-electric cars – were also inside Escobar's fence. So, too, was the real jail: a 2-metre by 3-metre, concrete-walled underground dungeon for special guests.

Nearer the chicken wire of the outer perimeter was a waiting room for secret visitors, several luxurious wooden chalets for entertaining prostitutes, a vegetable garden with mature marijuana plants and two air-raid shelters. Escobar controlled the flow of visitors with a doorphone connected to a farm on the way from Envigado; telescopes were trained on the road. Among the local guards appointed, at least eleven were discovered to have criminal records; some were relatives of the inmates. The Cathedral was built and organized – by Escobar with the government's complicity – not to keep its prisoners in so much as to keep assassins out. Instead of seeking to protect society from a murderous villain, the jail existed to protect the villain himself. As such, the Cathedral was a microcosm of the Colombian justice system. Furthermore, far from Escobar being rehabilitated, it was Escobar who was setting about the rehabilitation of his empire.

By August 1991, after two months of confinement, the inmates had received more than 300 visitors. Many of them, like the guards, had long criminal records and some were under arrest warrants; the government claimed these belonged to namesakes. Apart from judicial officials, regional authorities, relatives, regional beauty queens and prostitutes, they were also visited by Father García Herreros and two soccer heroes, including the national team goalkeeper, René Higuita. (Father García's demand for the Escobar bounty money of $800,000, which he promised to split with the 'University of Peace', i.e. the Cathedral, had been refused. He was now attempting to establish peace talks with another priest, Manuel Pérez, the guerrilla leader of the Maoist-style National Liberation Army (ELN). In the meantime, he was summoned to the jail for a marriage ceremony.) Many visitors entered the compound secretly, hidden in lorries; the soldiers were bribed to conduct the most fleeting of searches. Escobar and his men took brief excursions in the same manner.

'There were at least a hundred workers going in and out every day,' said an army intelligence officer with the Fourth Brigade. 'It was impossible to search them well and most of the external control was in Escobar's hands anyway. The Ministry of Justice was told what was going on but it permitted Escobar to have everything he wanted. Escobar gave the soldiers blankets to keep them warm and cheques to cash at his offices in Envigado. We had to force the soldiers to give it all back.' According to one of the inmates' lawyers, when he spoke of the conditions to Gaviria's second justice minister and his deputy, 'they just burst out laughing like irresponsible little boys'. President Gaviria himself – whose former campaign security chief, Colonel José Homero Rodríguez, was later made warden of the Cathedral – was advised several times of the irregularities by a furious DEA.

Colombia became an international laughing stock both for the leniency of the anticipated sentence and for the luxuriousness of the jail. Most of the country's leaders closed ranks in declaring that the state had triumphed over Escobar and in belittling the drug-traffickers' influence on Colombia as a whole. The gap between fact and fiction was to grow ever wider. The Conservative Party had become openly tolerant of the traffickers since the mysterious kidnapping and release of its future presidential candidate, Andrés Pastrana, in 1988. Under President Gaviria, the Liberals – who had suffered far more violence than the Conservatives – bowed too. While Ernesto Samper, Gaviria's first minister of development and his presidential successor, claimed that Escobar's 'surrender' should be evaluated not by the number of years he would spend in jail but by the tranquillity and foreign investment it would bring Colombia, the architect of the legal process that had led to it launched a tirade against the United States. Jaime Giraldo, who resigned as minister of justice shortly after Escobar moved into the Cathedral, boasted that Colombia had seized more cocaine than any other country and accused the North American 'distributors' of earning one hundred times more than the cocaine producers. That was a lie: according to the DEA, by 1990 the first, second and even third layer of distributors in the USA and Europe were usually Latin Americans, mostly Colombians.

Nevertheless, in condemning US hypocrisy over the marijuana trade, Giraldo touched a nerve. 'A few years ago the United States urged a fight against marijuana in Colombia, and we eradicated the crops and fumigated them with paraquat, and now that same country is the world's primary marijuana producer,' he said. 'Let them apply against marijuana the same campaign they insist we apply against cocaine.'

It was the bullet-scarred Enrique Parejo, the former minister of justice who had narrowly escaped assassination one snowy morning in Hungary, who spoke the home truths; so did the loved ones of Escobar's innocent victims. 'Can one honestly speak of the surrender of the drug traffickers to the state? Would it not be more exact to speak of the submission of the state to the will of the criminals?' asked Parejo. 'Essential values have been sacrificed in return for some apparent and fleeting successes. The damage being done to the national judicial system, in exchange for some ephemeral successes, may be very big.' Parejo harangued the political parties, their leaders and the authorities for their 'attitude of benevolence' towards organized crime and drugs trafficking in particular. 'I would go much further,' he added. 'There was a complacency by the whole of society, and when it wanted to react, it realized the problem had grown so much that it was a great deal more difficult.'

The widow of the *El Espectador* editor, Guillermo Cano,

declared: 'President Gaviria said his measures would fortify justice, and what happened was the opposite. He gave the drug traffickers so many privileges that ... they are going to be confident that in killing innocent people they will have more advantages than if they behave honestly.'

Parejo promptly received death threats. These followed the murder of Henry Pérez, the leader of the main paramilitary squads who had turned against Escobar, and of other witnesses who could testify against him. While Father García dismissed Parejo's death threat claims as 'exaggerated', Giraldo immediately exonerated Escobar of all responsibility for the Pérez killing in spite of abundant evidence to the contrary. 'The hypothesis ... does not seem to me logical,' he said. 'It is ingenuous to think that a person who intends to go on breaking the law puts himself in jail.' The ingenuousness, if it were that, was entirely the minister's. His successor, Fernando Carrillo, put the finishing touches to the coat of whitewash. 'The country knows that drugs terrorism has been stopped and that the drugs traffickers are behind bars,' he insisted.

The only bars in the Cathedral were those opened and shut by Escobar, for his own personal protection. And from behind them he continued to run his criminal empire – as did the traffickers in Cali, Bogotá and the rest of Colombia. According to Javier Peña, the head of the DEA's Medellín office, Escobar was sending up to 10,000 kilograms of cocaine a month through Mexico and the Caribbean Sea. In the United States, by the time it had been distributed and cut, that was worth up to $200 million on the street. The shipments were organized by about half a dozen men who had offices in Medellín and regularly visited Escobar in jail. At the same time, Escobar enforced taxes and commissions upon other traffickers. These tithes were demanded on the grounds that it was he who had spearheaded the business, he who had launched and won the war against extradition, and he who had sacrificed his freedom in order that peace could be made and the trafficking go on as before. Any local cocaine smuggler who sought to evade him had to leave Antioquia and hide. The Cali cartel and other independent groups, which were only too happy to provide asylum, expanded accordingly.

The Cathedral became stocked with computers, fax machines, radio telephones, beeper/message units and, according to a congressional investigative commission set up the following year, no fewer than eleven telephone lines. Just outside his bedroom, Escobar also kept an aviary. It was not that Escobar had developed a sudden interest in birdlife: the pigeons served a dual purpose, as guardians and message couriers. According to a trusted lawyer permitted just once into Escobar's inner sanctum, the drugs lord kept his money under the pigeons in order to be alerted by their noise should anyone approach. Above Escobar's kingsize bed, on which there rested a woolly monkey, was a ceramic wall portrait of the Virgin Mary. Nearby was a candle-lit shrine. Escobar 'wanted' posters, a snapshot of himself and his son in front of the White House, a Ché Guevara picture and a caricature of Escobar from *Hustler* magazine completed the decoration – apart from the photographs of four policemen he vowed to kill, including General Maza Márquez and the colonel whom Escobar claimed had tortured his men and pushed them out of helicopters, Oscar Peláez. Among Escobar's books were several Bibles, a life of Jesus Christ and novels by Graham Greene and the Colombian Nobel literature prize winner, Gabriel García Márquez. There was also a photograph of Escobar dressed up as his hero, the bloodthirsty Mexican bandit and revolutionary, Pancho Villa.

Apart from his brother Roberto, Escobar's closest confidant inside the Cathedral was John Jairo Velásquez Vásquez, nicknamed 'Popeye'. He allowed himself to be interviewed in Bogotá's main jail in September 1993. Popeye's cell in the sparkling, maximum security wing resembled a comfortable bedsit, with its own modern shower unit, smart stereo system and satellite television. Short, cheerful, rather baby-faced and with large, white, perfect teeth, Popeye was a self-confessed mass murderer (not that he would admit it to the authorities, and not that they would ever be able to prove it). His first contract hit – for which he claimed he was paid about $5,000 – was to kill the owner of a small bus company on behalf of a family who were being extorted. In classic Medellín style, Popeye shot him down from a motorcycle in the city centre. 'I was simply carrying out justice, I did it well and so I progressed to work for one of Pablo's men,' he said, offering me a soft drink.

'There are two kinds of *pistoleros*,' he continued, 'those from the poor neighbourhoods who kill anybody without a bodyguard for little cash, and the *finos* who live and eat well like the upper class, have pretty women and carry out the heavy jobs, on people with bodyguards. If it goes wrong, you pay for it, if it goes well – nobody left alive after a delicate job – you acquire status. *Pistoleros* are the backbone of the trafficking organizations, seeing that cash is paid, seeing that the boss's children are not kidnapped. I was mainly a driver, but I asked for work to show that I was *guapo* [brave], and won Pablo's trust.'

After detailed denials of Escobar's involvement in the murders of the Patriotic Union leaders, of M-19's Carlos Pizarro, and, rather less convincingly, of Galán – which he blamed on Rodríguez Gacha and General Maza Márquez – Popeye enthused about his *patron*: 'Pablo is incredibly calm and cold, really *guapo*. The only time he loses his cool is when his family is in danger. He has no fear of authority – he likes politics and realizes that's what's screwed him up. He likes power: the cash from cocaine has a social function for him. He was always the hard one, while his cousin was the financier.' (One old friend of Escobar's endorsed this view, telling the US magazine *Vanity Fair*: 'Pablo likes money, sure, but most of all he likes power. I once asked Pablo which woman in the world he would most like to make love to. He replied, "Margaret Thatcher".')

Life in the Cathedral was fun. 'There was lots of soccer, Pablo is very good at it,' said Popeye, who wore a baseball cap and a diamond ring. He scorned claims that Escobar only stopped the game when his side was winning. 'We had lots of visitors, there were games and parties, a wedding – and Hallowe'en, when I drew the short straw to dress up as a prostitute.' The latter incident led to Popeye, a former police officer cadet, being characterized by the DEA as a bisexual transvestite. Escobar, added Popeye, delighted in 'taking the piss out of you'. To illustrate the Doctor's subtle good humour, he described a trick played on one of the younger inmates: 'The guy gave Pablo a coffee. Pablo pretended to fall sick and sent for the nurse, who was let in on the joke and brought serum. Pablo played the part of a dying man. The poor guy got paler and paler and paler until finally we all burst out laughing—'

There was a knock on the blue metal door. The sound of ping-pong came from the lobby as the door opened and Popeye popped out to receive a beeper message. Again, maximum security went hand in hand with maximum luxury: money was the skeleton key that fitted all locks. 'If this were a country where the law resolved disputes, there would not be violence,' declared Popeye on his return. 'The only justice comes with a gun, as everyone is forced to take the law into their own hands. It is a culture of death here. It has never hurt me to kill anyone: I'm a professional, I do it coldly, it's something normal.' He had three brothers: an accountant, a clerk and a sociologist. Popeye was not a pathological killer; he suffered no mental disorder. Popeye was an entirely rational human being responding in a cold-blooded, mercenary manner to a society in which human life was no longer sacrosanct. His instincts were simply those of a marksman and a hunter. The fact that his prey were not pheasants and foxes meant nothing to him. Nor did it appear to matter much to Colombia: Popeye expected to be out of jail within two years. 'I love you so much,' said the words on the little grey teddy bear he had been given by his girlfriend.

On the way out of Bogotá's model jail, whose main passage smelled of excrement, a van arrived with new inmates. One of the men stumbled as he stepped out of the back, falling heavily to the ground. Another man, connected by handcuffs, came hurtling down on top of him, swearing his head off; so did a third. Like paper cut-out figures who possessed all the pathos of Breughel's blind men falling into a stream, they embodied the chilling impotence of people pulled remorselessly, compulsively, into a society's gravitational moral decline.

Escobar became increasingly paranoid about his security. On the one hand, the government was accumulating and developing homicide processes against him, which could severely increase his sentence. And, as if in response to Cuba's offer to provide incriminating evidence against him to the Colombian government, Escobar volunteered to give evidence against Fidel Castro's friend, General Noriega, who was standing trial in Miami after being grabbed during the US invasion of Panama. In exchange, and in the hope of making the evidence become invalid abroad, Escobar requested the United States hand over any evidence it had against him to Colombia. The United States rejected the offer. Most other foreign governments proved equally unwilling to share their proofs with the Colombian justice system.

On the other hand, and more concretely, Escobar was worried about being kidnapped by the USA or bombed by the Cali cartel. Unusual incidents involving small US aircraft overhead occurred at least three times; on one occasion, the Cathedral's army guards were so touchy that they took a shot at one, damaging an engine. Although the DEA admitted it indulged in some aerial surveillance, it denied there were ever plans to kidnap Escobar. (The suspicion was not so far-fetched: the North Americans had plucked drug traffickers out of Mexico, Honduras and Venezuela, not to mention Panama.) The head of the DEA's Medellín office, Javier Peña, said: 'Half the Colombian police wanted us to grab Escobar and make him suffer, and the other half wanted to kill him. It was just talk. Escobar was always afraid the US would kill him, which is why he never wanted to murder Americans or DEA people – as happened in Mexico – although his *sicarios* didn't care.'

The threat from Escobar's rivals in Cali was by far the gravest.

CHECKMATE FOR THE CHESS PLAYER (1991–93)

Two months after Escobar's torture and murder of Ariel Otero – who had replaced Henry Pérez as Puerto Boyacá's main paramilitary leader, then handed over his weapons and sought the protection of the Rodríguez Orejuelas – it emerged that the Cali cartel had bought at least four 230-kilogram 'cluster' bombs from military officers in El Salvador. The officers were led by Colonel Roberto Leiva. Meanwhile, one of Otero's henchmen confirmed he had been contracted by the Rodríguez Orejuelas and Pacho Herrera to participate in the assassination of Escobar and that it had been decided to bomb the Cathedral.

The plot was exposed in March 1992, after one of the stolen MK-82 bombs was discovered by El Salvador anti-drug agents. In spite of determined efforts by the Colombian secret police to deny any links between the bombs and the Cali cartel, they did admit that the aircraft flying the bombs had mysteriously eluded Colombian airforce fighter jets in the drug barons' heartland, the Valle del Cauca department. The aircraft reappeared in El Salvador – without the bombs. The Salvadorans claimed they had been paid $4 million for the bombs by the Cali cartel. These claims were partially corroborated in El Salvador by the proving of their links with the cartel's envoys. El Salvador was a major transit route for cocaine. In Colombia, although the 'cluster' bombs became linked to the trigger-man who had shot Luis Carlos Galán and who had worked for the Cali cartel after Rodríguez Gacha's death, Jaime Rueda Rocha, they were never found.

It was at least the fifth time that foreign military men had participated in plans to kill Escobar. Apart from the disastrous helicopter raid by the British mercenaries in March 1989, two other attempts were reportedly made by former US army officers in May and June that year – one of them involving an Israeli and a radio-operated model airplane which, packed with explosive, was intended to be dropped on Escobar at his Nápoles estate. Each attempt on Escobar's life was contracted by members of the Cali cartel, who were reportedly offering $1.5m to his successful assassin. Colonel Homero Rodríguez, the warden of the Cathedral, claimed that he told President Gaviria that the Cali traffickers offered him $10 million to collaborate in the bombing of the jail.

While Escobar was rebuilding his empire and initiating an internal purge of debtors and suspected traitors, as well as witnesses against him, the traffickers in the Valle del Cauca were expanding their trade and revealing how viciously they, too, could behave. Cocaine production, according to the DEA, had doubled since the government launched its offensive against the Medellín cartel in 1989. Coca-leaf plantations were springing up ever faster in the remoter parts of Colombia, and the Cali cartel in particular was starting to push its refining operations beyond the border and to develop more complex smuggling routes. At the same time, the Cali traffickers were at the forefront of the thrust into the new markets in eastern Europe.

The head of the DEA in Colombia, Joe Toft, said: 'The Cali cartel was always much more efficient and businesslike than Escobar, who was like a bull in a china shop. Even if Escobar had been out and about – which he was anyway for all practical purposes although the government would never admit he ran the Cathedral – it would have been just a matter of time before they took over from Medellín.' While tightening their grip on New York, the Cali traffickers were exporting violence there, too. Police reported that homicide rates in Queens, the nub of the cartel's New York distribution networks, had doubled since 1985 and that a third of its 357 killings in 1992 were related to drug trafficking. Among them was that of Manuel de Dios Unanue, a Cuban-born journalist dedicated to exposing the Cali cartel's stranglehold in Queens' Jackson Heights district. In March 1992 he was shot dead in a restaurant. The Rodríguez Orejuelas' longtime colleague, José Santacruz Londoño, was accused of ordering the murder.

Colombia's illicit drug industry was also diversifying strongly into heroin. Again, this was mainly in the hands of the traffickers in the Valle del Cauca, which was surrounded by the three departments where plantations of opium poppies were heavily concentrated: Tolima to the east, Huila to the south east, and

Cauca to the south. If there were a heartland, it was the mountainous slopes of Huila, above the valleys populated by the Páez Indians. Colombia's opium-poppy cultivation, which although documented since the mid 1980s had at that time been officially denied by the United States, boomed between 1991 and 1992. According to figures supplied by the United Nations International Drug Control Programme (UNDCP), by 1992 Colombia was growing more than 17,000 hectares of poppies and the crop was spreading fast to other departments. Some estimates suggested there were up to 30,000 hectares, with Colombia overtaking Mexico to become the world's third largest heroin producer. The plantations were often small, difficult to detect and violently defended: heroin prices per kilogram were far higher than cocaine, and the profit margins far greater. One hectare of opium poppies produced enough gum for about 1 kilogram of heroin – worth between $130,000 and $170,000 on arrival in the United States – twice a year. That compared with about $25,000 for a kilogram of cocaine. Asian chemists, mostly from India, Pakistan and Sri Lanka, arrived in Colombia to boost production levels. During raids on laboratories in Cali, Bogotá and small towns in Huila and Tolima in 1992, police found heroin of 90 per cent purity. The drug was mainly being exported by 'mules' who swallowed it or placed it up their rectums and vaginas. The UNDCP estimated that, by the early 1990s, Colombia was producing about 10 per cent of the heroin in the world and, in Latin America, challenging Mexico's regional supremacy in the market.

The growth of the heroin industry coincided with a rash of sadistic murders in the Valle del Cauca to the north of Cali. Scores of bodies were being washed up on the banks of the river Cauca, their heads and fingertips often sliced off in order to hide their identities, in what appeared to be a systematic campaign to wipe out anybody suspected of dissenting with the drug traffickers' rule. One priest, from the town of Trujillo, was found to have been castrated and to have had his arms and legs broken before execution. The area was dominated by the Urdinola family, particularly Iván Urdinola, who was famous for biting and pulling off the ears of people who incurred his displeasure. One ranch owner, a politician who claimed his steward was killed by Iván Urdinola, said: 'Within a few years Colombia will be in the hands of the mafia; in the Valle del Cauca itself, nobody any longer dares to speak out against the traffickers. They will dominate politics, the police, the justice system and business.' After surrendering to the authorities in a deal for which a senior member of the newly created public prosecutor's office was alleged to have been paid a few million US dollars, Iván Urdinola was expected to spend no more than four years in jail.

According to the DEA, Urdinola was an associate of the Rodríguez Orejuela brothers, José Santacruz Londoño and Pacho Herrera – the kingpins of the Cali cartel. 'There was no evidence to suggest the Medellín crowd ever got into heroin, although they did try,' said Toft. 'But the Urdinolas are widely known to be involved and there is a lot of evidence to suggest complicity by the Rodríguez Orejuelas. The heroin business could not have grown so much without the blessing of the main Cali cartel leaders, and they would not have given their blessing just for the hell of it. They would be getting their percentage.' Meanwhile, after Escobar's imprisonment, the Cali patriarch, Gilberto Rodríguez Orejuela, brazenly proclaimed his own innocence to *Time* magazine in the only interview ever conceded by the man whose flair for brutally shrewd, ice-cool planning had won him the underworld nickname of the Chess Player.

In fact, Rodríguez Orejuela had started out like Escobar, as a kidnapper. Brought up in Cali's working-class Obrero district, like Escobar the brothers also sympathized with the guerrillas. So did their lifetime partner, José Santacruz Londoño. A former left-wing student activist in Cali recalled: 'They were friends of the founders of the ELN [National Liberation Army], so much so that they took part in the [1969] kidnap of two Swiss men to finance the ELN.' The source, who worked for one of Gaviria's presidential advisory councils, claimed that the Rodríguez Orejuelas were handed the ransom money by the kidnap organizer, Luis Fernando Tamayo, before Tamayo was captured. When freed from jail a few years later, Tamayo was promptly murdered. Not only did Gilberto Rodríguez Orejuela and his accomplices keep the money – 12 million pesos (about $700,000), their first working capital – but a crucial witness to their past had been removed. Among their other friends from the Obrero district was Armando Holguín. After becoming a lawyer, Holguín went on to form part of the legal team that helped Gilberto Rodríguez Orejuela to be extradited from Spain to Colombia rather than to the United States. He also fought against extradition as a delegate to the Constituent Assembly.

'The Rodríguez Orejuelas' honeymoon with the left broke up when they got rich and opted to join the political élite,' said my friend, in an upstairs bar in central Bogotá. 'We felt and saw how they extended their power in industry and commerce as well as land. It was thanks to their capital that the sugar industry recovered.' When asked by *Time* magazine about the kidnapping – he was arrested over the Swiss case – Gilberto Rodríguez Orejuela replied obtusely: 'This is not logical. I was chairman of the board of directors of a bank in Colombia and president of . . . a bank in Panama [with Jorge Luis Ochoa].' His banking and pharmaceutical business activities had, in fact, begun several years later. 'Can you explain to me how I could get official blessings for these businesses if I had a criminal past?' he challenged. Perhaps by then it was a question of the dog that did not bark in the night: 'In the early 1980s,' said my friend in the bar, 'the cartel intervened on behalf of an important industrialist whose son was kidnapped by the ELN. They killed a lot of people in the hunt for him and held a dozen ELN militants until he was freed. My mate was the ELN negotiator.'

While Escobar tried openly to impose himself on the very closed and clannish Antioquia élite, the Rodríguez Orejuelas set about wooing the rather more porous upper classes in the Valle del Cauca by offering their economic and political support with respectful discretion. The Rodríguez Orejuelas led from behind. And while Escobar was believed to have bought nothing more than his high school graduation certificate, Miguel Rodríguez

Orejuela was alleged to have used a stooge – who later worked for the brothers in the Cartagena customs – to graduate in law at Cali's University of Santiago (where in recognition of his donations he was later granted an honorary doctorate). The Cali leaders had more style. And nobody in the Colombian government – police, politicians or judicial officials – wanted to touch them.

By the time Escobar was in the Cathedral, the DEA estimated that Cali families were producing up to 70 per cent of the cocaine reaching the United States. Their smuggling methods were ingenious, their organizational systems were complex but efficient, and their internal discipline was intractable. With the early exception of the Urdinolas, debtors simply disappeared, without any of the messy, exemplary violence of the Medellín mob: word of mouth was sufficient. The head of the DEA, Robert Bonner, was already calling the Cali cartel 'the most powerful criminal organization in the world'. To the intense anger of the DEA as well as Escobar, once Escobar had moved into the Cathedral the Colombian government hardly lifted a finger against the traffickers it pointedly addressed as the *señores* or 'gentlemen' of Cali.

'Hardly any attempt was being made to grab the Rodríguez Orejuelas and Co.,' said Joe Toft, Colombia's DEA chief. 'It seemed that the government did not want anything to do with the kingpins of the cartel. Laboratories were raided and seizures were made, but for the cartel these could just be written off as business expenses. Some of the raids targeting their financial operations seemed successful, but often we later found out the take was smaller than it should have been because somebody was tipped off.' Escobar, in a bulletin from the Extraditables issued in March 1992, voiced the same complaint: 'We do not see any action being taken by the anti-drug authorities against the *señores* Rodríguez Orejuela.' The government, claimed Escobar, was behaving 'in a biased manner in favour of a group of criminals carrying on with the drugs business on a huge scale'.

*

By early 1992 the government was no longer able to turn a blind eye to Escobar's activities in the Cathedral. In February, the jacuzzis were removed. Two months later, the Ministry of Justice started to build a third, electrified fence and a corridor for land mines. Cameras were to be installed. However, after the workers were beaten up by Escobar's fellow inmates the security improvements were suspended – and Escobar celebrated his first anniversary in captivity outside the compound, in an Envigado club. At the same time – having already ordered the killings of dozens of his enemies from his hilltop kingdom – Escobar was denounced before the public prosecutor's office for kidnapping, torturing and murdering some of his oldest and closest allies within the jail itself.

Escobar was becoming paranoid about betrayal, of any kind. After beating the state, Escobar's certainty in his own power and judicial invincibility had returned with a vengeance. This accompanied the increasingly sanctimonious nature of his belief that the entire Colombian drug trade owed him a lasting debt because he had won its war and paid the price with his liberty. Escobar's martyrish self-righteousness aggravated the suspiciousness of a mafia leader customarily alert to signs of faltering allegiances from his subjects. Escobar became an embittered tyrant whose conviction that Colombia would never call him to account for his crimes encouraged him to give free rein to his instinct for waging a blood-letting purge. 'He was mad, irrational, an animal,' said one senior police officer.

The flashpoint was the finding of $23 million – in cash – rotting in a garage in the town of Itagüí, bordering Envigado. The money belonged to the Moncada and Galeano families, cocaine traffickers who had worked alongside Escobar for more than a decade and who were among his best friends. During the first year of their leader's sojourn in the Cathedral, they had religiously paid Escobar his dues from their own smuggling as well as organized shipments for Escobar himself; both families regularly visited the Doctor to receive their orders. In May, however, they were said to have attempted suspending part of Escobar's protection quota.

The multi-million dollar stash was discovered by one of Escobar's top *sicarios*, Mario Alberto Castaño or *El Chopo*, in late June. How it was discovered and what happened next was a matter of a very nasty discussion. With or without Escobar's blessing, and whether it was found by accident or by torturing one of Galeano's henchmen, *El Chopo*'s men stole the hoard on his boss's behalf. According to Popeye, the Galeanos responded by kidnapping and killing the girlfriend and sister of one of the thieves, *El Nato*; when the thieves volunteered to return the cash in exchange for the women, a rendezvous took place with Gerardo Moncada and Fernando Galeano; when the thieves and their men – who numbered about twenty – were told the women were already dead, Moncada and Galeano were murdered themselves and Escobar let the thieves keep the money. According to the Moncada and Galeano families, after one of the twenty men they had kidnapped on suspicion of involvement was identified by the two women who had witnessed the theft, Gerardo Moncada and Fernando Galeano visited Escobar in the Cathedral. They were concealed in the van bearing the inmates' food supplies – and all but eaten alive by their master. After being reprimanded by Escobar for holding out on him, they were shot dead by Escobar's bodyguards. Moncada was also said to have been tortured. Police reported that Moncada's fingernails were yanked out and an electric drill driven into his knees in order to extract from him the identities of the frontmen holding his assets.

During the following fortnight, in July 1992, Escobar's *sicarios* hunted down, kidnapped and killed about two dozen men from the Moncada/Galeano organization. Properties, aircraft, bank accounts and cattle worth hundreds of millions of dollars were transferred at gunpoint in the Cathedral into the names of Escobar's own frontmen and *sicarios*. The victims' families were forced to pay money for their loved ones' bodies to be returned. They were then double-crossed: many corpses were never found.

The survivors fled Medellín. Several headed straight into the waiting arms of the Rodríguez Orejuelas in Cali, who were strongly suspected of having helped to provoke the Moncadas' and Galeanos' play for independence in the first place. The Cali barons demanded one condition for their assistance: that the public prosecutor's office be informed of the slaughter.

Openly confronted with judicial evidence indicating that Escobar had converted the Cathedral into the day-to-day headquarters of what was probably still one of the world's biggest drug-smuggling syndicates – police believed Escobar was continuing to trade alongside the Ochoa brothers – the government was finally obliged to intervene. The man who became the scourge of Escobar was Gustavo de Greiff, a sixty-three-year-old pipe smoker with a fatherly presence who had just been appointed Colombia's first chief prosecutor. Undere the new constitution, his role had been divorced from that of attorney general as part of a switch from the declaratory, Napoleonic judicial system towards the inquisitional, Anglo-Saxon one. Another constitutional change had been the loss of the Supreme Court's independence in July 1991. Instead of being a self-elected body whose magistrates enjoyed life appointments, eight-year tenures were imposed and the appointments fell under the sway of the president and Congress. The politicization rippled down and throughout the legal hierarchy. De Greiff, who had been chosen by the Supreme Court although he had no experience of penal law, had made his name as a civil lawyer defending Jaime Michelsen Uribe, the former financial magnate who had laundered money for the Medellín cartel before fleeing Colombian justice and being sentenced to jail in connection with his collapsed banking empire.

Prompted by de Greiff's investigations into the murders in the Cathedral, the government decided to transfer Escobar to a military jail until such time as his Envigado holiday camp had been transformed into an authentic maximum security prison. The drugs lord was having none of it. Fearful both of kidnap by the US – that month the abduction of foreign suspects abroad had been legally ratified by the US Supreme Court – and an assassination attempt by the police or the Cali cartel, he was also unwilling to sacrifice his current freedoms. A few hours after the first warning of mysterious troop movements, Escobar walked out of the Cathedral as calmly as a bishop leaving Mass.

The operation to move Escobar was bungled from the beginning. The commander of the Fourth Brigade, General Gustavo Pardo, and the young vice minister of justice, Eduardo Mendoza, received different orders. While the general had been told simply to take over the Cathedral, Mendoza had been ordered to have Escobar transferred to a military barracks. While the vice minister pretended to Escobar that the army was only going to increase its security control over the Cathedral, Escobar heard over the radio that he was going to be transferred. Mendoza was promptly seized as a hostage: 'I've always wanted to kill a vice minister,' said Popeye, stroking his face with the barrel of an Uzi sub-machine-gun. While the vice minister and the director of prisons, Colonel Hernando Navas, were held by five of the inmates, Escobar paid off an army sergeant and strolled out with his brother and the rest of his henchmen through a hole in the outer fence. At around 1.30 a.m., 22 July, Colombia's number-one drugs baron and terrorist escaped, effortlessly, into the forest. About a day later, by which time it was reported that six of the jail's (Escobar's) prison guards had been shot dead while putting up a fight in the pretence that Escobar was still there, the government realized they had escaped. Another day later, Escobar promised to hand himself in again if he were allowed to remain in the Cathedral with the protection of a United Nations guard. Escobar was back on the run. President Gaviria, meanwhile, was forced to miss the celebrations in Madrid marking the 500th year since Christopher Colombus' discovery of the Americas.

Medellín in 1992 was a much richer city than when Escobar had started out as a robber of gravestones and cars more than two decades earlier. Although its population had more than doubled to 1.8 million, the city had finally caught up with the tide of rural migrants that had swamped its northern hillsides as well as its surrounding municipalities. The so-called communes suffered nothing like the poverty and physical hardship of the equivalent neighbourhoods in other Latin American cities such as Lima, La Paz or Sao Paolo. Nearly every dwelling now enjoyed electricity, mains water and drainage. Sixty per cent of homes in the poor northern districts even had telephones, and most of the streets were paved. Industrial growth, fuelled by a renewed construction boom – in turn helped by cocaine money – was twice the national average between the last half of 1992 and the first half of 1993. This forced unemployment down from 15.2 per cent to a relatively respectable 12.2 per cent over the same period.

Yet murder rates had inexorably risen. Initially peaking in 1991 with 6,838 murders in the city itself, which was 300 per cent more than in 1987, by 1993 the figure had jumped again to 7,074. Poverty was not the problem. Crime as a whole had simply become legitimate in a society where at all levels it carried minimum social stigma and where huge income differentials generated colossal resentment and ambition by those at the lower end of the scale. Human life had ceased to hold much meaning; murder was a part of getting rich and defending yourself, or of resolving disputes.

Fabian, a fatherless, eighteen-year-old mulatto in Medellín's north-eastern Nuevo Horizonte district, dismissed death as a matter of minor importance. 'It happens to everyone sooner or later, so why worry?' he asked as we climbed the streets under a burning sun. 'What's more worrying is the everyday – finding work and getting enough to eat.' He worked as a taxidermist. A few minutes later, while I chatted to a woman who lived near a corner where, at the height of the violence, plainclothes policemen had gunned down card-playing youths in broad daylight, Fabian rushed inside, pale and shaking with terror. 'Don't let them kill me, don't let them kill me!' he begged, as Doña Nina made the sign of the cross and I listened for shouts and footsteps behind him, hoping there was an escape route at the back. God Speaks

Today declared the front of the family bible on the bookshelf. Nobody entered. Doña Nina clutched Fabian to her bosom as his mumbles slowly ceased and his eyes regained their focus. He had suffered a nervous fit.

By 1993, the city's youth was not only severely traumatized by the violence; it was also punch-drunk by the spectacle of corpses. In order to make a killing exemplary, the killers had to shock. Hence, the bodies were often disfigured. Since the late 1980s, self-defence groups had been springing up in the communes to combat the gangs of assassins and thieving hoodlums caught up in turf wars in which innocent people also died in the crossfire. The leadership of these militia groups was gradually hijacked by ELN guerrillas as well as former rebels from the Popular Liberation Army (EPL), whose main faction had laid down its arms in 1990. The militia provided the guerrillas with a political machine, offering security and justice, through which they could continue their local struggles for power. Thieves and drug users were routinely executed if militia warnings were ignored. To get their message across, the militias in the Aranjuez district – where Escobar's gang, the Priscos, had used to operate – inserted plastic knives and forks into the victims' knife wounds. The intention was to illustrate that the corpses were *desechables*: worthless throwaways.

Homero was a typical *desechable*. Only ten years old, he begged, stole, sniffed glue and smoked marijuana; he said he let himself be buggered in exchange for $7. Homero had been threatened by both police and militia before being rescued by Salesian priests who ran a rehabilitation school in the north-western suburbs. Escobar was his hero. 'Pablo is very intelligent, a very good man,' he said. 'Pablo has given clothes and money to poor people. His bodyguards are the bad ones.' A fifteen-year-old companion added: 'The police are jealous of Pablo. He wanted to be a prestigious politician and that screwed him.'

A little later, I spoke with a group of eighteen-year-olds who had also sought refuge with the Salesians. Nelson described his first kill. 'The militia provoked war – they wanted to dominate the district, like us. It fell to me to kill a militia member to show I could be one of the gang. It was easy. I smoked some *basuko* and shot one in the back with a rifle.' Gang contracts were for robberies of shops, homes, banks and cars as well as for murders. 'I earned $700 for robbing a boutique,' said Nelson's friend, Carlos, fingering his necklace; it bore the image of one of the *sicarios*' favourite saints, San Judas Tadeo. 'As soon as I had the money, I spent it – on alcohol, women, clothes, Nike training shoes.'

Earning 'fast' money had become an obsession that touched all classes. The *paisa* work-and-save ethic had been rocked by the cocaine bonanza. There was a tendency to scorn the average wage, to want everything now or never. Cocaine had touched everybody's lives. Few families came out undamaged; few businesses turned the money away. And, worryingly for the future, it was as if the level of educational prowess in Antioquia had deteriorated in direct relation to the influx of investment by the drug traffickers. Until the 1970s, the department had led the country in the ICFES university entrance exams. By 1993, Antioquia had sunk to twenty-second place; it was followed by the Amazon departments, the most backward in Colombia. The lure of fast money had helped to drain schools and universities of their talent. Meanwhile, according to Alberto Echavarría, the departmental president of the National Association of Industries, cocaine money had probably bought up to 30 per cent of the debt paper issued on Medellín's stock exchange in the 1990s.

With the execution of most of the leading members of the Moncada and Galeano families, which was meant to be a lesson to other mafia mortals, Escobar suddenly found himself not only out of jail but out in the cold. With Rodríguez Gacha dead, with the Ochoas playing goody-two-shoes while their handsome, maximum security jail was built in Itagüí, with the families of the Moncadas and Galeanos baying for revenge and with the government's patience exhausted by the international shame and disgrace caused by his escape from the Cathedral, Escobar had hardly anywhere to turn. His credit had run out. Past political godfathers, who had forged links with cocaine sponsors in Cali anyway, could no longer touch him. At the same time, Escobar was entering a liquidity crisis.

The proximity of politicians to the Cali drugs cartel was potently illustrated by a police raid in the north of the Valle del Cauca in the first half of 1992. A photograph was found showing Iván Urdinola, the ear-biting chief of the cocaine clan that was also reported to be exporting heroin, embracing Misael Pastrana, the former president whose son Andrés was preparing for his own presidential bid.

The government's response to Escobar's new surrender demands was to launch the biggest manhunt in the history of Colombia. President Gaviria described the escape, which revealed the farcical nature of the jail conditions to which he and his ministers had originally agreed, as a 'challenge to the state and the whole of society'. Initial attempts to locate the fugitive involved the deployment in north-west Colombia of six US aircraft, including four Hercules transport planes, equipped with infra-red detection devices. The government offered a $1 million reward for information leading to Escobar's capture. The DEA and US authorities added another $2.7 million. The Moncada and Galeano families promised $1.5 million more – although they wanted him dead. The explosion of a car bomb outside one of Escobar's Medellín properties, the Monterrey shopping centre, wounding several passers-by and wrecking about twenty vehicles, heralded the start of a bombing campaign by his mafia enemies which in the months ahead destroyed dozens of Escobar's buildings and ranches.

Escobar continued to send shipments of cocaine through his few remaining allies in Medellín. The DEA and police claimed that he also received financial contributions from the Ochoa brothers. To throw his pursuers off his scent, he paid people to provide false but convincing information on his whereabouts, thereby wasting days of police and army time. Meanwhile, Escobar reverted to his *sicario* war on the police: he was reported to be behind the killings of dozens of detectives from Colombia's secret police organizations. Simultaneously, again playing the same game as before his confinement, in order to soften up the government Escobar ordered some of his fellow fugitives from the Cathedral to turn themselves in once more. Popeye and Escobar's brother, Roberto, were among those who in October were dispatched to the same jail as the Ochoas. Surrendering was no easy process: Escobar's men and their families were being hunted down and killed in an all-out vendetta by his former allies and the secret police. So hazardous was it to surrender without being murdered in the process that one of Escobar's lackeys presented himself before the public prosecutor's office in Antioquia dressed up as a monk.

Escobar's Medellín mafia enemies joined forces firstly with Fidel Castaño, the vicious right-wing paramilitary leader who also broke with Escobar over the Moncada and Galeano murders – for which, like Lehder, he referred to Escobar as the Monster – and secondly with the 'gentlemen' of Cali, whose contribution was mainly financial. The security forces were also united against him: the police could now count on the unswerving support of the army, which had been humiliated by Escobar's escape. Together, the Elite Force of police and the army's Fourth Brigade mounted a 600-man Search Force backed by another 2,400 soldiers and detectives. The objective was not to capture Escobar, but to kill him, as few of its officers denied in private. Scanners and triangulation equipment to trace radio and telephone calls were operated twenty-four hours a day. By the end of November, nearly 3,000 homes had been raided in and around Medellín, more than 1,000 people arrested and one of Escobar's top bodyguards killed. The manhunt coincided with a crackdown on the FARC and ELN guerrillas following a rebel bombing campaign in response to the government's refusal to renew peace talks. In such a climate, Escobar's chances of surrender were slim; by December, he was reported to have aborted at least two attempts to hand himself in at the Itagüí jail because he feared the Search Force would kill him before he made it inside.

By Christmas, Escobar was stepping up his war again. A car bomb, although possibly the work of the ELN, blew up fourteen people, including ten policemen, after a football match in Medellín. A police captain was shot dead after his home was bombed in an operation personally directed by Escobar in which his sixteen-year-old son, Juan Pablo, was later accused of taking part. ('The witnesses changed their story when they were bribed and threatened by his dad,' said a DEA source. 'The kid was there.' A senior member of the DAS state security police claimed that Juan Pablo – 'a nasty piece of work' – had actually joined in the shooting.) As more bombs exploded – usually aimed at the police – Escobar found that some of his key bodyguards were giving evidence against him to the chief prosecutor's office as well as providing valuable information to the Search Force. At the same time as his charge sheet lengthened with murders and kidnaps, increasing his potential jail sentence, anybody who attempted to mediate for him, such as lawyers and local politicians, was shot or bombed by his enemies.

Even as the rope tightened, Escobar lashed out. They were the thrashings of a desperate beast. In what proved to be no more than an impotent, bilious threat, the Doctor warned that if the 'tortures and disappearances' were not halted, he would detonate 10,000 kilograms of dynamite outside the chief prosecutor's office. In mid January 1993, he announced that 'in the search for peace' he was going to launch the Rebel Antioquia group; it was another vain attempt to be granted guerrilla rather than terrorist status. All Escobar wanted was to return to jail. However, the government, determined to clear its name nationally and internationally, was no longer willing to negotiate.

In forming Rebel Antioquia, Escobar hoped to rally the support of the Medellín militia groups. With the exception of some of those linked to the ELN, few rose to the occasion. And the gangs of hoodlums that once had supported him were in complete disarray. After two bombs in northern Bogotá, which killed nobody, the Rebel Antioquia group was never heard of again. The capture of the *sicarios* responsible, along with 1,200 kilograms of dynamite, pointed straight to Escobar and won him further public loathing. With the fall of extradition he was bereft of a nationalist cause: Pablo Escobar was seen to be fighting for nobody but himself. His only remaining supporters were his family, most of Envigado and the hordes of delinquents and poor, ill-educated people in Medellín who still viewed him as a hero who had struck gold in the streets and fear into the hearts of governments whose authority they held in contempt.

Encouraged by the initial success of its witness protection scheme, which, coupled with generous payments to informants, was allowing the Search Force to amass data, raid properties, seize bank accounts and slowly cut Escobar off from his remaining contacts, the government raised the official reward for his capture to nearly $7 million. That figure included contributions from the DEA, FBI, CIA and Interpol. Within hours of Escobar's first Bogotá bomb of the year, car bombs exploded outside the buildings where his mother and wife lived in Medellín. Attacks on other family properties followed. Behind these blasts was the paramilitary group based around the Moncada and Galeano families which by now called itself the Pepes, the Spanish acronym for People Persecuted by Pablo Escobar. The Pepes, with the backing of the Cali cartel leaders, upped their bounty for Escobar to $5 million. With a total of $12 million on his head, Escobar had passed within a decade from being one of the richest men in the world to its most wanted.

The Cali cartel was also reported to be working directly with the office of the chief prosecutor, Gustavo de Greiff, by providing information. In return, the cartel was left alone. According to the DEA, police raids in the Valle del Cauca were often stillborn because it was believed information had leaked out of the chief prosecutor's office, which processed the requests for search warrants. 'Too many people knew of an upcoming raid, and the take [detentions or evidence recovered] just wasn't there,' said a DEA agent. De Greiff's office, he added, 'would hold on to information without giving us the warrant, so the information became useless'. A Cali cartel source later claimed that a deal had been cut.

In February, Escobar hit back with more car bombs in Bogotá, killing four people and wounding more than 100. The Pepes promptly fire-bombed one of his mansions in Medellín and went on to destroy a ranch belonging to Escobar's wife, his sister's art gallery, a private entertainment complex and, most painful of all for Escobar, his collection of vintage cars including six Rolls-Royces. It was reported that the Pepes had already killed more than forty of Escobar's people and caused up to a dozen others to be arrested by tipping off the Search Force. As his men either fled, handed themselves in, were captured or were murdered, Escobar was left more and more isolated and increasingly dependent on novice *sicarios*. His bodyguard was reduced to a handful of men at a time when he was gradually abandoning radio and telephone communications in favour of foot messengers and when, as his liquidity crisis worsened with the surveillance, seizure or destruction of his available assets, he was regularly organizing kidnaps of local businessmen, former colleagues and their families in order to keep himself afloat. 'He feels cornered,' said one of Escobar's former workers. 'But he's a warrior who will fight until the end. He will never accept losing.'

Escobar's fears for his family launched the saga that eventually led to his entrapment. In February, when Juan Pablo and Manuela attempted to board a flight for Miami – their US visas were curiously in order – they were stopped because they lacked a written note from their father authorizing their departure. The USA cancelled their visas, as well as those of their accompanying cousins, and reminded the world that when new ones were issued for minors both parents were required at the embassy. 'We are suffering in thinking that my father is going to be captured or killed,' said Juan Pablo at Medellín's international airport. 'But God has given him an ability always to come out on top. I love him and I would like to help him in this war.' When Escobar offered to surrender if his family were given asylum, the USA refused.

Each time Escobar felt thwarted in his bid to hand himself in, he replied with dynamite. In turn, the Pepes hit back harder. After the Search Force blocked one possible surrender – involving the participation of Monseñor Darío Castrillón, a bishop who had always smiled kindly on the drug traffickers – by conducting operations in the given area of Rionegro, Escobar exploded another large bomb in northern Bogotá that killed nine people. The following day, the Pepes machine-gunned the lawyer who had worked side by side with Escobar for more than a decade, Guido Parra, and his son.

Parra was among at least five lawyers killed during the Pepes' systematic elimination of Escobar's remaining network. 'The Pepes are mad fanatics,' one black, bullnecked lawyer on Escobar's payroll declared to me, *sotto voce* and scared, in a smart downtown office in Medellín. Salomón Lozano was shot dead six weeks later, in July. By September 1993, the Pepes, under the military leadership of Fidel Castaño and working mostly with information provided by the Moncada and Galeano families, had killed more than 80 people. Although strongly denied by the Search Force, it was also suspected that the Pepes were being used by the police to conduct their dirty work. In a letter to Escobar about the Pepes attacks, his mother Hermilda wrote: 'The trick of staging [police] checkpoints in the same point where they [the Pepes] are going to commit villainies goes on.' Escobar's protests to the chief prosecutor's office about the Pepes were effectively ignored. 'Initially, we thought the Pepes were a vigilante bunch of heroes,' said the DEA's Joe Toft, 'but then it became very evident that they were nothing more than puppets with strings pulled by the Cali cartel.'

In an attempt to defend his family, Escobar installed them in an apartment building in Medellín's rich residential district of El Poblado. Supposedly, they were to be protected by the chief prosecutor's office. However, in October, only weeks after his immediate family, his in-laws and his cousins had moved in, they were attacked by gunfire and a grenade. Their police cordon, through which the assailants escaped with as much ease as they had gone in, was clearly very permeable. In trying to inflict maximum psychological damage on the family, the Pepes went beyond merely destroying their ranches and commercial property. In August, a young stallion owned by Roberto Escobar was found forlornly tied to a tree near a liquor factory off Medellín's southern highway. Terremoto, or Earthquake, was one of the finest paso colombiano horses in the country. He earned more than $600,000 each time he covered a mare and was worth about $1 million. Earthquake, whose trainer had already been shot, had been kidnapped from the stables of the Ochoa brothers. It was no wonder that Earthquake was found looking forlorn. Both his testicles were missing.

The day after Terremoto was found castrated, I took a bus to the small town of La Ceja, south east of Medellín. Scapulary necklaces were offered by children who boarded the bus at the journey's start. Later, a little wistfully, I rather regretted turning one down.

La Ceja lies at the heart of a fertile band of hills famed for their dairy produce. The town also featured within the labyrinth of dots and lines indicating the possible whereabouts of Pablo Escobar on the map at the Search Force headquarters. It was Pablo's country – and the home of his father, Abel de Jesús.

The large, white Spanish colonial square was swimming in sunlight as I stepped off the bus. Although it was a Sunday, the shops were open and the pavements packed with people and traders. The church bells were ringing for Mass. A drunk waved his arms in a frantic attempt to regain the equilibrium upon which his legs had given up in despair. I entered the rectory.

'Don Abel is a good man, a simple peasant who has no problems with anyone,' said one priest, sitting in the courtyard. Little yellow birds chattered and perched on the bench; the church bells rang. Like so many *paisas*, the priest was ineffably polite, charming and helpful. It could lull you into a false sense of security.

The head of the Search Force, Colonel Hugo Martínez Póveda,

had affirmed that Abel de Jesús, unlike his wife – from whom he had long since separated – had nothing to do with his son's activities. Joaquín Vallejo, Pablo Escobar's godfather, had asserted the same. 'He's not very bright – a peasant – but good.'

Don Abel de Jesús lived not on his farm but just seven blocks above the square, I was told. In a white house opposite a white convent.

Two old men were sitting out on the terrace as I approached what appeared to be the place Father Pedro had described. It was an attractive, one-storey building faced in stucco. Turn of the century. No, never heard of him, said the grisly, grey-haired man. Lives out in the countryside, said the other one with the moustache. I carried on up the hill.

Upon further inquiry, an elderly gentleman with a stick pointed me back down again. I tried another white house. This time its occupant, a short, smiling lady, showed me the way herself. I was back at the terrace, now deserted. I pressed the doorbell. After a long delay, a younger man came out, declaring that the owner had lived there fourteen years, that they had the papers to prove it and that people were tricking me. Meanwhile, a fawn-coloured jeep drew up, driven by a thug who looked as if his face had been chewed and spat out by a Rottweiler. The owner's driver, I was informed. A gun barrel stuck out from under his seat.

We walked up the street, my companion demanding to know who'd been 'misleading' me. He was rude to the smiling lady. The priest was a liar, he said: or was I calling him one? He was suddenly aggressive. As I started to suggest that either the world was upside down or maybe he was doing his duty in protecting Don Abel, and that I was simply a journalist, the jeep appeared at a corner 50 metres away. He dashed for it. After a five-second talk with the thug, he climbed in and they vanished.

It was time to leave, and seven lengthy blocks back to the square. The jeep materialized, stationary, in a side street. I shrugged, waved and walked on. Reaching the square, I crossed it and swiftly bargained an expensive taxi ride back to Medellín.

Forty kilometres later, after the winding hillside curves and the giddy plunge into Medellín's valley, I made the taxi leave me by a roundabout. As it sped off and I dropped out of sight, the fawn-coloured jeep swept up from behind, chasing the taxi into the underpass.

Maybe Don Abel was no more than a 'good' peasant, but he was obviously a very scared one.

The last of the bombs had been in April. As US surveillance aircraft flew high above Antioquia, as helicopters buzzed over the city at night, as Search Force checkpoints appeared and disappeared, Escobar's main lieutenants either deserted him or were picked off one by one – killed, not captured – until only he remained. The yellow, blue, green and orange dots indicating his presence, his properties, his hideouts and his routes on the black-and-white wall map at the Search Force headquarters evolved, at a constantly quickening pace, into a complex matrix through which there emerged a portrait of the fugitive.

Colonel Martínez Póveda was the Search Force leader. Tall, elegant and handsome, his unruffleable good humour belied the tremendous national and international pressure to which he was subject. His men had survived a mass poisoning attempt by a bribed cook, several had committed suicide and every movement from the barracks was known to be reported to Escobar. As a security precaution, none of the Search Force members were from Medellín. The colonel described his prey: 'Escobar started off as a kidnapper – he has done it all over the world, from Italy to Japan. All his life he has been an expert at hiding people and an expert in protecting himself. That is what gave him his power in the drugs trade. Now, he is using the same local hideouts where he held his victims in order to conceal himself, and he knows the area like the back of his hand.'

So ingenious were Escobar's niches and hideouts that US experts using electronic detection equipment failed to find any of his secret places in the Cathedral. However, when his former henchmen offered their assistance, they found them all. Once the Search Force understood the false walls and floors operated by everything from clothes hooks to bathroom taps, many of Escobar's old hideouts became useless. He opted for ordinary, rented accommodation instead, moving between houses every few days. His family, while liaising with the chief prosecutor's office over his possible surrender, regularly provided him with information on the car number plates of the secret police. The information was sent by messengers. Radio and telephone calls were used by Escobar only for personal matters – and kept to within a few seconds, too short for the police's direction-scanner equipment to get an accurate fix on even their general location. He travelled in ambulances and funeral vans but mostly in taxis. Envigado remained his fortress, where almost nobody breathed a word against him and where his old friend, Jorge Mesa, the mayor, ruled with a rod of iron.

Mesa, who was investigated for the murders carried out by the Department of Security and Control and under grave threat from the Pepes, declined to be interviewed. 'The Different Community, Land of Peace and Culture', proclaimed a municipal poster portraying a land of milk and honey. 'There is no drug trafficking in Envigado and the traffickers have not invested here,' said the director of the House of Culture, Amalia Gómez, a striking Amazon of a woman with vivid red fingernails, wearing a shiny green dress. If she had said otherwise, she would probably have lost her job, or worse. 'It used to be a paradise here but I am now terrified,' said another resident. The bishop, with his splendidly refurbished white church, refused to talk. Earlier interviewees now evaded contact.

Whenever it was suspected that Escobar might hand himself in to the Envigado council, the town was invaded by the Search Force. The same was true around Itagüí's maximum security jail, whose nearby streets were occupied upon the slightest rumour of his surrender there. On one occasion, as troops turned over a woman's home after several hundred police and soldiers had arrived at dawn to raid every house near the prison, the victim asked with sleepy innocence: 'What's the matter? Has somebody lost something?'

The Cali cartel, which according to a government human rights official as well as an important business associate of Escobar's, was paying the Pepes $5 million every two months, thrived on the anti-Escobar crusade. Their arch enemy had become the nation's scapegoat. Not only was Escobar cornered, but so were Colombian and US anti-drug resources. The *caleños* were free to grab Escobar's routes and to traffic as they pleased. Their main reason to wish Escobar dead, quite apart from the hatred they bore him, was their gnawing worry that otherwise he might somehow engineer a miraculous comeback from within another jail. The Escobar myth still inspired Antioquia's great unwashed. Another factor was the Cali cartel's fear that the besieged drugs lord could provide incriminating evidence against them.

The government seemed to share a similar concern. In April, prison guards were reported by a senior human rights official to have ransacked Roberto Escobar's jail cell. According to the source, documents were stolen with evidence compromising the Rodríguez Orejuelas which Escobar's brother intended to hand over to the USA. 'The search was so irregular that the public prosecutor from Bogotá withdrew from the scene and a complaint was placed with the attorney general,' said the human rights official. 'The government was obviously participating in the war between the cartels.' Similarly, a lawyer specializing in international affairs alleged privately that in a police raid on the home of a professional colleague, Escobar's entire defence file was stolen. 'Among other things, the file contained a full set of documents referring to General Maza Márquez,' said the lawyer.

Escobar came within a whisker of capture on 11 October. The police scanners had picked up his voice near the rural village of Aguas Frías, just above Medellín's western suburb of Belén, after an informant advised them that Escobar was in the area and that he was being protected by an ELN-linked urban militia. Nearby was the land that Escobar had donated to Father García. However, the scanners were tricked by the hilly terrain and the encircling operation was misfocused. With hundreds of police and soldiers converging in small platoons on the valley and the surrounding pine forests, Escobar, whose small farmhouse lay at the valley head, was tipped off as to their movements. Later, it was also suggested that the helicopters had been sent in too soon and that Escobar was alerted by their noise. He fled an estimated fifteen minutes before his house was raided.

Based on the description given by the two women who had been looking after Escobar, Colonel Martínez Póveda announced over short-wave radio, as his men settled down for the night: 'The target is wearing a red shirt, black jeans and tennis shoes. His hair is short, he has a light beard and no moustache.' The hair, beard and moustache details proved to be lies.

In spite of an intensive hunt over the following days, in which the helicopters bombarded the forests with grenades and tear-gas canisters, and loosed off round after round of machine-gun fire into the trees, Escobar vanished. The exhausted police and soldiers, who once again had come so near and once again had been made to look like fools, would heartily have agreed with the sentiments expressed in the Cambalache tango recorded on one of the cassettes discovered amongst Escobar's abandoned belongings: 'The world is full of pig shit —'

Letters that were also found there indicated that Escobar's wife, María Victoria, was becoming increasingly desperate. Winning asylum for the family was the government's bait in persuading Escobar to show his head and surrender. But nobody trusted the other party not to play a double game. His wife wrote to Escobar: 'I don't want you to make errors but, if there is nowhere to go, I feel safer with you. We will shut ourselves in ... whatever.' Led to believe by the chief prosecutor's office that Germany would accept them, on 27 November María Victoria suddenly flew with her children to Frankfurt. Whether or not there had existed an agreement, Escobar did not come out of hiding and two days later the family was sent back to Colombia. By then, even the Vatican was trying to mediate.

Instead of returning to Medellín, the family installed themselves in a hotel complex in central Bogotá. Their telephone calls were easy to monitor: the hotel, the Residencias Tequendama, was owned by the army. Escobar, meanwhile, had moved into a rather gaudy, two-storey house in the middle-class district of La América, in west Medellín. Heavy iron bars covered its windows and the mottled grey marble facing was haphazardly broken up with shiny splodges of black stone. The second-floor terrace hung over the street, looking out on a drainage canal from whose tired, grassy banks there nevertheless sprang a respectable line of trees. The house backed directly on to a bungalow, its red roof tiles sunk between rough, breeze-block walls climbing up on either side.

La América district was surprisingly violent. One month earlier, while happening to live just opposite Escobar's hideout – it was here that I had abandoned the taxi being chased by the thugs who were protecting Escobar's father – I had witnessed a motorbike theft at gunpoint along the same canal, and on another occasion been kept awake by a running street battle in the hours before dawn.

December 1st was Escobar's forty-fourth birthday. True to form, he called his family for a few seconds. Although he was heard loud and clear in Bogotá, he kept the conversation too brief for the scanners to pick him up in Medellín. The following day, however, at 1.30 p.m., he called again. This time, as his wife brought him up to date with the family's latest offer of asylum – from El Salvador – Escobar delayed too long. The scanners at the Search Force base in north Medellín locked on to his call. As the seconds ticked by, the young lieutenant operating the tracer equipment narrowed down the radius of the source to about 800 metres. One hour later, Escobar telephoned his family again. The police lieutenant identified the exact source of the call. A seventeen-man assault force in civilian clothes had already moved into the area. Once given the address, they took up position to the front and the back of the house. Five burst in through the main door.

CHECKMATE FOR THE CHESS PLAYER (1991–93)

Escobar's bodyguard, Alvaro de Jesús Agudelo, alias the Lemon and formerly his mother's chauffeur, was killed by machine-gun fire after racing over the roof tiles of the bungalow behind and jumping into the street. Escobar, emptying his Sig-Sauer pistol as he took the same route across the roof, never even reached the edge. His left shoulder blade already fractured by the 2-metre jump on to the roof, three bullets pierced his head, his lungs and his thigh as his corpulent, barefooted frame crashed to the tiles. It was 3.03 p.m., 2 December. After nearly 11,000 raids since his escape from the Cathedral, the Search Force had finally got their man.

Colombia had rid itself not just of the brutal killer of hundreds of its judges, politicians, policemen, delinquents and innocent civilians. Colombia had not just eliminated the man who, in his bid to protect his trade and to overturn extradition, had waged a war against the state and generated unprecedented corruption. It had also wiped its conscience clean. The age of drugs terrorism was over, at least for the moment. But a new age of drugs trafficking had only just begun. By now, the pragmatic tolerance of Colombian society had asserted itself. It was tired of terrorist violence. If the rest of the world wanted to buy cocaine, marijuana and heroin, then let the trades continue. In the meantime, powerful sectors of the state found themselves in hock to the leaders of the Cali cartel, the nice guys. The gentlemen.

CHAPTER TEN

WHITEWASH FOR THE WORLD (1994–)

The city of Cali lies 450 kilometres south of Medellín, pressed up against Colombia's westernmost mountain range on the other side of the hot, fertile plains sprawling towards the jungle and the Pacific Ocean. Cali, whose traditional wealth is founded on sugar, is the gateway to the country's busiest port, Buenaventura, which handles more than 60 per cent of Colombia's official exports. By 1993, rural migration had helped Cali to overtake Medellín as the second largest city, with a population of 1.8 million. Transactions on the stock market, which was only launched in 1983, had also outstripped those of its older, northern rival; so had its share of Latin America's cocaine exports, of which by late 1993 the department of the Valle del Cauca was now estimated by the DEA to have an 80 per cent control.

So extensive was the city's domination by the Cali cartel, and so dense its intelligence and counter-intelligence networks, that a CIA report likened their own working conditions to those behind the Iron Curtain during the Cold War. Taxis, the nicer hotels, the airport, the bus terminal, telephone companies and all service-oriented, private and public entities were 'locked up' by the cartel, said a DEA agent.

The appearance of any foreigner or outsider, especially if he seemed too inquisitive, was liable to be reported back to a central security force. This consisted of the leaders of the bodyguard and driver teams assigned to each member of the main drug-trafficking families; many of the leaders were former military and police officers. Every member of the family was identified by a code, which was formed by a letter denoting the family and a number for the individual. Houses, offices and streets were coded in a similar way. Anybody who triggered the interest of the central security force was investigated and followed; information was solicited, particularly from hotels, on his movements and business. If interpreted to be a potential nuisance, the target was unsubtly scared out of the city; if that failed, he was kidnapped and killed, with the job usually contracted out to *sicarios*.

The number of murders in Cali was rising steeply. In 1992, violent deaths had risen by 60 per cent over 1990, according to official figures. In 1993, the city morgue reported that homicides increased by another 15 per cent, to 2,064. Although that was still one third the homicide rate of Medellín, whose population was nearly the same size as Cali's, it naturally omitted victims whose bodies vanished. One of the most popular spots to dump corpses was at the foot of the giant statue of Jesus Christ in the mountains overlooking the city. At the same time, and in spite of apparent efforts by the cartel leaders to restrain the behaviour, the newly rich thugs revelled in their money and firepower.

Cali, which had been famed as a peaceful city, was turning into a re-run of Medellín during the early 1980s. Gleaming landrovers were driven at breakneck speed by *traquetos* – an onomatopoeic term to describe the sound of the machine-guns toted by the *sicarios*, bodyguards and other junior members of the business – who shot anybody who triggered their wrath. If you scratched their vehicle, they would demand a new one. Plaster models of smiling traffic policemen designed to draw attention to road hazards were riddled with bullet holes. Stories abounded of the rapes and murders, by the *mágicos* (big-time traffickers) and their gangs, of girls laughingly grabbed at gunpoint from their boyfriends in discotheques. Pedestrians were liable to be shot from moving cars for target practice (which was probably why the model policemen suffered). Fear kept everybody silent.

The rough justice meted out by the gentlemen of the Cali cartel was recounted by a landowner near the town of Sevilla in the north of the valley. In early 1994, said the landowner, thieves were foolish enough to steal a drug trafficker's 1,500-kilogram prize bull, slaughter it and sell off the meat. Over the next twenty days, fifteen bodies belonging to the thieves, the owner of the slaughterhouse and the local butchers who had bought the joints of the carcass were discovered in their doorways with their hands cut off and their eyes scooped out. Everybody knew who ordered the massacre, but in public nobody uttered a word.

Yet it was money as much as fear that protected the cartel leaders. Their cash did more than purchase the loyalty of Cali's individual policemen. Allegedly, the salaried bribes came with the jobs themselves. 'All our information was that the chief downwards got something,' said one US official. 'A new person in a post received the payment automatically.' The DEA considered the Search Force itself, which was a separate body from the local police, so corrupt and incompetent that it hardly worked with it. Cali as a whole was beholden to the cartel. Cocaine money was simply pouring into the department's economy, mainly through construction. In 1992 the regional building federation, Camacol, reported that development permits were granted for 36 per cent more land in the Valle del Cauca than in the previous year. Local cement supplies failed to keep up with demand. In 1993, when property prices rose by a third, licensed construction increased by a further 18 per cent. Meanwhile, it was reported that more than 150 construction workers were murdered in July 1994; as with Escobar, it was suspected that most had been killed on the orders of drug traffickers as a security device after building their secret hideouts.

As in the rest of Colombia, the drugs mafia were believed to be at the heart of the construction boom; their intermediaries invested the cash with agencies which in turn pumped it into dozens of high-rise, residential and commercial developments. According to a Cali cartel source, 'Hernán', the *mágicos* were behind at least a third of the building in Cali; a spokeswoman from Camacol refused to comment. Apart from their role in the construction boom, which itself hugely boosted all other sectors, the traffickers also expanded available credit. Alberto Ramos, a lecturer at Cali's Universidad Libre, wrote in late 1993: 'Although the banking system is not theirs, the *caleño* peripheral-banking market is the most powerful in the country; they have created their own financial companies, managing about 150,000 million pesos [$190 million] a year in loans.'

The Search Force headquarters was perched on a dusty mound in Cali's foothills, to the west of the city. Formerly a police cavalry training camp and boasting a swimming-pool surrounded by palm-trees, its appearance and atmosphere was more that of a country club than of a crack police commando unit hunting down some of the world's most wanted criminals. The Search Force was much smaller than its Medellín counterpart and, during the eight months since its inception in January 1994, its senior officers said that it had carried out a mere 200 raids on offices, houses, flats and ranches. In the eighteen months that Pablo Escobar was on the run from the Cathedral, the Medellín force carried out more than 11,000. The radio/telephone tracing and triangulation equipment that finally tracked Escobar down had not yet been sent to Cali, and Colombia's rewards for information leading to the capture of the Rodríguez Orejuelas and their colleagues varied between a derisory $125,000 and $250,000 – compared with the several million US dollars it offered for the leader of the Medellín cartel.

A police colonel leading the Search Force, whose telephone rang only twice in two hours – and who received just three messages during that time – said: 'The rewards are so small that we never get any information from informants. We receive no collaboration, nobody fights with us. There is a lack of political will at all levels.' So low was the level of preparedness that when his general telephoned, the colonel could not even find a pen to take notes. The DEA claimed that the main reason for the lack of informants was that the Search Force was riddled with informers.

*

The music thumped into the brain. Not for nothing was the discotheque called the Auditorium. Cali's bright young things were throbbing with cocaine, rum and salsa music. Beautiful women with long hair and tiny skirts thronged the galleries running along the sides of the hall; men were fewer, and more casually dressed, although no less expensively. The wide dance floor at the end was dwarfed by a video screen above showing frenzied, kaleidoscopic images. Full moons exploded into stars which sucked viewers into their orbit and then raced off with them into infinity. If you wanted to keep your balance, it was best to look the other way.

'The nightmare is only seen by those with their eyes open,' somebody was saying. Except that the voice belonged elsewhere, not to that time and place where the combination of music, sex, money and drugs drove out reason and reduced a person's moral willpower to pulp. Not to that ecstatic, mass state of pleasure enslavement in which the spoilsports who clung on to their senses ran every risk of being bulldozed by their peers. No, the voice belonged to an outsider; to somebody able to afford the luxury of peeping over the precipice without being propelled over the edge by the gravitational pull of a lifetime's compromises. In that dark, heaving and contented discotheque, a microcosm of the nightmare, you shut your eyes. Or joined in and jumped over the edge.

My host, a slim and handsome homosexual with immaculate fingernails who worked for the cocaine organization of *El Chupeta*, gestured towards a lively but not particularly eye-catching girl who had just taken a seat at a nearby table with a group of friends. It was the daughter of José Santacruz Londoño, the main partner of the Rodríguez Orejuelas and allegedly the blood-thirstiest – as well as the most educated – of the trio. In spite of her father being wanted by police on at least three continents for murder and drugs trafficking, and in spite of him being one of the cartel kingpins supposedly hunted by the Search Force in Cali, Milena not only remained a social starlet enjoying the courtship of her friends: she also felt sufficiently secure to spend his money in public with no fear of coming under surveillance that would lead back to him.

WHITEWASH FOR THE WORLD (1994-)

'The Search Force has changed our lives very little,' said my companion 'Hernan', whose job was to arrange the secret merry-go-round of apartments enabling senior members in his organization to remain at least a dozen steps ahead of their pursuers. 'Although the big bosses themselves no longer go out in public much, it is no problem for them to get around and to throw parties at their homes.' Hernán did not, however, recommend that I introduced myself to Milena. 'It would create a bad atmosphere and we wouldn't leave here alone,' he muttered, pursing his lips. The Auditorium was his lair, nevertheless. Unlike others, we were waved through at the entrance without being frisked for guns.

Cocaine could be bought discreetly over the bar – by known customers such as Hernan – at about $5 a gram. Although everybody knew that most people were stoned on it, snorting the white powder which had injected the city and the country with more money than any other single product in the last decade was still restricted to the lavatories. It was a question of image. Neither friends, nor the proprietors, nor the police were thereby compromised. They could all simulate blissful ignorance and hence let the mutually profitable show go on. What the eye did not see the law did not touch. Behaviour was distorted and compartmentalized – as in any efficient criminal organization – for the protection of the perceived common good. Hypocrisy and deceit had become everyday norms in defence of a trade that was internationally vilified.

Hernán was offering me cocaine in a small paper packet. Did I want some? The music hammered away and where once there had been stars now there were giant tulips leaping above the dancers' heads. In that place, in that time, in that company, the temptation was irresistible. Having studiously avoided the drug in Colombia out of principle and out of disgust for the bloodshed and corruption around it, snorting cocaine in the market's Mecca seemed at least a semi-legitimate investigative exercise. I took the packet and went downstairs, trying to look as little like a gringo as possible. The men's lavatories were spacious, clean and uncrowded. There was a queue for the cubicles, but people emerged quickly enough, sniffing to clear their nasal passages or wiping their moustaches. My turn; I shut the door, tipped a few specks of cocaine on to a coin, and inhaled. The blast of springtime was a cross between taking a cold plunge and a shot of whisky. It was immediately exhilarating; 'delicioso' as Hernán would say. But I did not repeat it.

Making my way back upstairs, where Milena's party had by now disappeared, it occurred to me that apart from the legal status there was only one important difference between shots of whisky and snorts of cocaine. While the former substance was an old and trusted friend, the latter was a cultural upstart. Both were psychologically addictive. However, whereas my education had prepared me for alcohol – and warned about the dangers of excess and alcoholism – pot and cocaine had been satanized. Why?

It was not just because they were illegal. 'Drugs' were associated with unconventional, rebellious and even politically subversive – i.e. left-wing or anarchist – behaviour. In the 1960s and 1970s, First World societies experienced tremendous cultural, political and philosophical torment. That era of deep self-questioning, overshadowed by the Cold War with the Soviet Union, was embodied by drugs and rock music. The middle-aged middle classes were scared. At the same time, the mood of excitement, uncertainty and self-analysis was intrinsically dangerous; it led weaker or unhappier people down dark alleys from which they did not always have the strength to return. Too often, they deliberately self-destructed. Although it was the nastier illicit substances – crack-cocaine and heroin – that usually helped them to jump the wall, there were many other ways, alcohol among them. After the first publicized cases, drug deaths were essentially suicides: the victims chose to ignore the red lights knowing they would crash. And the death of an 'addict' seemed to mark the triumph of middle-aged, middle-class values. It provided simple, I-told-you-so reassurance as well as a finger-wagging warning to others to keep to the straight and narrow. In reality, however, the death of an 'addict' marked the failure of those values. Demonizing drugs was a way of deflecting and reversing the blame. By the 1980s, the demon had whipped the main First World governments into a frenzy of action to stem the flow of cocaine and heroin from Latin America, the Middle East and Asia. In countries such as Colombia, where the income from cocaine was as fundamental as the rule of law was feeble, and which had the bloodiest modern history on the continent, the inevitable had occurred. The trade in the illicit white powder had protected itself. In the process, that sparkling dust I had just snorted through my nose had wreaked unimaginable death and corruption.

'It's a question of atmosphere,' said Hernán, looking to the future. 'Pablo created a bad atmosphere by killing politicians [the police and innocent civilians went unmentioned]. Here, we work with them. We want people to be discreet, no showing off with jewellery and flashy cars, no messy bodies in the streets, you understand?'

It was the classic Cali cartel line, denying all responsibility for the terrorist war whose fruits of victory were ultimately theirs. 'But is the money worth the violence?' I asked. 'Does the law itself matter to anybody?'

'*Hombre*, there is a death culture, you must understand that. If somebody betrays you, you send for them to be *quebrado* [broken]; it's normal. You cannot complain to the police, so what else do you do, how do you maintain your power?'

A few days later, a DEA agent gave a graphic description of how Hernán's boss, *El Chupeta*, habitually maintained *his* power. 'He sat there while one of his guys hacked a man's penis off and stuffed it into the victim's mouth, in front of the man's wife. His limbs were then chopped off, from the fingers and hands upwards, until he died.' While Escobar flaunted his corpses, the Cali traffickers hid them. Often, the bodies were reportedly cut up into small pieces with chain-saws, before being thrown into the river Cauca, swept downstream and thrown up on the banks to be eaten by wild dogs and Colombia's ubiquitous vultures. At other times, the bodies were simply buried on the traffickers' vast estates. 'We had information that one trafficker in the north of the Valle del Cauca used to bring poor people on to his ranch, release them and hunt them down with guns like wild animals,' said the agent, as an afterthought.

'The cartel's political penetration in Cali is total,' said another DEA agent. 'If there is an exception, I haven't seen it – in the whole of the Valle del Cauca.' Among the local politicians connected with the cocaine traffickers was Manuel Francisco Becerra, a board member of the América soccer club for several years under the vice presidency of Miguel Rodríguez Orejuela, whose family were the club's main shareholders. After being governor of Valle del Cauca and Colombia's auditor general, Becerra was considering running for the presidency in 1998. There was also Armando Holguín, a teenage friend of the Rodríguez Orejuelas in the Obrero district, who was elected to the Senate in 1994.

The intrusion of politicians intent on defending the interests of the Cali drug traffickers was by no means discreet. In early 1993, a small group of politicians reportedly visited the director general of the national police, General Miguel Antonio Gómez Padilla, to ask why he was upsetting Cali's tranquillity by molesting honest, law-abiding citizens. The general, whose force had begun to refocus its efforts against the Cali cartel, smartly kicked them out of his office. Among the group, allegedly, was a former friend and political patron of Escobar's, an immensely powerful Liberal congressman who later narrowly failed to be elected president of the Senate.

Congress itself reflected the power of the drug traffickers. While some Colombian journalists claimed privately that up to half of the 264 congressmen owed their seats at least partly to cocaine money – the trade's aim being to dominate the key parliamentary commissions – the DEA's estimate was nearer three quarters. Ernesto Samper, the president who succeeded César Gaviria in August 1994, insisted that the number of congressmen backed by drug traffickers was no higher than six. The Senate's tolerance towards the trade became strikingly evident in November 1993, when most of the senators abandoned their chamber in order to torpedo a bill regulating the confiscation and inheritance of drug-traffickers' assets. The Senate had already approved an amendment effectively gutting a law against illicit enrichment. Other signs of the way the wind was blowing among Colombia's legislative and judicial institutions included the Constitutional Court's legalization of cocaine and marijuana consumption in May 1994.

Most galling of all to the north Americans were the actions of the chief prosecutor, Gustavo de Greiff. Not only did de Greiff provoke US anger by coming out in favour of legalizing the drugs trade, but they also believed he was kowtowing to the leaders of the Cali cartel. A cartel source who worked for El Chupeta – reputed by police to be one of the youngest, richest and most violent of the traffickers, and a close friend of Iván Urdinola – endorsed the DEA claim that de Greiff was keeping to a deal. 'The chief prosecutor worked with and used the cartel in hunting down Pablo Escobar,' said the source, speaking over a meat sandwich off a palm-lined boulevard in central Cali. 'So, it was understood he would not go after them.' A former, senior member of the public prosecutor's office in Cali added: 'No attempt was made to chase the traffickers there. Everybody knew who and even where they were, but we were ordered to leave them alone.'

Although Gustavo de Greiff denied he had ever met the Rodríguez Orejuelas, the chief prosecutor's signature allegedly appeared alongside Gilberto Rodríguez Orejuela's in documents relating to an airline of which they were co-owners in 1987. According to a lawyer involved with the airline in Villavicencio – a strategic centre for cocaine flights in the Llanos Orientales or eastern plains – de Greiff had a minor stake in the airline before and after it was taken over by the Chess Player. 'What sickened me most was not de Greiff's business relationship, which might simply have been coincidental,' said the lawyer, over a glass of *aguardiente* in his modest Bogotá home. 'It was listening to the man then hailed as the moral saviour of the country lie about the connection.'

In January 1994, de Greiff issued certificates amounting to safe-conduct passes to five Cali cartel leaders, including *El Chupeta* and Pacho Herrera, claiming that there was not enough evidence to arrest them. The following month, an increasingly irate US Justice Department stopped sharing evidence with de Greiff's office after it emerged that some of the witnesses were being threatened. In April, the US State Department sent a protest note to the Colombian government after de Greiff interfered on behalf of a Medellín cartel *sicario* being tried in New York for the bombing of the Avianca airplane that killed 107 people, including some US citizens. The following month, after publicly referring to the Rodríguez Orejuelas as *Doctor* Gilberto and *Don* Miguel, de Greiff declared there were no warrants out for the former's arrest. He was immediately contradicted by the attorney general. National Police files showed that at the time there were a total of seven warrants for the brothers – on charges ranging from drugs trafficking to terrorism and homicide. De Greiff's battle with the United States touched off Colombian nationalism, which was already being fomented after embarrassing claims made before a US Congress committee in April by a former member of the Medellín cartel. The trafficker, Gabriel Taboada, said that former presidents Belisario Betancur and Julio César Turbay Ayala – whom he referred to by a nickname, 'the dancer of Cúcuta', alluding to a scandalous party in that city attended by Turbay while he was president – both received funds from drugs traffickers.

The two main contenders in the 1994 presidential elections, whose second round was in June, were Ernesto Samper and Andrés Pastrana. The former had been present when a presidential campaign donation was recieved from the Medellín cartel by Alfonso López Michelsen in 1982; Samper was the campaign treasurer. In October 1993, Samper was warned by the US assistant Secretary of State for International Narcotics Matters, Robert Gelbard, that the US was worried by indications that Samper's campaign was receiving funds from the Cali drug lords. Unsolicited or not, the cartel's support for Samper's candidature was obvious in Cali. 'The cartel had a three-line whip out to get him elected,' said a foreign banker. 'They were picking up people in lorries to take them to vote.' (The election run-off was close: Samper won with a margin of just 1.7 per cent.) A cartel source admitted: 'We wanted Samper to win because he had been pro-legalization and said there would not be another drugs war.' Even Escobar's former henchman, 'Popeye', was pro-Samper: 'He has never confronted the mafia, Samper is very intelligent,' he said. 'Perhaps he will do it once in power, but not beforehand in order to avoid problems for himself.' In Cali, Samper propaganda signboards were posted all over properties whose real owners were known to be the Rodríguez Orejuelas. His name featured alongside that of Armando Holguín, the teenage friend of the cartel leaders who was elected a Liberal senator. 'There was loads of cartel cash going into Samper's campaign,' said my cartel source, 'the Rodríguez Orejuelas only denied it because they did not want to damage him.'

Pastrana, meanwhile, was compromised by the arrest of a cousin in Miami. The cousin, Gustavo Pastrana, was allegedly laundering drugs money which he told an undercover DEA agent that he was sending to Colombia for Andrés Pastrana's electoral campaign. The cousin was Colombia's councillor in its Uruguayan embassy and a political nominee of Andrés Pastrana's during the government of President Gaviria.

Drugs were hardly mentioned in Colombia during the presidential campaign – during which one of the main candidates attended the birthday party of Miguel Rodríguez Orejuela's eldest daughter, María Fernanda, in late August 1993, according to another guest there. Even a curious meeting at the home of Alberto Giraldo, the journalist and political lackey famed for acting as the Rodríguez Orejuelas' public relations manager and who had an extraordinary capacity to gather together Colombia's most influential statesmen, attracted little attention. Giraldo was the sycophant who openly proclaimed himself the intermediary of the Cali cartel leaders and who was married to the sister of Juan José Bellini, the head of the national soccer league association and a long-time associate of Miguel Rodríguez Orejuela on the board of the América team. Although it was common knowledge that the Rodríguez Orejuelas were Giraldo's principal meal ticket, Colombia's leading politicians ate out of his hand.

Giraldo's flat in Bogotá was where General Maza Márquez, who came fifth in the election's first round – the general was also beaten by the one-legged, former M-19 guerrilla leader, Antonio Navarro, and a self-styled 'witch', Regina Betancourt – pledged his second-round electoral support to Samper. Although the meeting place was strange enough, it assumed far greater significance two days after Pastrana – whose father, a former president, was also revealed to have recently attended a lunch there hosted by Giraldo – narrowly lost the election. Cassette recordings were made public of several telephone conversations between Giraldo and the Rodríguez Orejuela brothers. In the tapes, Samper, and particularly General Maza Márquez, were among those implicated in apparently having received campaign funds from the Rodríguez Orejuelas in a political culture famous for its marketing of votes and favours.

The exchanges were oblique and idiosyncratic, the recording quality excellent.

'I spoke with Maza,' said Giraldo. 'That has improved dramatically and after what I told him, hmmm? But I hope you give it to me in cash.'

'*Tranquilo*,' replied Gilberto Rodríguez Orejuela.

In a separate conversation, after Giraldo enthused about 'the thing with Miguel', Gilberto Rodríguez Orejuela responded: 'With Miguel? You mean with Maza?'

'Yes,' said Giraldo. A little later, Giraldo added: 'But I want to tell you that I spoke with the man . . . the trip to Santa Marta was very good . . . everybody was there. Miguel called me this morning to say to me, "About that situation with *La Prensa* [the Pastrana family newspaper, which had denounced Giraldo's meeting with the general] they are sons of bitches."'

Although the general later proclaimed his innocence – thumping his chest as the man who had been targeted by successive car bombs during the war against the Medellín cartel and declaring that nobody else in the world had combated drugs trafficking with as much fortitude as he had – his reputation was ruined.

Debate focused, however, on the references to the campaign of Samper himself.

'How goes the thing with Samper, *hombre?*' Miguel Rodríguez Orejuela asked Giraldo.

'Well, everything depends on you. What a strange thing, no?' the journalist answered.

The pair went on to discuss Santiago Medina, the treasurer of Samper's campaign, who, according to Rodríguez Orejuela, had been to visit them.

'Look,' said Giraldo, 'the reality is that they need 5 billion [$6.25 million], of which they have got hold of two. They need 3 [$3.75 million] from you.'

Rodríguez Orejuela said matter-of-factly: 'It's already there. That's dealt with.'

Other senior Liberal figures referred to included César Villegas, a personal and business friend of Samper's who had been investigated for illicit enrichment after working for the civil air authority and who had intervened on behalf of Gilberto Rodríguez Orejuela with a justice minister designate in 1991.

Andrés Pastrana's campaign did not escape unscathed. In a conversation between the most uncouth of the Rodríguez Orejuela brothers, Jorge Eliécer, and a slavish simpleton named Omar, a drunken Rodríguez Orejuela declared: 'That gonorrhea [Pastrana] is a prostitute and is beginning to talk about hot money and I don't know what . . . because we didn't give him one peso and he sent a request for it. You know what? He was simply told, "I'm siding with the other Señor [Samper], we are not even giving you shit. You are going to lose."'

In publicly disseminating the first cassette – four were eventually released, apparently by a group of police officers frustrated by the silence and corruption of their superiors – Pastrana incurred the wrath of a nation. Colombia was once again in the dock. Its international reputation was at stake, its president-elect crippled from the start. Samper's photograph featured in *Time* magazine with the headline 'Narco-candidate?' and a quote from a DEA source condemning the US and Colombian governments for failing to act in spite of being aware of the tapes: 'Nobody did a thing. They allowed this grotesque parody [of an election] to happen. Everybody, including the government of the United States, is participating in this cover-up.'

While a US congressman said that 'this guy [Samper] has a long history of connections with the traffickers', Robert Gelbard himself, the US assistant Secretary of State for International Narcotics Matters, warned that, if the accusations were true, they 'would obviously have the most serious effect on . . . any kind of bilateral relationship'. US congressional officials were also reported to have been advised that the CIA believed Samper knew his campaign managers had not only asked for but had received money from the Cali cartel leaders.

According to the United Press International news agency, based on interviews with US officials, 'the government of Bill Clinton concluded that the president elect of Colombia, Ernesto Samper, accepted more than $3.5 million dollars in contributions to his electoral campaign from powerful drugs traffickers'. Meanwhile, the *Miami Herald* reported that a DEA informant identified as María, who had worked for the Cali traffickers, said that she had 'organized a meeting in 1990 at the request of Samper, between him and two leaders of the Cali cartel, Miguel Rodríguez Orejuela and Gilberto Rodríguez Orejuela, in which Samper received six cases which contained $800,000 in cash'. According to the article, María claimed that Samper had promised to fight to overturn extradition in return for the campaign money. Samper threatened to sue the newspaper. Without retracting its story, the *Miami Herald* turned against the US government and demanded it came up with more evidence.

Joe Toft, the head of the DEA in Colombia, explained the DEA's own dilemma in releasing more evidence: 'A lot of information is highly classified and its release would be breaking US law. The tapes are a significant piece of evidence against Samper but only one piece among many.' One of those pieces was the pocket telephone book belonging to Gilberto Rodríguez Orejuela, discovered in his Madrid apartment when he was arrested in November 1984. The book contained Ernesto Samper's name and number; just above it was the home number of Alberto Santo-fimio, and above that the number of the wife of José Santacruz Londoño, Amparo. Samper's details also appeared in a Rodríguez Orejuela diary seized by police in the Valle del Cauca in early 1992. A senior member of the US State Department said: 'Relations with Colombia were heading for a breakdown. It is better to have an imperfect co-operation in fighting drugs than none at all. We cannot stop Samper being president but we'll sure be watching what he does.'

Gustavo de Greiff, the chief prosecutor whose daughter Mónica was initially Samper's campaign treasurer and had recently been named Samper's adviser on international affairs, scotched any formal investigation on the grounds that the tapes were edited, that they were recorded illegally, and that they did not constitute proof of any wrongdoing. 'The tapes were made, I think, to foster an obscure plot against the country,' he said. 'It is obvious that neither campaign accepted funds.' The only crime committed, declared de Greiff, had been to tap the telephones. In other words, in their vain attempt to expose drug-related corruption by intercepting telephone calls illicitly in order to avoid security leaks, it was only the police who had committed the crime. De Greiff himself was mentioned on the tapes; an apparent reference to him was linked to a discussion about a bribe.

So far as several of the politicians apparently incriminated by the tape recordings were concerned, Alberto Giraldo and the Rodríguez Orejuelas had simply become engaged in a massive case of mistaken identity. The conspirators must have been discussing other people with the same name, they shrugged or fulminated. Santiago Medina doubted the tape existed (after de Greiff's decision, Samper's treasurer was judicially correct) before claiming that, in the following exchange, 'four' was 'a number that [could] mean many things, four envoys, four letters, four messages':

Giraldo: 'I am going to meet Santiago Medina now ... They are counting on that money today.'

Rodríguez Orejuela: 'We've already sent them four, haven't we?

Giraldo: 'Yes, four.'

The blatant inconsistencies between some of the evidence on the tapes and the explanations of those involved were glossed over by the media, politicians and business leaders alike, who instead preferred to trumpet the virtues of Ernesto Samper and Colombian democracy.

'Every single donation was scrutinized by our campaign,' claimed Samper himself. 'It is safe to say that I took the strongest efforts in the history of our country to ensure no contributions were received from drugs traffickers.' In order to prove his point, the forty-three-year-old president-elect offered up for inspection the campaign's accounts, an offer which he reiterated again and again.

Few commentators ventured to suggest in public that, in the event of the Rodríguez Orejuelas' having funded the Liberals, it was hardly likely that their names would appear in the campaign books. After all, neither was there any record of the Medellín cartel's payment to López Michelsen when Samper was his campaign treasurer twelve years earlier. 'The truth is that Andrés Pastrana and Ernesto Samper are immune to that sordid world [of drug traffickers],' concluded *Semana* magazine, as it joined in the national conspiracy of humbug among the Colombian élite. The conspiracy was broken only by a handful of figures. Among them was the former justice minister, Enrique Parejo, who condemned those who were 'more interested in showing solidarity with the country than with establishing the truth'.

The outgoing president, César Gaviria, had been handed the cassette by Pastrana on the eve of the second round of the election. As with the video showing Pablo Escobar's lawyer bribing a member of the constituent assembly, initially he kept silent. Once the cassette became public two nights after Samper's victory, Gaviria moved on to the attack – against those who were damaging the country's reputation. 'When Colombia's image is tarnished abroad, the cartels triumph,' he said. 'When our political leadership receives attacks on its credibility, the cartels triumph.' Two weeks later, the perfidious slur on anybody who dared to question the integrity of the country's political élite was followed by an intemperate harangue against the 'hypocrisy' of 'the international community'. Gaviria contended: 'No country; no government, no official; nobody has the moral authority to question us, to look us in the eyes and tell us that we do not do enough in the fight against the drug cartels ... it seems ironic that they want to apply to us the toughness that they are not capable of applying to their own cartels, to their own manufacturers of arms and precursor chemicals or to their own banks.' While ignoring that the penalties and controls in Europe and the USA for drug taking, drug dealing, money laundering and arms exporting were considerably tougher than in Colombia – and were generally applied a good deal more stringently – these were the words of the man who had orchestrated the legislation whereby the Ochoa brothers, the main colleagues of Pablo Escobar, would be free in two years' time.

Muzzling any criticism at home was reinforced by a warning from the minister of communications, William Jaramillo – himself once compromised by a photograph showing him to have flown aboard one of Escobar's private aircraft – who reminded radio and television stations that since 1993 it was illegal to broadcast interviews with drug traffickers. The warning was clearly aimed at the broadcasts of any further cassettes. Meanwhile, a prestigious television news programme, QAP, of which a cousin of

Samper's was a senior editor, had granted several minutes to the rantings of a person claiming to represent a group called Death to the Cali Cartel. The man threatened to kill, among others, Samper and de Greiff. He claimed to represent up to 180 armed men. Not only did some members of QAP believe it was a put-up job by the Liberals. But, when somebody suggested the programme might be fined if the rantings were broadcast, the response was, according to one insider: 'It doesn't matter, it will distract attention from the narco-cassettes.'

Perhaps the most extraordinary whitewash was that promoted by *El Espectador*, which by now was a shadow of its former self after falling under the influence of one of Samper's main financiers, the international business magnate, Julio Mario Santodomingo. An opinion poll asked Colombians if they thought the country was a 'narco-democracy' – a word invented by US officials, with Colombia in mind, to describe a state whose democracy was dominated by drugs traffickers. While 51 per cent of those questioned replied 'No', as many as 43 per cent responded 'Yes'. In Cali itself, the answer 'Yes' was given by a resounding 87 per cent. *El Espectador*'s poll headline was: 'Colombia is not a narco-democracy.'

Under pressure from Colombia's anti-drugs police, who worked quite separately from both the local police and the Search Force set up in early 1994, the Cali cartel had moved most of its cocaine laboratories out of the Valle del Cauca. The laboratories had also been shifted in order to provide window dressing for a surrender deal by between 75 and 100 of the region's major traffickers, led by Gilberto Rodríguez Orejuela. The surrender deal, which was first mooted in mid 1993, was being brokered for the state by the chief prosecutor, de Greiff. Under a final draft agreement, Gilberto Rodríguez Orejuela and Iván Urdinola's brother, Julio Fabio, faced just four years in jail as well as a string of benefits; no mass surrender was mentioned. The pair promised to abandon the drugs trade and demanded that the state recognize the contribution they had made 'to the security forces in the capture and death of several traffickers linked to the Medellín cartel'. Reportedly, the initiative was only frustrated, in March 1994, by the political ambitions of President Gaviria, who was relying on US support for his candidature as president of the Organisation of American States.

In what was seen as an attempt to placate the US government, which gave Samper a private dressing-down in New York on his way to Europe and delayed its courtesy message of congratulation to the president-elect for more than three weeks, Search Force raids were stepped up on the Cali cartel's homes, ranches and offices in the Valle del Cauca. During the raids, cartel payrolls were discovered featuring the names of more than 100 members of Cali's metropolitan and secret police. The defence minister, Fernando Botero, announced that half of Cali's police force had been punished because of the disclosures. (Fernando Botero's father, of the same name, was Colombia's most famous artist, a *paisa* acclaimed for his paintings mocking the newly moneyed middle classes, whom he depicted as fat, childlike and vulgar.) Fifty-four officers were fired. Among those implicated was the chief of operations, Lieutenant Colonel Julio César Rodríguez. Another payroll featured Eduardo Mestre, a former Conservative senator already embroiled in the scandal of the cassettes, a former auditor general, Rodolfo González, and a former president of the Chamber of Deputies, Norberto Morales, who had fought against extradition. The army was also compromised: a list of nineteen officers was found on a retired major, Guillermo Pallomari, who was alleged to be a former chief of security for the Rodríguez Orejuelas currently administering their army bribes.

However, Pallomari was freed a day after his capture. His release followed hot on the heels of that of a cousin of Iván Urdinola's, Héctor Jairo Urdinola, who had recently been caught with 100 kilograms of cocaine. That same week, General Octavio Vargas, the director general of the national police, was shunned while visiting the DEA in Washington after it emerged that on the latest cassette to enter circulation he, too, appeared to be linked with the Cali cartel. Conversations between Giraldo and the Rodríguez Orejuelas indicated their proximity to a senior member of the security forces named Benetín, which according to the DEA was the cartel's pseudonym for General Vargas. The identity behind the pseudonym was hardly disputed. Once again, however, in spite of detailed discussion regarding the handing over to Benetín of a 'packet' and about what was required of him in return – an end to the police raids 'until January or February' – it was said there was no proof that the 'packet' had actually been received by the general. His snubbing by the head of the DEA, Thomas Constantine had, understandably, caught Colombian nationalism on the raw. As with Samper, the country rallied furiously behind him.

'It was the biggest fuck-up the DEA ever made in its handling of relations with a foreign police department,' said the DEA's Colombia chief, Joe Toft, who subsequently resigned from the DEA. 'The Colombian police were humiliated. They did not care about the truth, they wanted to protect the institution. That is why there is no hope in really doing something here. But I could work with Vargas. Guilty or not, he is nothing compared to Samper. Vargas is just a small player. The new president's the real issue.' In Toft's opinion, Samper was 'dirty and received the cash'.

Two months later, in September, Samper's government re-affirmed General Vargas in his post; sent the DEA's preferred senior police officer, General Rosso José Serrano, to a desk job in Washington; retired the chief of the DIJIN secret police, General Jairo Rodríguez, who was held responsible – wrongly – for the cassettes; replaced the latter with the colonel who had led the Search Force against Escobar allegedly with the direct assistance of the Cali cartel, Hugo Martínez Póveda, and promoted to sub-director of the national police General Guillermo Diettes, a former chief of Cali's metropolitan police force. So brazenly corrupt were the Cali police under Diettes that a retired army captain arrested by the chief prosecutor's regional office and alleged to be a key cartel security chief was switched for somebody else while being held in a police cell. The retired captain, Jorge Rojas, was young, bearded and white; the stand-in who was presented by police at the public prosecutor's office the following day was elderly, beardless and black. As sub-director of the national police, Diettes became responsible for the Cali cartel Search Force. Joe Toft said: 'Every cop in Colombia knows how powerful the cartel kingpins are, and how dangerous. How can one expect the police or any law enforcement entity to go after the guys knowing full well that the government will not stand by them, that the political will is completely lacking?'

Samper's vice president, Humberto de la Calle, was also compromised through his wife, Rosalba, according to a French organization called the Geopolitical Observatory of Drugs. In June 1994 the organization's director, Alain Labrousse, accused de la Calle's wife of conducting illegal business with the Cali cartel while she was secretary general and, later, director of the government medical authority, Cajanal, between June 1988 and March 1991. An investigation by a Cajanal commission supported by the state security police, DAS, concluded that during her management Cajanal had sold medicines that were out-of-date, fake, over-priced or non-existent. Not only was it claimed that eighteen of the pharmaceutical laboratories supplying Cajanal were fictitious, but that they had also imported large quantities of cocaine precursor chemicals through the port of Buenaventura in the Valle del Cauca. Most of the cheques paid by Cajanal to these laboratories were said to have been endorsed by the same person. Authentic medicines were bought mainly from the Rodríguez Orejuelas' chain of discount chemists, Drogas La Rebaja. A reported request from the investigating commission that Humberto de la Calle, the minister of interior, should resign in order for witnesses not to feel intimidated, was turned down. In August 1992 the commission's lawyer, Isabel Romero, was shot dead by *sicarios*. A few weeks later, the prosecutor in the attorney general's office in charge of the case, Rocío Velez, was also gunned down with his driver and bodyguards. Humberto de la Calle, who as interior minister had contributed to the cover-up over the video tape showing Escobar's lawyer bribing a member of the Constituent Assembly, claimed the French report was 'delirious'. The case against de la Calle's wife was closed by de Greiff's office in July 1994 after his election as vice-president.

Although with Pablo Escobar's death Colombia had hoped to expiate much of its past by removing the central protagonist of the drugs war, drugs trafficking has flourished in the country like never before. According to United Nations estimates, Colombia has overtaken Bolivia as the second biggest supplier of coca paste after Peru. René Saa-Vidal, the director of the UN's Drug Control Programme in Colombia, said in September 1994: 'There are at least 60,000 hectares of coca plantations here, of which a fifth is large scale, commercial production, and the coca is now top quality.' If regional agricultural authorities were to be believed, the true area was more than 86,000 hectares. Both the local market in coca paste and the international market in cocaine were saturated. The price of coca base fluctuated around $1,000 a kilogram in Colombia and the wholesale price of cocaine in the main US cities hovered around a mere $10,000. These figures compared with $19,000 and $55,000 respectively in 1982, according to DEA figures. Unlike in the 1980s, when the international price jumped after local trade setbacks, Escobar's death altered it not a jot. Market size, diversification and sophistication appeared to have rendered it immune. At the same time, marijuana and heroin production were booming in Colombia – and causing so much deforestation that there was drought on the La Guajira peninsula and, in the Huila department, an avalanche following an earth tremor – which resulted in the death of about 1,500 Páez Indians.

Similarly, Colombia's violence and corruption was as rampant as before. In Medellín itself, the number of murders had dropped since the peak of 7,074 in 1993. Between January and August 1994, the murder rate was about 10 per cent lower than over the same period in 1993, according to the city morgue; however, it appeared to be shooting up in the latter half of the year. In Cali, however, homicides in the first half of 1994 increased by nearly 6 per cent. Nationally, the annual murder rate in 1994 was running at about 85 per 100,000 people. Colombia was still the most violent peace-time country in the world; the rate was more than three times higher than the runner-up, Brazil.

It was a country so saturated by violence that its long-distance buses played the most gruesome video films imaginable – albeit made mostly in the USA – in front of passengers of all ages. By way of celebrating Colombia's historic 5–0 soccer victory over Argentina in Buenos Aires in late 1993, 98 people were killed in the brawls at home; the atmosphere was electric with drunken aggression. Human life held so little value that a taxi driver would shoot a passenger over a 30 cent fare disagreement: because of the 'insult'. Ransom-kidnapping was commonplace, too. According to foreign security specialists, the incidence in Colombia of the crime in which Escobar cut his teeth continued to be the highest in the world – more than 1500 a year, about half of which were carried out by guerrillas.

The cultural and endemic nature of Colombian violence ensured that its perpetrators enjoyed extraordinary impunity. Its criminal justice system was so feeble that neither Rodríguez Gacha nor Escobar were ever convicted for drugs trafficking in Colombia. Hence, it was hardly likely that the country's political and economic leaders would be effectively punished for any wrong doings of theirs. The national planning director, Armando Montenegro, disclosed in April 1994 that the chances of a criminal not being punished were 97 per cent and that a judge issued an average of only fifteen sentences a year. And according to the prisons authority, between 1992 and September 1994, one prisoner escaped on average every forty-eight hours.

The judicial system appeared to reflect public and government tolerance. Few were bothered by the fact that within a handful of years the Ochoa brothers, Popeye and Iván Urdinola – criminals whom everybody knew, even if the judges were ignorant, had killed or participated in the ordering of the killings of hundreds of people – would all be released from jail because of plea bargaining and sentence reductions that made a mockery of the penal system. Few were unduly concerned that the so-called popular militia that were replacing the gangs in Medellín were intimately linked with the guerrilla groups – and that their pacts with the government handed official power to groups whose loose and jaded left-wing ideology was mainly a cloak for extortion. Few, indeed, were troubled by the murder of street children by policemen and shopkeepers, which occasionally caused the briefest of public stirs but little heartache or self-questioning.

Perhaps because of life's very precariousness, the country seemed to suffer from collective amnesia. But perhaps that amnesia also stemmed in some way from a sense of collective guilt. As Colombia's soccer captain, 'Pibe' Valderrama, said after corruption allegations following the surprise early knock-out of his 1994 World Cup side: 'In this country, you have to investigate everyone.'

Looking back over the last two decades, one television journalist in Medellín observed: 'The whole of Antioquia's political class was involved with Escobar until the persecution came. Then, they distanced themselves from him as far as they could.' Too many people wished the past to be forgotten; too many people wanted the present to be smothered, too. People in glasshouses do not throw stones.

In such a climate, and with the new constitution being interpreted in such a way that it fiercely restricted the freedom of a media that was already too closely tied to the politicians, there was scarcely a murmur when former Escobar protectors such as Alberto Santofimio sought the Senate presidency, or when Jorge Mesa, the four-times mayor of Envigado who had worked with Escobar until the very end, stood for the governorship of Antioquia; or when Manuel Francisco Becerra, a close associate of Miguel Rodríguez Orejuela, disclosed his ambitions to stand for the presidency. And, when the former president, Alfonso López Michelsen – who had been described as the godfather of the Medellín cartel, accepted their support and negotiated for them – lectured on Dracula at the mock castle confiscated from the estate of a dead Escobar associate, Camilo Zapata, was anybody struck by the irony? Probably not. This was, after all, a country where, on being advised by recorded message that you had won more than $1,000 in a telephone lottery, you discovered the prize to be a discount burial lot.

While honest judges, prosecutors, police, airport controllers, other public servants and local politicians continued to be threatened and killed by drug traffickers, there was rarely any sense of outrage. How little society cared was demonstrated by how little it sought to punish those culprits as well as those who aided and abetted them in their business. Yet such tolerance was true for all crimes. 'The way in which we [bribe to] get our driver's licences creates the silent consensus for drugs trafficking,' said a prominent lawyer. 'Nobody respects the law – if you can get around it you're right on, that's *malicia indigena* [native cunning].' A researcher at the Centre of Investigation and Popular Education (CINEP) in Bogotá, Ricardo Vargas, asserted: 'Big capital accumulation in Colombia has always been illicit and been accompanied by violence. Drug trafficking is no different.'

Crime bore little social stigma. Where drug traffickers were rejected by society's élite, and excluded from their schools and clubs, it had more to do with their lower-class backgrounds than with the crimes they had committed. By the same token, the Ochoa brothers, who came from a good Antioquia family, retained a certain status there. Horses bred in the family stables, marked with the number eight for 'ocho', could be seen at any weekend *cabalgata* or riding trek. The Ochoas' father, Fabio, whose former stables in Envigado were described as a front for drug dealing by Colonel Augusto Bahamón of the Fourth Brigade, enjoyed great popularity at his new stables and restaurant complex outside Bogotá. Even in Escobar's case, his money had won him acceptance until the going got tough.

It was Colombia's permissiveness that enabled drug trafficking to dig profound social roots in a manner that it had not, for instance, in Peru, where in cases of top-level corruption the newspapers and television news programmes generally clung like dogs to the accused. Quite apart from the prison terms offered to Colombia's biggest, confessed drug traffickers, sentences were so lenient for those who could afford to defend themselves that in April 1994, one former senator, convicted for holding 2,472 identity cards in a ballot-rigging scam, was ordered to plant trees. Meanwhile, in May, a nun who expelled a troublesome pupil from school was sentenced to a week in jail for exceeding her authority and bringing the pupil into disrepute.

The tolerance and the refusal by Colombians to be imposed upon – by the law, by another country, or by anybody – was reflected in a judicial system under which corruption investigations were bogged down almost interminably by legal technicalities and interpretations that went mostly in favour of the accused. When the fourth most senior member of the attorney general's office, Guillermo Villa Alzate, was suspended in September 1993, after compromising tape recordings emerged of conversations between himself and the Rodríguez Orejuelas, his investigators were still stymied a year later following the submission of sixty-four objections to the evidence. That was before the case even reached the public prosecutor. Eventually, however, he did at last lose his job. Colombia's permissiveness was such that the family came before the law: parents, spouses, children, brothers and sisters were not obliged to denounce a crime committed by one of them. The development of mafia families was inevitable.

Gabriel García Márquez, in a seminal speech to mark a report for the president by the Commission of the Wise Ones in July 1994, described Colombia as 'a dense and indecipherable fatherland where the implausible is the only measure of reality.' He added:

The very idea of easy money puts us into a frenzy. We have in the same heart the same quantity of political resentment and historical forgetfulness . . . We have an almost irrational love for life but we kill each other in our longings to live. The author of the most terrible crimes is defeated because of a sentimental weakness . . . We are two countries at the same time: one on paper and one in reality ... In every one of us there cohabits, in the most arbitrary way, justice and impunity; we are fanatics of legalism, but wide awake in our soul we bear an expert, pettyfogging lawyer to cheat the laws without breaking them, or to break them without punishment ... The bad image of the country abroad angers us, but we do not dare to admit that the reality is worse ... We always want a little more than what we have ... much more than within the law, and we get it however we can: even against the law.

Pablo Escobar's personal legacy was estimated at the time of his death by Fernando Brito, the director of DAS, the state security police, to be about $2 billion. However, the properties, aircraft, paper companies, accounts and financial instruments in Colombia and abroad that were known or suspected to belong to him featured mostly in the names of frontmen or *testaferros*. A three-way battle ensued between the state, Escobar's widow and children, and his imprisoned brother, Roberto, to identify the Doctor's assets, to remove them from the *testaferros* and to claim them for themselves.

While the vultures fought over the carrion, Colombia's economy struggled to swallow the huge inflows of foreign cash after the relaxation of exchange controls and an amnesty for repatriated capital in mid 1991. The moves were part of the country's free-market revolution. Oddly enough, one of the Extraditables' demands had been for just such an amnesty on their foreign capital. As with an another demand – that the government should seek to repatriate Colombian prisoners from abroad – both had become a reality. According to one central bank board member, Salomón Kalmanovitz, by the end of 1992 about $4 billion had been brought back into the country, representing nearly 60 per cent of that year's legal exports. In an attempt to dampen the resulting revaluation of the local currency, in 1991 the central bank increased foreign reserves by $1.9 billion – the equivalent of Colombia's entire monetary base. Although the inflows subsequently decreased, their sustained pressure severely depressed the dollar's value, damaging exports and domestic industry while sucking in imports and creating a grave current account deficit. These inflows came over and above the drug money already entering the economy through contraband, the use of false or fictitious invoices for exports and imports, and other means.

In reducing supervision, the reforms in exchange controls were a gift for the drugs traffickers. Apart from the immediate, no-questions-asked amnesty provided for the return of capital previously held illegally by Colombians in foreign accounts, many more channels were opened up through which to launder hard cash in spite of tighter bank restrictions in themselves. Determining how much of the instantly 'repatriated' money derived from cocaine, marijuana and heroin sales was impossible. However, Colombia's economic liberalization, in which the supervision of imports by customs was also effectively abolished, offered a golden opportunity for the fusion of the country's official and underground economies. Illicit, second-floor banks – common throughout the banking system but exemplified by the operations exposed at the BCCI subsidiary in 1987 – folded effortlessly into their mother banks or re-emerged as separate financial entities. Without proper customs supervision, imports and exports invoices were even more effortlessly falsified, and contraband became so endemic it was almost the norm. The sub-director of the National Directorate of Taxes and Customs (DIAN), Mauricio Rodríguez, calculated that $2.4 billion was laundered through contraband between mid 1991 and mid 1993.

By 1994, Colombia's economy had enjoyed such extra-ordinary growth that no fewer than three of its biggest magnates, Luis Carlos Sarmiento (whose Banco de Occidente had been convicted of laundering $411 million), Julio Mario Santodomingo and Carlos Ardila Lülle, were included in the list of US dollar billionaires published in *Forbes* magazine. Although Santodomingo's name had appeared since 1992, the only Colombians previously to feature in the list had been Escobar, Rodríguez Gacha and Jorge Luis Ochoa.

In spite of Colombia being endowed with vast natural resources, entrepreneurial ingenuity and a long tradition of responsible macro-economic management, the country's gathering financial prosperity owed an enormous amount to its drugs trade. The loosely estimated $5 billion a year earned by Colombians through their control over the cocaine business (never mind marijuana and heroin) at home, in Bolivia and Peru, and at much of the street-level in the United States and even Europe, reached every corner of the domestic economy. In 1993, that sum – which was at the higher end of estimates that nevertheless minimized local coca-leaf production and excluded Colombians' dominance in the trade abroad – was the equivalent of 10 per cent of Colombia's GDP and 70 per cent of its legal exports. To pretend that such money could be sterilized from the economy was absurd. So huge were the sums floating around that in 1994 a hard cash offer was made with drugs money – and turned down – for the Colombian subsidiary of a Venezuelan bank. 'Businessmen in illegal psycho-active drugs may easily become the dominant economic group in the country,' wrote Francisco Thoumi, a refreshingly independent-minded Colombian economist. 'Even more: a proportion of the capital generated illegally is actually the property of individuals who are not easily identified with the illegal psycho-active drugs industry, and therefore the industry's real impact on the Colombian economy exceeds that caused by those who may be identified as drugs traffickers now or in the past.'

Yet if Colombia provided the kaleidoscopic mixture of historical, geographical, ethical and cultural conditions for the cocaine trade to prosper in the face of international law and opprobrium, the developed world was more than content to supply the trade with the consumers, the necessary production chemicals and the weapons with which to regulate and protect itself. Bankers mainly in the United States and Europe were also only too happy to mop up the profits. The vast bulk of the earnings from the global drugs trade – estimated at anything from $250 to $500 billion – remained in the First World. It was also the First World governments that benefited from the improved capacity of Colombia, Peru and Bolivia to pay off their foreign debt with the flood of cocaine dollars cheaply soaked up by their central banks. With the opening up of the countries' economies in the early 1990s, foreign investment also poured in, particularly to Colombia and Peru. The investors turned a blind eye to the impact of cocaine on regional growth. During the previous decade, representatives of some European financial institutions had been so eager to attract drug money that they had come asking for it from a governor of Antioquia. Now, merchant banks preferred blatantly to skate over the surface by, in one exemplary case, contenting themselves with the figures for Colombia's exceptionally high per capita cement production without noting that cement was a primary ingredient in cocaine-making and that up to 30 per cent of construction was estimated to be financed by drugs cash.

Money laundering, a skill that soon became a very lucrative international service, was not itself a crime in the US until 1986. Unusual, big cash surpluses in Los Angeles and Miami banks during the 1980s were believed by the DEA to be directly linked to the cash-rich cocaine trade: Los Angeles' surplus rose from $343 million in 1981 to $5 billion in 1991. Laws and regulations were so slack that among the US institutions discovered to have been used without their knowledge by Pablo Escobar were Chemical Bank, Continental Bank International, Morgan Guaranty Trust and Wells Fargo.

Although a concerted, global battle against money laundering started with the launch of the Financial Action Task Force by the Group of Seven industrial countries and the European Community in 1989, by then the laundering methods employed were growing ever more sophisticated. Hard cash wholesale transactions were being abandoned in order to avoid easily traceable deposits. With the Cali cartel now depicted by the CIA, albeit perhaps with some hyperbole, as the biggest criminal organization in the world – gradually seizing the initiative in Europe from the Italian mafia families with which it was intricately allied – it had ample capacity to conceal drug payments electronically transferred through its national and international labyrinth of legitimate companies. At the same time, with the regulatory screws being turned in the world's established financial markets just when Latin America was opening up its own economies, the cash moved closer to home – where it could also count on better protection. In Venezuela, which reputedly had become Latin America's main money-laundering centre, $21 billion was being washed a year in 1994, declared Leyda Briceño de Febres, of the country's Institute for Higher Studies in National Defence. Citing a Bank of England official, *The Economist* wrote in June that year: 'Fighting money laundering is like pushing on a balloon – you simply displace the activity to wherever there is least resistance.'

Law-enforcement authorities in the United States and Europe have long complained that the war against drugs lacks the necessary, full-blooded, international political commitment. In April 1988, a Democratic senator dedicated to the drugs battle, John Kerry, told a US Senate Foreign Relations subcommittee investigating Panama, Central America and cocaine: 'Stopping drug trafficking into the United States has been a secondary US foreign policy objective. It has been sacrificed repeatedly for other political goals.' Such goals were usually trade relations and the confrontation with Communism. As the threat of Communism receded in the wake of the Cold War and as foreign markets flung open their doors, trade relations came bursting to the fore. In August 1994, after three successive US ambassadors with a background in national security had served in Colombia, the administration of President Bill Clinton – the man who had smoked pot but not inhaled it – slipped Myles Frechette, a trade expert, into the job. 'Drugs trafficking suddenly became priority number five,' commented Joe Toft, Colombia's outgoing DEA chief.

Again, at least in the mid-term until money-laundering regulations conceivably caught up, the globalization of international markets was itself beneficial to the drugs trade. It was feared that the NAFTA free-trade agreement would see Mexico's major role as a drug route, producer and money launderer increase all the more. And in Europe, where drugs trafficking was facilitated by the lifting of internal European Union frontier controls, the supply of cocaine was expanding dramatically with the massive new sales and routing opportunities afforded by the collapse of the Soviet Union at a time when the US market was saturated.

No longer was it only the First World's fondness for cocaine and other drugs that made its war on them abroad reek of hypocrisy. The illegality of drugs also ran against the grain of the *laissez-faire* economics sweeping the globe. Free-market gurus such as Milton Friedman, of the University of Chicago, and Sir Alan Walters, a key personal adviser of Britain's former prime minister, Margaret Thatcher, were not alone among leading opinion formers in favouring some manner of legalization. Friedman's position was founded, as he told a Bogotá conference in October 1993, on 'moral' grounds. 'What right does the government have to tell me what I inject myself?' he asked. 'Hang gliding is more dangerous than pot smoking. It is a question of civil liberties: prohibition has no ethical justification.' In common with other pro-legalizers, Friedman claimed that prohibition increased the profits and stimulated violent crime and corruption – which simply expanded with the imposition of prohibitive controls. 'Most of the terrible things blamed on drugs are the result of the war on drugs rather than the drugs themselves,' he said.

The moral basis of the US-inspired war against drugs has never been understood by Colombia, which views the crusade as puritanical and hysterical – as well as hypocritical. Colombia considers domestic cocaine consumption a minor problem. Surveys by United Nations-backed groups in Medellín indicated that although it cost only $5 a gramme (the same price as six bags of rice), cocaine users taking at least one snort a year had remained at around just 3 per cent of the population between 1987 and 1993. Total users in the United States, according to its 1993 National Household Survey on Drug Abuse, represented around 2.2 per cent in spite of the price being about fifteen times higher for a much diluted and dirtier product. Although Medellín's rate of *basuko* use – also about 3 per cent – was much greater than in the United States, where consumption had stabilized, it was in marked decline. There was a learning curve: street children saw the damage that *basuko* did to their peers and elders. Many, therefore, stuck to inhaling glue, a cheaper habit if only marginally less damaging.

The lower cost of cocaine therefore – which would be much lower after legalization – did not in itself appear to increase demand over the long term. Indeed, although the price in the United States fell by a third between 1985 and 1993, education and changing social attitudes saw that the number of occasional users also dropped – by as much as 63 per cent according to the US Health Department's national household survey. 'An informed citizenry is the best protection against drug abuse,' said Ethan Nadelmann, a former Princeton University lecturer. The effectiveness of anti-tobacco publicity campaigns in greatly reducing cigarette smoking in the United States and Europe, as well as the failure of crack to get a grip at least in Britain and Holland because of the nightmarish publicity the drug received before its arrival, proved that education worked. People learned what was good for them.

In spite of the billions of dollars a year that had been spent for more than a decade in the attempt to crush the international drugs trade by repressive, militaristic means, cocaine was cheaper and more abundant than ever before. Its low price was reflected worldwide in the higher quantities seized, which were usually estimated to be a mere tenth of the amount actually hitting the markets (although some credit needed to be given for greater policing efficiency). In 1993, US customs – the agency which seizes the most cocaine there – impounded 80,000 kilograms, nearly ten times as much as in 1983. Within the European Union, total cocaine seizures increased forty-two times to 16,800 kilograms between 1982 and 1991. By 1994, the DEA and the US Department of State estimated that up to 1 million kilograms of cocaine was being exported annually from Latin America. The war on supply had palpably failed.

Attempting to stem the cocaine trade had proved futile in that it had neither reduced the quantity reaching the streets nor had any perceptible impact on the level of cocaine use – which was influenced more by education, fashion and peer pressure than the lure of the drug's strikingly lower price. The trade was constantly reinventing itself. Drug routes and smuggling methods proliferated; so did money-laundering systems. No sooner had one precursor chemical been blocked off from Colombia, such as MEK in early 1994, than another had taken its place: by August, five non-controlled substitute chemicals had flooded the market and cocaine production was back to normal. So great was the economic and political clout of the trade that it had had no problem interwining itself with outwardly respectable activities and people until, aided by greed and fear, it had become the single biggest power broker in Colombia.

In September 1994, a few days after the recently departed US ambassador, Morris Busby, said on CNN that the Cali drug mafias formed the world's biggest multinational 'with bigger profits than Texaco, Boeing and Pepsi', Joe Toft, who had just resigned, publicly declared Colombia a 'narco-democracy'. Admitting he was sad and frustrated that the traffickers' power had snowballed during his six and a half years in Bogotá, Toft told various Colombian newspapers and television stations that the traffickers' institutional penetration and capacity for intimidation, as well as the leakage of information, made it impossible for the Colombian police and the DEA to succeed. The global effort against drugs, he said, was insufficient. Toft's agents, accustomed to being 'burned' by people they had closely trusted, and dogged by the sense that they were swimming against a tidal wave, were not optimistic. Tough cops, used to risking their lives against the white menace, they, too, were beginning to stress education as the better strategy. They, too, had suffered corruption in Colombia, as elsewhere: at least two agents had been suspended on suspicion of taking bribes.

Meanwhile, as the Colombian drug barons shipped out marijuana and cocaine using techniques that were ever more sophisticated, they were running up against competition from the European and US manufacturers of new, illicit, synthetic drugs. The most fashionable was Ecstasy, or methylenedioxymethamphetamine, a synthetized, lightly hallucinogenic amphetamine that provoked euphoria as well as boosting adrenalin, reducing inhibitions and increasing sexual libido. So far, there was little evidence of the drug producing physical addiction. The dozen or so deaths a year caused by Ecstasy in Britain were brought on mostly by exhaustion. The drug, which was made mainly in Holland, was especially fashionable among teenagers. Colombia's cocaine trade confronted a similar challenge to that faced fifteen years earlier by the country's marijuana business, which had been undermined by US pot cultivation and the discovery of cocaine as much as by the sweeping destruction of the marijuana plantations. Ecstasy was produced close to its consumers and appeared to be safer than cocaine. In Holland itself, a 1990 government household survey indicated that by then the cocaine consumption rate had been easily outstripped by that for Ecstasy, which, nevertheless, was still only 1 per cent.

Recognizing the impossibility of stemming illicit drugs supplies whilst consumer demand exists, and recognizing the potential of reversing that demand by waging serious campaigns against drugs abuse and by trusting in the fickleness of fashion and in most healthy people's sense of self-preservation, US and European governments may find that to adopt a pragmatic approach to illicit drugs would prove far more effective than their traditionally emotive and dogmatic one. In February 1994, a government summary of Holland's drug policy stated: 'The central objective is to restrict as much as possible the risks that drug abuse present to drug abusers themselves, their immediate environment and society as a whole. These risks ... are dependent not only on the psychotropic or other properties of the substance, but primarily on the type of user, the reasons for use and the circumstances in which the drugs are taken.' In 1991, in spite of Holland's liberal attitude towards drug users, illicit drugs were the primary and secondary cause of the deaths of only seventy-four residents.

'The government tries to ensure that drug users are not caused more harm by prosecution and imprisonment than by the use of drugs themselves,' asserted the same Dutch document. By the same token, perhaps the First World governments should have endeavoured to ensure that persecuting drugs traffickers in an historically lawless, developing country such as Colombia did not cause more harm than the use of the drugs themselves. Colombia's tragic and remorseless level of unblinking violence and corruption originated from the scale of the illicit business proportionate to its economy; its people's scorn for a hopelessly ineffective justice system; its frontier mentality and political fiefdoms, generated by chaotic, ongoing colonization and weak central government; its tradition of banditry; and its consequent gambling spirit, greed, permissiveness and scant regard for human life. Furthermore, the cocaine boom exacerbated social and class tensions by bringing unimaginable riches within reach of the poor. The cash excited feverish ambition, and with it, jealousy and resentment. When excluded by an élite that was more than happy to partake of the profits of the trade if not to dabble in the trade itself, the *magicos* and *mulas* tended to become vengeful and bullying.

Ironically, in late 1993 the pragmatic approach was openly vaunted by the US surgeon general, Joycelyn Elders, whose son, Kevin, was convicted of selling 48 grams of cocaine, and then in 1994 by Colombia's chief prosecutor, Gustavo de Greiff. Both announced their support for legalizing the drugs trade. Although jeered at for their evident self-interest – in de Greiff's case because his country produced the drugs – their positions reflected an inescapable reality and their voices joined the mounting chorus of support for such a move. Among the world's leading publications in favour of legalization were the *New York Times* and *The Economist*. In the United States, even a former secretary of state, George Shultz, was moving in favour of the control and legalization of drugs. In June 1994 the secretary general of Interpol, Raymond Kendall, declared he favoured the depenalization of drugs use, which was half-way there. Several British judges and senior police officers agreed. Other European countries, such as

Germany and Italy, had already recently decriminalized personal drugs use to some degree.

While the sea change of opinion started to occur – the pot smoking of President Clinton and his vice president, Al Gore, was no impediment to their taking office – it was European and North American politicians who balked. They did not want to have the courage to confront the hysterical dinosaurs who still blindly identified illegal drugs as the source of all evil (a line that the CIA was happy to push in finding itself a new role after the Cold War) and the vast, multinational government industry that had built itself up around drugs prohibition. Every day the drugs trade remained illegal, the murderous barons behind it in Colombia simply grew richer and more powerful and the whitewash continued.

EPILOGUE

On June 9 1995, Gilberto Rodríguez Orejuela was captured in Cali by Colombian police. He was arrested in the affluent neighbourhood of Santa Mónica after the attempts to hunt down himself and his cartel colleagues had been dramatically stepped up by President Samper, who following continued revelations over how the drug traffickers had helped to finance his campaign was fighting to salvage his sullied image domestically as well as internationally. The thinly bearded Rodríguez Orejuela was discovered hiding in a wardrobe after police were tipped off by an informant. He surrendered peacefully and handed over three handguns, according to the Defence Minister, Fernando Botero.

Rodríguez Orejuela, who was flown to Bogota's La Picota jail where police helicopters buzzed overhead and tanks stood guard outside, was captured only months after a reorganization of senior police officers in which General José Serrano, a trusted ally of the DEA, had been appointed chief of the national police. Raids in Cali had been increased, at least a dozen congressmen were being investigated by the chief prosecutor, Alfonso Valdivieso, and million-pound rewards advertised for the capture of the cartel ringleaders.

Police claimed initially that the informant who had led them to Rodríguez Orejuela was an infiltrator. Among the other, more unlikely, versions circulating in Colombia was that Alberto Giraldo, the Cali frontman who had recently turned himself in, had himself shopped his paymaster.

However, it may have been that the arrest was linked to the issuing

333

of drug charges against fifty-nine people earlier in the week by the US government. Among those charged in what was the biggest judicial operation to date against the Cali cocaine traffickers' network, were six US lawyers. Most remarkably, these included the former chief of the Reagan-era Justice Department's Office of International Affairs, Michael Abbell. Until 1984, Abbell had been responsible for trying to extradite traffickers from Colombia; thereafter, he was alleged to have stepped beyond the law while serving as counsel to the Cali cartel leaders. Two former federal prosecutors in Florida, Donald Ferguson and Joel Rosenthal, were also named as advisers to the drug barons. Ferguson was accused of paying hush money to arrested cartel members, while Rosenthal pleaded guilty to money laundering. It was also alleged that the US lawyers had passed on death threats to the jailed cartel men as well as threats to their family. Abbell himself was accused of pressurizing one Miami middleman to file a false affidavit clearing Gilberto Rodríguez Orejuela. In the plea bargaining that was already taking place, to shop Rodríguez Orejuela would have been a formidable bargaining chip for anybody able to do so.

The arrest of Rodríguez Orejuela and the indictments in the United States were huge blows to the Cali traffickers. However, if he were to win the full benefits available under Colombia's penal code after being indicted and convicted, Rodríguez Orejuela possibly faced no more than four years in jail.

A day after Rodríguez Orejuela's capture, Colombia was pitched back into violence reminiscent of the worst in the drug wars. A ten-kilogram bomb filled with shrapnel exploded in the Parque San Antonio in downtown Medellín. At least twenty-nine people were killed and more than two hundred injured. The bomb, which had been planted among crowds celebrating a Caribbean music festival, shattered a bird sculpture by the Defence Minister's father, Fernando Botero. Although it was reported that FARC guerrillas claimed responsibility for the slaughter – the bird was said to be the target, the human victims an accident – some feared that the bomb represented a reprisal against the government for the drug leader's capture rather than an act of rage over stuttering peace talks. Whoever lay behind it, Colombia was once again plunged into mass bloodshed and uncertainty.

BIBLIOGRAPHY

Books

Anonymous: *Un Narco se Confiesa y Acusa*, Editorial Colombia Nuestra, Bogotá, 1989

Arango, Mario: *Los Funerales de Antioquia La Grande*, Editorial J. M. Arango, Medellín, 1990

Arrieta, Carlos Gustavo; Orjuela, Luis Javier; Palacio Eduardo Sarmiento; Tokatlian, Juan Gabriel: *Narcotráfico en Colombia, Dimensiones políticas, económicas, jurídicas e internacionales*, Universidad de los Andes and Tercer Mundo Editores, Bogotá, 1990

Bahamón Dussán, Augusto: *Mi Guerra en Medellín*, Intermedio Editores, Bogotá, 1992

Cañón M., Luis: *El Patrón. Vida y Muerte de Pablo Escobar*, Planeta Colombiana Editorial S.A., Bogotá, 1994

Castillo, Fabio: *La Coca Nostra*, Editorial Documentos Periodísticos, Bogotá, 1991

Castillo, Fabio: *Los Jinetes de la Cocaina*, Editorial Documentos Periodisticos, Bogotá, 1987

Cortés, Fernando: *Rodríguez Gacha 'El Mexicano'*, Intermedio Editores, Santafé de Bogotá, 1993

Ehrenfeld, Rachel. *Evil Money, Encounters along the Money Trail*, HarperCollins, New York, 1992

Galán Medellín, Rafael: *El Crimen de Abril, lo que no se ha revelado del proceso*, ECOE Ediciones, Bogotá, 1986

García Sayan, Diego (ed.): *Coca, Cocaína y Narcotráfico, Laberinto en los Andes*, Comision Andina de Juristas, Lima, 1989

Gómez, Ignacio and Giraldo, Juan Carlos: *El Returno de Pablo Escobar*, Editorial La Oveja Negra, Bogotá, 1992

Grupo Editorial 87: *En que momento se jodió Medellín*, Editorial Oveja Negra and Editorial Milla Batres, Bogotá, 1991

BIBLIOGRAPHY

Gugliotta, Guy and Leen, Jeff: *Kings of Cocaine*, Simon & Schuster, 1989

Guzmán Campos, Germán: *La Violencía en Colombia*, Ediciones Progreso, Cali, 1968

Hargreaves, Clare: *Snowfields. The War on Cocaine in the Andes*, Zed Books and Holmes & Meier, London, 1992

Júbiz Hazbum, Alberto, 'Yo no maté a Galán', Estudio Tres Graficas, Bogotá, 1993

Krauthausen, Ciro and Sarmiento, Luis Fernando: *Cocaína & Co, un mercado ilegal por dentro*, Universidad Nacional de Colombia and Tercer Mundo Editores, Bogotá, 1991

McAleese, Peter: *No Mean Soldier, The Autobiography of a Professional Fighting Man*, Orion, London, 1993

Medina Gallego, Carlos: *Autodefensas, Paramilítares Y Narcotráfico En Colombia. Origen, Desarrollo y Consolidación. El Caso 'Puerto Boyacá'*, Editorial Documentos Periodísticos, Bogotá, 1990

Mermelstein, Max: *El Hombre Que Hizo Llover Coca*, Intermedio Editores, Bogotá, 1993

Osorio Lizarazo, José Antonio: *Gaitán: Vida, Muerte y Permanente Presencia*, Carlos Valencia Editores, Bogotá, 1982

Parsons, James: *Urabá: Salida de Antioquia Al Mar*, Traducido bajo la dirección del Instituto de Integración Cultural con los auspicios del Banco de la Republica ye de la Corporacíón Regional de Desarrollo de Urabá CORPURABA

Pearce, Jenny: *Colombia, Inside the Labyrinth*, Latin America Bureau, London, 1990

Rodríguez, Juan Ignacio (unidad investigativa compuesta por varios periodistas): *Los Amos del Juego*, Tecimpre, Bogotá, 1989

Salazar J., Alonso: *No Nacimos Pa Semilla*, Centro de Investigación y Educación Popular, CINEP, Bogotá, 1990

Salazar J., Alfonso and Jaramillo, Ana María: *Medellín, Las Subculturas del Narcotráfico*, Centro de Investigación y Educación Popular, CINEP, Bogotá, 1992

Samper, Ernesto and others: *Legalización de la Marihuana*, Asociación Nacional de Instituciones Financieras, Bogotá

Thoumi, Francisco: *Economía, Política y Narcotráfico*, Tercero Mundo Editores, Bogotá, 1994

Tokatlian, Juan G. and Bagley, Bruce M: *Economía y Política del Narcotráfico*, Ediciones Uniandes and CEREC, Bogotá, 1990

Velásquez, Jorge Enrique: *Cómo me infiltré y engañé al Cartel*, Editorial Oveja Negra, 1993

BIBLIOGRAPHY

Reports and unpublished studies

Permanent Subcommittee on Investigations of the Committee on Governmental Affairs, United States Senate. Arms Trafficking, Mercenaries and Drug Cartels. Washington, 1991

Zamora, Luis Carlos. Chemicals used in the Production of Dangerous Drugs, Review of the National Directorate of Dangerous Drugs. Bogotá, January 1993

Medellín: En el Camino de la Concertación. Presidencia de la República, Programa Presidencial para Medellín y su Area Metropolitana. Informe de Gestión, 1990–1992.

Medellín: Reencuentro con el Futuro. Presidencia de la República, Dirección Programa Presidencial para Medellín y el Area Metropolitana, Departmento Nacional de Planeación. Bogotá, 1991

Petersen, Robert. History of Cocaine, Investigation Divison, National Institute on Drug Abuse, United States

Uribe, María Teresa. La Territorialidad de los Conflictos y de la Violencia en Antioquia. Universidad de Antioquia, Colombia

Melo, Jorge Orlando. Consideraciones generales sobre el impacto de la violencia en la historia reciente del pais. Presidencia de la República, Programa Presidencial para Medellín y su Area Metropolitana. Bogotá, 1990

Maza Márquez, Miguel. Modus Operandi de Pablo Escobar. Departamento Administrativo de Seguridad, 1991

Colombía 1993 Annual Country Report. United Nations International Drug Control Programme. Bogotá, 1994

Kalmanovitz, Salomón. Análisis Macroeconómico del Narcotráfico en la Economía Colombiana. Centro de Investigaciones para el Desarrollo, Universidad Nacional de Colombia. Bogotá, 1992

Magazine and newspaper articles

Musto, David: 'Opium, Cocaine and Marijuana in American History', Scientific American, July, 1991

Kalmanovitz, Salomón: 'La economía del narcotráfico en Colombia', Economía Colombiana, February–March, 1990

Sarmiento, Libardo: 'Narcotráfico y sector agropecuario en Colombia', Economía Colombiana, February–March, 1990.

INDEX

INDEX

INDEX

WHITEWASH

INDEX